MEDIEVAL PAPALISM

BY THE SAME AUTHOR
THE MEDIEVAL IDEA OF LAW

The Maitland Memorial Lectures
Delivered in the University of Cambridge in Lent Term 1948

MEDIEVAL PAPALISM

THE POLITICAL THEORIES OF THE MEDIEVAL CANONISTS

by

WALTER ULLMANN
J.U.D., F.R.Hist.S.
Lecturer in Medieval History in the University of Leeds

METHUEN & CO. LTD., LONDON
36 Essex Street, Strand, W.C.2

First published in 1949

MATRI SUAE

PREFACE

THE political concepts of the medieval canonists—a species of mankind that is virtually known only to librarians—are hidden in dust-covered and worm-eaten tomes which have been relegated to sanctuaries usually inaccessible to the average student of mediveal history. With the breakdown of the medieval world the canonists and their doctrines were consigned to an oblivion that is at once unfathomable and undeserved. I believe that the reason for the extremely scanty attention paid nowadays to the canonists is that their ideas lie, as it were, in the shadowy no-man's-land between history and law. The historian is somewhat hesitant to overstep the boundaries fixed by tradition and custom. The lawyer, on his part, does not feel at ease when called upon to deal with politics and especially with the history of political thought. Each has a valid excuse for refraining from steeping himself in the wealth of material that confronts us in the works of the medieval canonists. The medieval "oceanus juris" extends far beyond the frontiers somewhat shyly set by contemporary legal thought. To anybody who has once wetted his feet on the shores of that vast and illimitable "oceanus juris" it must be clear that the floods, once allowed to break the dykes, are capable of infiltrating into spheres which were commonly thought to be beyond the pale of any canonistic influence. The field of political theory in particular is one that is the least immune from this influence. All history is a "seamless webb" was one of Maitland's happy phrases, and the present is part of it as well as the past. No apter demonstration of the unity of history can be found than the records of political ideas. It may very well be that modern ears are but faintly responsive to canonistic phraseology, but once stripped of inessentials, this phraseology may be the medium for conveying a large part of our Western heritage.

A lawyer converted to history, Maitland's chief aim was to show the development of the Western mind. As a pathfinder he was the first amongst modern scholars to examine *ex professo* that no-man's-land which lies between history and law. It is not only in his investigations into the constitutional framework and the institutional history of associations, but also—and perhaps to a still greater extent—in his researches into ecclesiastical history that Maitland, "with his genial penetration",[1] showed the immense importance of that no-man's-land. It is, to be sure, an unfortunate fact that the line of research so clearly marked out by the master, has not aroused that enthusiasm which it so richly deserved. I was therefore deeply sensible of the honour which the Managers of the Frederic William Maitland Memorial Fund bestowed upon me by inviting me to lecture on a subject connected with my researches. Indeed, I was fully conscious, not only of this great honour, but also of the very great responsibility which had thereby been placed upon me. For even the remotest connexion with Maitland's name must produce feelings of awe in the heart of every mortal. Who would not be prouder and, at the same time, feel the burden of responsibility more heavily than he who fascinated by everything that the name of Maitland implies, as yet is able to see only dimly the bright light of his star that is at once motive, aim and reason for his researches? Therefore, when I chose "Medieval Papalism" as the title of these lectures, it was with the avowed intention of attempting a small opening in the dykes of that vast "oceanus medievalis juris" so that the perennial, constructive value of the human plan and purpose in medieval times might be viewed from an angle undeservedly neglected.

These lectures are here presented in a slightly expanded form. They are primarily intended to indicate a hitherto little-trodden tract of medieval political thinking. The quite overpowering mass of untouched material necessitated that these lectures should be introductory in character. It is one of those inexplicable phenomena of modern historiography that these untapped sources seem destined to remain of a mere antiquarian interest. The wealth of canonistic material that confronts us in cathedral and college libraries is one more proof of the richness of medieval intellectual life, and also of the great interest which English scholars, in times gone by, must have had in canonistic studies. Since within the history of political thought the canonists have not yet found the position that is due to them, this book may serve as a very modest and humble

[1] Professor Knowles in his inaugural lecture *The Prospects of Medieval Studies*, p. 18.

contribution towards this end. The introductory character compelled me to select, firstly, only the very fundamental and basic aspects of canonistic political thought, and, secondly, those canonists who can be considered typical and representative of the schools. I have tried to give a survey of canonistic political thinking from the second half of the twelfth century down to the end of the fourteenth century. In view of the vast medieval literature, the material presented here is infinitesimal.

I am anxious to express my sincerest thanks to the Managers of the Frederic William Maitland Memorial Fund for the grant they have so generously advanced to meet the necessary expenses of collecting the material. In particular I would like to thank Professor H. A. Hollond, of Trinity College, Professor M. D. Knowles, of Peterhouse, and Professor Helen Cam, formerly of Girton College, for the very kind interest they have taken in my work.

To a number of librarians I am very much indebted for the readiness with which they met my requests. In the first place I am desirous of expressing my sincere thanks to Mr. H. M. Adams, the Librarian of Trinity College, for his patience, tolerance and constant friendly help. My special thanks are due to the Librarian of Durham Cathedral Library, Professor S. L. Greenslade, and the Cathedral Chapter, for the loan of some very valuable MSS.; also to Professor C. Jenkins and Dr. Irene Churchill for the loan of MSS. from the Library of Lambeth Palace. I must furthermore thank Professor G. Le Bras, of the University of Paris, and Mlle Margaret Boulet, of the Bibliothèque Nationale, for procuring photostats of a MS.; to Mlle Boulet I am also indebted for much helpful information. My thanks are also due to Sir Ivor Atkins, the Librarian of Worcester Cathedral Library; Canon W. H. Kynaston, the Librarian of Lincoln Cathedral Library; Chancellor F. Harrison, the Librarian of York Minster Library, for giving me access to their libraries. To the Librarian of Pembroke College, Mr. H. J. Habbakuk, the University Library in Cambridge, the Keeper of MSS. of the University Library of Edinburgh, the officials of the British Museum, the Keeper of MSS. of the National Bibliothek, Vienna, the Librarians of the Badische Landes Bibliothek, Karlsruhe, of the

Laurenziana, Florence, and of the Cistercian Monastery, Zwettl, I offer my thanks for their allowing me to procure photostatic copies of a number of MSS. and tracts.

I am grateful to Professor John Le Patourel and Professor C. R. Cheney for their valuable suggestions. The numerous references to his works in the footnotes make my debt to Professor Stephan Kuttner sufficiently evident.

This preface would be incomplete, were I not to express my affectionate thanks to my wife for the infinite care with which she has assisted me to get the TS. into shape.

W. U.

June, 1948

CONTENTS

Chapter		Page
I	CANONISTS AND CANONISTIC SCHOLARSHIP	1
II	THE CANONISTS AND NATURAL LAW	38
III	THE POPE AND NATURAL LAW	50
IV	PAPAL PLENITUDE OF POWER: THE IDEA	76
V	WORLD MONARCHY	114
VI	POPE AND EMPEROR	138
	APPENDIX	199
	LIST OF MANUSCRIPTS CITED	217
	INDEX	221

ABBREVIATIONS

Com.	=*Commentaria.*
Comp. I, II, III, IV	=*Compilatio Prima, Secunda,* etc.
D 4, D 8	=Manuscript in Durham Cathedral Library (D 4: C III 4; D 8: C III 8).
Gl. ord.	=*Glossa Ordinaria.*
LB	=Manuscript in the Library of Lambeth Palace.
LC	=Manuscript in Lincoln Cathedral Library.
P	=Manuscript in the Library of Pembroke College, Cambridge.
SB	=*Sitzungsberichte.*
Spec.	=*Speculum Judiciale,* Guilelmus Durantis, ed. Basle, 1574.
Tractatus	=*Tractatus Illustrium Jurisconsultorum,* ed. Venice 1584-86.
T	=Manuscript in the Library of Trinity College, Cambridge.
W	=Manuscript (Folio) in Worcester Cathedral Library.
Zeitschrift, kanon. Abt.	=*Zeitschrift der Savigny Stiftung für Rechtsgeschichte, Kanonistische Abteilung.*

PRINTED EDITIONS FREQUENTLY CITED:

Alvarus Pelagius, *De Planctu Ecclesiae,* Venice, 1560.
Antonius de Butrio, *Commentaria in V Libros Decretalium,* Venice, 1578.
Archdeacon (Guido de Baysio), *Rosarium seu in Decretorum Volumen Commentaria,* Venice, 1577.
Archdeacon (Guido de Baysio), *Apparatus in Sextum,* Venice, 1503.
Bartholomaeus Brixiensis, *Glossa Ordinaria in Decretum,* Venice, 1499.

Bartolus, *Commentaria in Codicem et Digestum Vetus*, Lyons, 1523.
Bernardus Parmensis, *Glossa Ordinaria in Decretales*, Venice, 1514.
Cynus, *Commentaria in Codicem et Digestum Vetus*, Francfort, 1578.
Glossa Ordinaria Decretum, 1471.
Glossa Ordinaria (Bernardus Parmensis), *Decretales*, Venice, 1514.
Glossa Ordinaria (Johannes Andreae), *Sextus*, Lyons, 1523.
Glossa Ordinaria (Johannes Andreae), *Clementinae*, Paris, 1503.
Glossa Ordinaria (Zenzelinus de Cassanis), *Extravagantes Johannis*, Paris, 1503.
Goffredus de Trano, *Summa in Titulos Decretalium*, Venice, 1586.
Hostiensis (Henricus de Segusia), *Summa Titulorum*, Cologne, 1612.
Innocent IV, *Commentaria in V Libros Decretalium*, Venice, 1578.
Johannes Andreae, *Novella in V Libros Decretalium*, Venice, 1581.
Johannes Andreae, *Novella in Sextum*, Lyons, 1527.
Johannes Andreae, *Glossa in Clementinas*, Paris, 1503.
Panormitanus, *Commentaria in Decretales*, Lyons, 1512.
Petrus de Ancharano, *Lectura super Sexto Decretalium*, Lyons, 1543.
Zabarella, *Super Decretales*, Cologne, 1602.
  In Clementinas Commentaria, Cologne, 1602.

CHAPTER I

CANONISTS AND CANONISTIC SCHOLARSHIP

"THE ideal of the golden age of the canonists," said the late A. L. Smith in his Ford lectures, "was to make a working reality of the kingdom of God upon earth; to express the laws of that kingdom in a coherent, all-embracing code, to enforce that code upon the still half-heathen kingdoms of this world. An ideal truly, and predestined to fail, but a noble ideal".[1] This passage succinctly and concisely sums up the literary efforts of several generations of canonists and other jurists who took up their pens for the promotion of papalist aims. This of course is a generalization, but it is certainly true that the history of the Middle Ages, ever since Hildebrand ascended to the headship of the Western Church and re-orientated its policy by his characteristic strong-mindedness, exhibits the traits of two irreconcilable ideologies, commonly epitomized in "empire versus papacy". Whether imperialist or papalist—the two terms are not always identical with civilian and canonist—the external policy of emperor and pope was but the concrete manifestation of an ideological contest that was fought out behind the curtain of world-shaking events. What we see in the actions of the Innocents, Gregories, Bonifaces and other notable ecclesiastical rulers, was but the execution of a policy, insistently, sometimes persuasively, not seldom extravagantly, propounded by the teachers and interpreters of the canon law. Perhaps in no other age of the history of mankind did the law play such a paramount role as in the centuries after Gregory VII. For the whole struggle between emperor and pope centred in the law.

It is perhaps symptomatic of the present state of historiography that this basis of the contest, indeed its *conditio sine qua non*, is a topic upon which far too little energy is spent. To take only a very recent example, the Carlyles in their great six-volumed work devoted only a negligible space to the canonistic teachings. Indeed, contemporary presentations of medieval

[1] *Church and State in the Middle Ages*, p. 51.

political thought are apt to be very misleading. The works of medieval philosophers, theologians and publicists are given disproportionate prominence, and apart from some stereotyped, casual references to Innocent IV and Hostiensis, we hear nothing of those who—unlike the philosophers—really created a political theory and made politics. For what the theologians and their colleagues said, was but a residuum of canonistic theory: canonistic political thought had long been formulated and had clearly taken on a definite pattern, when the publicists, philosophers and theologians entered the arena of political controversy. But whilst modern theology and philosophy in some respects shows a certain kinship to its medieval predecessor, the canonists left no heirs.

The understanding and adequate comprehension of the centuries-long contest presupposes the knowledge of the ideas which were formulated somewhat inconspicuously in the legal laboratories of the canonists, and which exhibited themselves so conspicuously in official papal policy. It may be stated with confidence that no political action can be fully understood without prior understanding of the law which itself merely crystallizes the true state of mind of its authors. Popes as statesmen had to reckon with a given set of circumstances and hence had to adjust themselves to concrete reality: whilst the canonists merrily, and sometimes irresponsibly, put forward their claims unhampered by considerations of expediency, practical wisdom or diplomacy, working in the serene atmosphere of an august theory. Hence we frequently observe a gulf between the theoretical claim of the canonists and the practical execution of papal policy. To be sure, whenever papal policy lagged behind the theoretical design of the canonists, it was not from opposition to canonistic doctrine, but from considerations of practical politics. In fact, the secret of the—at least temporary—success of the medieval papacy lay in the ingenious adaptation and accommodation of canonistic theory to the temper of the time.[1]

The popes who set their seal to the history of the Middle

[1] See the very pertinent remarks of Fritz Kern, *Gottesgnadentum und Widerstandsrecht*, p. 233, note 429: "Das Eigentümliche der Priestermacht ist eben eine der Zeitlage sich anpassende Verknüpfung unverjährbarer Ansprüche und Theorien mit dem politisch Erreichbaren. Auf der Kunst dieser Verknüpfung beruht der Erfolg der päpstlichen Interventionsansprüche von Gregor VII bis auf Bonifaz VIII."

Ages were all canonists of great repute; and the very few who were not, were surrounded by a circle of canonists whose advice was as decisive as the sentence of the pope himself. Thus, decrees of the popes were no mere orders to regulate the conduct of the clergy and so forth: they were far more, for they bore the imprint of the sanctity of the law. Alexander III acquired great fame as a canonist when he was known as Magister Rolandus; shortly after him Magister Albertus, also of the Bolognese school, ascended to the papal throne as Gregory VIII.[1] The great glossator, Huguccio, was the influential teacher of Innocent III, who himself proved an outstanding canonist and worthy pupil of his great master. And we should note in parenthesis here that this pope first promulgated his own collection of decretals (the *Compilatio Tertia*) not as law, as it would have befitted a supreme legislator, but as so-called directives to the canonists at Bologna. "I send them to you," said Innocent III addressing the professors in Bologna, "that you may be able to apply them when need arises, in court and in the lecture hall."[2] We witness a very similar procedure on the part of his successor Honorius III, when he issued the *Compilatio Quinta* in 1226[3] to Master Tancred at Bologna and to other professors[4] urging them to use these decretals "tam in judiciis quam in scolis".[5] No words need be wasted about the canonistic

---

[1] On him see Professor S. Kuttner, *Repertorium der Kanonistik*, pp. 7, 10, 18, 47, and J. F. v. Schulte, "Die Glosse zum Dekret Gratians" in *Denkschriften der kaiserl. Akademie d. Wissenschaften* (phil. hist. Classe), vol. xxi, ii. pp. 37, 51.

[2] Potthast, *Regesta Pontificum Romanorum*, No. 4157. The wording of Innocent's bull transmitting this first official collection of decretals is strangely reminiscent of the wording used by Justinian in promulgating his *Codex*, see the constitution "Cordi nobis", § 2. H. Kantorowicz deduces from this not unintended similarity that thereby Innocent III desired to appear a papal Justinian, see "Das Principium Decretalium des Johannes de Deo" in *Zeitschrift, kanon. Abt.*, vol. xii, p. 429. It is noteworthy that the canonistic background of both Alexander III and Innocent III is quite neglected in the great work of J. Haller, *Das Papsttum, Idee und Wirklichkeit*, vol. iii, pp. 138 ff., 280 ff.

[3] Potthast, No. 7684. Kuttner, op. cit., p. 382, fixed the date of the promulgation as 2 May 1226.

[4] F. Savigny, *Geschichte des Römischen Rechts im Mittelalter*, vol. v., p. 118, note f, and A. Friedberg, *Quinque Compilationes Antiquae*, p. XXXV.

[5] See Potthast, No. 7684. The edition of the Vienna MS. 2077 by J. A. Riegger was not accessible to me. Gregory IX, Boniface VIII and Clement V followed these examples: they addressed their collections to the masters and students of Bologna.

scholarship of Gregory IX—the promulgator of the *Decretales*,[1] and who, as a former judge of appeal in the Roman curia, will be remembered for favouring the monks of Canterbury against their archbishops.[2] Throughout the Middle Ages Innocent IV as Sinibaldus Fliscus boasted of a renown equalled only by that of Bartolus of Sassoferrato. Whatever view one may take of Boniface VIII's policy, it is futile to cast doubt upon his qualities as a canonist, qualities manifesting themselves in his collection of the *Liber Sextus*. All these popes belonged to the thirteenth century—indeed a remarkable century that could pride itself upon this galaxy of rulers, themselves acknowledged authorities of the law. The fourteenth century marred though it was by the Avignonese adventure of the popes, also presents us with personalities who ranked high in the science of canon law. We need only refer to Clement V as the initiator of the collection of decretals known as *Clementinae*, and John XXII whose own collection, though no part of the *Corpus Juris Canonici*, unmistakably betrays the sure touch of the lawyer. Gregory XI, as he himself was proud of declaring publicly, had been a devoted pupil of the "lumen juris", that is, Baldus de Ubaldis. Aeneas Sylvius, better known perhaps as Pius II, left an indelible imprint upon political science which to him, as to so many of his predecessors, was but a branch of canonistic scholarship.

Next to these illustrious personages who, for good or evil, changed the face of Europe during their often astonishingly brief reigns, we must refer to the many cardinals and other high ecclesiastics, by whom the popes were surrounded and decisively influenced. Without these princes of the Church a medieval canonistic scholarship cannot be envisaged. And a number of them were very strong candidates for the pontificate. Henricus de Segusia, better known by his function as cardinal-bishop of Ostia (Hostiensis), was only prevented by illness from filling the vacant chair after Clement IV's death; perhaps the future relations between England and the papacy might have taken a different turn, if this canonist, the "juris utriusque monarcha", at one time the paid adviser and ambassador of King Henry

---

[1] For contemporary opinions on the collection and its value for canonistic scholarship, see A. Theiner, *Commentatio de Collectionibus et Decretalium Codice*, 1829, pp. 35–8.

[2] See *Epistolae Cantuarienses*, (R.S.), pp. 471–2, 476–7, 506–7.

III,[1] had become the occupant of the bishopric of Rome. Premature death prevented Cardinal Zabarella from ascending to the height of ecclesiastical power at a very critical time, and these examples could easily be multiplied. In passing we may mention the famous collectors of canons, Cardinal Deusdedit and Anselm of Lucca. Whilst little is known about the life of the former,[2] the latter's biography is preserved:[3] a nephew of Alexander II[4] he was particularly busy in North Italy during the great political conflicts at the time of Gregory VII. Then there was Magister Bernardus, the archdeacon of Compostella and professor at Bologna, who acquired fame as the collector of Innocentian decretals (1208) which came to be known as the *Collectio Romana* until superseded by Innocent's official collection, the already mentioned *Compilatio Tertia* (1210);[5] Cardinal Laborans, an able, though little known, canonist;[6] the Spanish bishop Laurentius whose *Apparatus* (written between 1210 and 1215) gained such universal acceptance, as is shown by the very frequent references to him in later works; the redactor of the official collection of decretals, Cardinal Petrus Beneventanus Collivaccinus;[7] the Bishop of Osma in

[1] On the somewhat mysterious circumstances of his departure from England, see Matthew Paris, *Chronica Majora*, vol. iv, pp. 33, 286, 351, 353, and Maitland, *Roman Canon Law in the Church of England*, p. 115. It is mere guessing to say that Hostiensis taught in an English school, cf. Schulte, *Quellen*, vol. ii, p. 124, P & M, vol. i, p. 122, and the late Kantorowicz, *Studies in the Glossators of Roman Law*, p. 91; see also Gaines Post, "A Romano-Canonical Maxim... in Bracton", in *Traditio*, vol. iv, (1946), p. 213.

[2] See W. Glanvell, *Die Kanonessammlung des Kardinals Deusdedit*, introduction, and P. Fournier and G. Le Bras, *Histoire des collections canoniques*, vol. ii, pp. 36 ff.

[3] See *Mon. Germ. Hist. (Scriptores)*, tom. xii, pp. 1–35.

[4] A. Fliche, *La Réforme Grégorienne et la Réconquête Chrétienne*, p. 185.

[5] See especially H. Singer, "Die Dekretalensammlung des Bernardus Compostellanus Antiquus" in *SB d. kaiserl. Akad. d. Wiss.* (phil. hist. Cl.), vol. clxxi, ii, pp. 1 ff., and Professor Kuttner. "Bernardus Compostellanus Antiquus" in *Traditio*, vol. i (1943), pp. 277 f. This Bernardus, should not of course be confused with his younger namesake who was a chaplain of Innocent IV, see Johannes Andreae, *Additio in Speculum*, III De inquisitione, § 1, and Professor G. Barraclough in *EHR*, vol. xxxix (1934), pp. 487-94, *idem*, in *Dictionnaire de Droit Canonique*, vol. ii, pp. 777 f.

[6] He was made a cardinal in 1173, see Eubel, *Hierarchia Catholica*, tom. i, p. 8, and S. Kuttner, *Repertorium*, p. 268. Cf. also A. Theiner, *Disquisitiones criticae in ... collectiones*, 1836, pp. 401 ff.

[7] See F. Heyer, "Über Petrus Collivaccinus" in *Zeitschrift, kanon. Abt.*, vol. vi (1916), pp. 395 ff.

Spain, Melendus, at one time teacher of canon law at Bologna and later at Vicenza (about 1209), unequalled in his knowledge "in utroque jure";[1] Raymundus de Pennaforte—"in utroque jure peritissimus"[2]—the compiler of the Gregorian collection. We may further mention Goffredus de Trano who became famous for the first *Summa* written on Gregory's *Decretals;* Richardus de Senis, the vice-chancellor of the Roman curia, who was one of the redactors of the *Liber Sextus;*[3] Johannes Monachus, a creation of the unhappy Celestine V, who was the first glossator of his later master's collection, and at the same time an active, though not always blameless politician and intermediary; the subtle, though not prolific Zenzelinus de Cassanis. Petrus Bertrandi, another luminary in the ranks of famous cardinals, wrote a tract whose importance unfortunately has not so far received due recognition.[4]

But we would create an entirely false impression if the idea gained ground that all the canonists were ecclesiastics. It is of course true that the overwhelming majority belonged to the clerical fold, and yet there was an influential minority of lay-

---

[1] See *infra* p. 15.

[2] As Ptolomy of Lucca styled him, see *Mon. Germ. Hist., Scriptores*, n.s. vol. viii, "Die Annalen des Tholomeus von Lucca", ed. B. Schmeidler, p. 122.

[3] See the decree of promulgation by Boniface VIII, "Sacrosanctae"; cf. also Schulte, *Quellen*, vol. ii, p. 35. Richard was professor at Naples, cf. H. Denifle, *Die Universitäten des Mittelalters*, vol. i, p. 436, and E. M. Meijers, *Juris interpretes saeculi XIII*, pp. 217 ff. He received the cardinal's hat in 1298, see Eubel, *Hierarchia Cathol.*, tom. i, p. 13. See also H. Finke, *Aus den Tagen Bonifaz' VIII*, p. 106, note 1, where the initium of the Munich copy of Richard's *Casus Sexti Decretalium* is reproduced. He died, according to Eubel, *Hierarchia Catholica*, tom. i, p. 13, 10 February 1314, but according to Chevalier, 26 February 1313. The former date seems to be the correct one, as a copy of his last will dated 27 January 1314 proves, see Professor Kuttner, "Bernardus Compostellanus" in *Traditio*, vol. i, p. 334, note 10. Would it be possible that Richard glossed some decretals of Clement V? The *Apparatus* on the *Clementinae* in LC 151, fol. 21-67 verso (hitherto unknown) shows isolated glosses which bear the siglum "rica".

[4] Apart from those mentioned in the text, the following canonists were also cardinals: Pelagius (whose siglum "p" frequently occurs in the *Apparatus* on *Comp. I* (LB 105)), Berengarius, Guilelmus de Mandagoto, Gabriel Capodilista, Panormitanus, Johannes Turrecremata. The following were bishops: Melendus, Jacobus de Albenga, Vincentius, the Speculator (Guilelmus Durantis), Egidius Mandalbertus, Guido de Terrena, Petrus Boherius, etc., etc. The episcopal canonists increased rapidly towards the end of the fourteenth century. The canonists who were archdeacons, canons, presbyters, papal chaplains, and so forth, are too numerous to be counted.

men. That is not to say that they were surpassed by their clerical brethren in the attempt to exalt the pope's position; as regards their political views, they lagged in no way behind the ecclesiastics. The lay element was almost entirely absent in the twelfth century; it slowly emerged in the thirteenth century and was firmly established in the fourteenth, especially after it was possible to graduate in both the civil and canon laws. Egidius Fuscararius, Dynus de Muxellano and Martinus de Fano may be taken as outstanding lay examples of the thirteenth century, whilst the fourteenth century possessed lay canonists who became most influential. Johannes Andreae, commonly referred to as "the fount and trumpet of the canon law",[2] Petrus de Ancharano, Johannes de Lignano, Antonius de Butrio, Johannes ab Imola—these were only a few of the better known personalities: Caspar Calderinus was as fertile in the field of canonistic scholarship as in the family sphere: he was survived by not less than eleven children, whilst his elder namesake Johannes Calderinus was married three times.

With all deference one may be justified in advancing the opinion—assuredly not novel, though in constant need of repetition—that medieval history cannot be fully grasped, if the academic activity of popes and cardinals is not taken into account. These personages were first and foremost canonists. Can one wonder that the policy of these popes who shaped the destiny of the empire, nay of Europe itself, was merely the translation of their own canonist teachings into the world of practical politics? Can one wonder, we must furthermore ask, that the interpretation of the canonist later became the final and absolute word of the vicar of God (the "vicarius Dei") as the popes were wont to style themselves?[3] Indeed, the over-

---

[1] In order to honour the memory of this canonist (who died 1289) the Bolognese statute which forbade the wearing of scarlet robes at funerals of the doctors of canon law, was cancelled; until then scarlet robes were allowed only at funerals of the doctors of civil law, see Schulte, *Quellen*, vol. ii, p. 140.

[2] Or, as a contemporary chronicler called him when lamenting his untimely death during the plague: "egregius doctor juris canonici", "Die Chronik Heinrichs Taube von Selbach" in *Mon. Germ. Hist.*, *Scriptores*, ed. H. Bresslau, n.s., vol. i, p. 59.

[3] A. Harnack, "Christus praesens—Vicarius Christi" in *SB d. preussischen Akademie d. Wissenschaften*, vol. xxxiv (1927), pp. 415-46, shows that in early medieval times this appellation was used for kings (at pp. 438-41). On the *rex-sacerdos* conception of the king especially under the Ottonians, in fact down to

whelming majority of canons embodied in the great collections came from the pen of popes who were fully-fledged canonists. Any attempt to understand medieval history without registering the theories of the canonists and of canon law itself, is doomed to be fruitless. It would be no less futile than trying to understand the French revolution without first probing its literary sources or trying to comprehend the policy of recent dictatorial régimes without a prior investigation of their ideological basis. Even at the risk of being tedious one must emphasize that the issue of empire versus papacy was a legal contest: the whole quarrel was fought in the arena of the law. When we speak of a medieval lawyer we should not compare the modern lawyer with his medieval ancestor. The terms law and lawyer comprised then a far larger field than they do now: law was a collective name for those branches of scholarship now rather loosely termed social sciences. And political science was wholly indistinguishable from legal science: politics and law were interchangeable terms in medieval days. Empire versus papacy was a constitutional quarrel: the canonists forged the weapons for the papacy, the legists or civilians for the empire. To expose the fundamental ideas underlying this contest was the business of the canonists (or legists), and our understanding of medieval history should benefit from an inquiry into these sources.

For the reconstruction of the canonistic political views—the very background and source of papal politics—cannot fail to provide a contribution to the history of diplomacy in the international government of Western Europe. If by history of diplomacy is understood an account, not only of the progress of international intercourse, but also—and this seems perhaps still more important and pertinent—the exposition of the motives and ideas underlying international actions, a reconstruction of canonistic political theory must appear an indispensable requirement to him who is anxious to understand the often complicated and sometimes apparently meaningless sequence of events. The examination of the genesis of papal political activity is bound to lead us into the canonistic camp; and in particular to the canon law books. A good deal of what nowadays constitutes the subject-matter in the so-called coloured

---

Henry II (1024), see G. Barraclough, *The Origins of Modern Germany*, 2nd ed., p. 33: "Whereas the bishops were merely the representatives of Christ, the king was the vicar of God the Father himself."

books, the blue, red, white, yellow books, issued by the various Foreign Offices, is contained in the medieval canon law collections. Would a serious study of nineteenth and twentieth centuries diplomatic and international relations be thought feasible without consulting government publications, including correspondence made accessible in the archives? The answer to the medieval counterpart suggests itself. Moreover, especially in regard to England, the recipients of papal bulls, letters, decrees, etc., were more often than not personages high up in the departments of Church and State. A mere glance at the Gregorian[1] collection will confirm the scope and quantity of diplomatic activity displayed by the medieval popes towards this country.

Although in the contest between Boniface VIII and Philip IV the protagonists appeared to be the publicists, the canonists had forged the weapons with which they fought. Beneath all the publicistic literature of the age one can clearly discern the canonistic groundwork and thought pattern. Moreover, it was they, and not the publicists, who, in cases of real importance, were made the spokesmen of curial policy, since the curial antagonists were all drawn from the legistic camp. Here the publicist stood little chance of a victory in a fight against the keen and sharp-edged arguments of the civilian. When, for once in a way, the contest between temporal and spiritual power was taken to the conference table, the pleas on either side were made by jurists, the canonist on the one hand, the legist on the other. Perhaps the best example is provided by the French equivalent of the Parliament of Merton (1236), that is, the assembly at Vincennes (1329), where the constitutional issue was to be thrashed out in the manner of a round-table conference. Our modern historians of political thought devote far too little attention to this momentous, though abortive, conference of which the whole proceedings are fully recorded. This council serves to illustrate my point that the canonist took the field, if the case was of sufficient importance.[2]

[1] Cf. the late Z. N. Brooke, "The effects of Becket's murder on papal authority in England", in *Cambridge Historical Journal*, vol. ii, pp. 213-228; idem, *The English Church and the Papacy*, pp. 213-14; P. and M., vol. i, pp. 115-16; cf. also the observations of A. Morey, *Bartholomew of Exeter*, pp. 76-7.

[2] Another case occurred in 1338 when Lewis of Bavaria summoned "legistas et canonistas valentissimos" to decide on the legitimacy of the pope's steps, see "Die Chronik Johanns von Winterthur" in *Mon. Germ. Hist.*, ed.

The medieval canonist was a jurist, politician, and statesman all in one. Moreover, the medieval history of this island provides frequent instances of conflicts between the temporal and spiritual powers. The men behind the visible stage were jurists,[1] and not the verbose personalities who made their entry into our current text books. The chancellors of medieval England were thoroughly trained in canon law, whilst the study of Roman law became of secondary importance. In fact, unlike canon law, Roman law, as such, was never wholly adopted in these lands. There is no gainsaying the fact that much of medieval English history would benefit if the canonistic background of these conflicts was given due recognition. But apart from these, there was much collaboration between ecclesiastical and secular officials, especially in the numerous thirteenth-century State councils and later parliaments. Both sides did a considerable amount of unacknowledged borrowing. The frequent meetings of high ecclesiastics with their temporal counterparts lent themselves so easily to fruitful exchanges of ideas. It is a mistake to assume that canon law and canonistic training were all kept in watertight compartments when bishops met their temporal counterparts. The concomitant intermixture of canonistic and civilian ideas was bound to show itself in legislation as well as in the development of the English constitution.[2]

Henry VIII is said to have initiated a new era in the history of England, but it is strangely forgotten that it was another Englishman who some three hundred years before Henry's time inaugurated the very ideas of papal supremacy against which Henry revolted. The English canonist Alanus was to a considerable extent responsible for the establishment of those political views which later found such pronounced expression in Innocent IV, Hostiensis, and the Archdeacon; one may say that the extreme ideas of papal plenitude of power in both the

---

F. Baethgen, n.s., vol. iii, pp. 157-58. Cf. also the remarks of Sir M. Powicke, "Reflections on the Medieval State" in *Transactions of the R. Hist. S.*, fourth series, vol. xix, p. 6.

[1] See now also Professor G. O. Sayles, *The Medieval Foundations of England*, pp. 456, 458.

[2] See Professor C. R. Cheney, *English Synodalia of the Thirteenth Century* pp. 144-45, and the remarks in S. E. Thorne's review in *Traditio*, vol. i, p. 418. See also *infra*, pp. 20 ff. and notes.

temporal and the spiritual field were the direct result of the English Alanus's teachings. It is indeed a remarkable coincidence, we may remark in parenthesis, that in the secular as well as in the clerical sphere two Englishmen were the chief sources of European thought: John of Salisbury, through the medium of a Neapolitan scholar, profoundly influenced sixteenth century political thought:[1] Alanus, through his glosses, shaped the ideas of curial politicians. It may suffice to say that the theory of political omnipotence of the pope as Boniface VIII propounded it in *Unam sanctam*, was to all extents and purposes set forth by Alanus in a gloss on a decretal.[2]

Of course, I do not wish to convey the impression that Alanus was the only great English canonist: a score of others are worthy to be ranked with him, such as the famous Richardus Anglicus (Richard de Lacy), one of the most celebrated masters of Bologna; Gilbertus; Johannes Galensis; Honorius whose pupil was Thomas of Marlborough and who[3] invoked Innocent III's help in his struggle for the archdeaconry of Richmond, the phases of which struggle are so vividly depicted by Roger Hoveden;[4] Thomas of Marlborough himself, who was a teacher of canon law at Oxford and a former pupil of Stephen Langton;[5] David of London;[6] and last, but not least, William of Drogheda.

---

[1] To the influence of John of Salisbury, outlined in "The influence of John of Salisbury" in *EHR*, 1944, pp. 384–92 should also be added: Alvarus Pelagius, *Speculum Regum* which referred to John's *Policraticus* extensively, see the historically important sections as transcribed by R. Scholz, *Unbekannte kirchenpolitische Streitschriften aus der Zeit Ludwigs des Bayern*, vol. ii, pp. 514-29. This tract of Alvarus was written between 1341 and 1344. For the source of another possible English influence see Appendix H.

[2] See *infra* ch. VI. That many English students flocked to the Italian law schools, especially during the thirteenth century is well known. Even as late as the second half of the fifteenth century we find a considerable number of English students studying at Italian schools, for Padua see J. R. Mitchell, in *Transactions of the R. Hist. S.*, fourth series vol xix, pp. 101-17. The number of doctorates taken in canon law is quite remarkable, see p. 117.

[3] See Thomas of Marlborough in *Chronicon Abbat. Evesham*, p. 126.

[4] See Roger Hoveden, *Chronica*, vol. iii, p. 298, vol. iv, pp. 9, 52, 158, 159, 177. Cf. also A. Hamilton Thompson, "The Registers of the Archdeaconry of Richmond" in *Yorkshire Archaeological Journal*, vol. xxv, pp. 131–5, and *Early Yorkshire Charters*, ed. Clay, vol. iv, pp. xxv–xxvi; see *Decretales*, III, vii. 6, viii. 7.

[5] Thomas, op. cit., p. 126, see also p. xxi note.

[6] See Z. N. Brooke, "The Register of David of London" in *Essays in History presented to R. L. Poole*, pp. 227-45, correcting the unfavourable opinion of Stubbs on David. Part of the MS. examined by Brooke is also examined by R. Poupardin,

Nor in this context should I fail to mention the English founder of the University of Vicenza, that is, Magister Robertus Anglicus, one of the leaders of the scholars migrating from Bologna,[1] and the occupant of the bishopric of Coventry, Gérard Pucelle, a former Parisian doctor and teacher of canon law.[2] Men of action rather than retiring scholars were canonists like Laurence of Somercote, the author of a practical and useful treatise on canonical elections,[3] Walter Suffield and

---

"Dix-huit lettres inédites d'Arnoul de Lisieux" in *Bibliothèque de l'Ecole des Chartes*, vol. lxiii (1902), pp. 352-73 where the two letters of Arnulf are printed, see also *The Letters of Arnulf of Lisieux* (Camden, third ser., vol. lxi, ed. F. Barlow), pp. 124-25. Master David is several times mentioned or referred to in the *Summa "Permissio Quaedam"* (Distinctiones Halenses), see Schulte, "Dritter Beitrag zur Geschichte der Literatur über das Dekret Gratians" in *SB d. kaiserl. Akad. d. Wiss.*, vol. lxv, pp. 64, 66, 72; on the *Summa* itself, see Kuttner, op. cit., pp. 192-94.

[1] See F. v. Savigny, *Geschichte*, etc., vol. iii, p. 307, note a, Rashdall, *The Universities of Europe in the Middle Ages*, ed. F. M. Powicke and A. B. Emden, vol. ii, p. 7; Mittarelli, *Annales Camaldunenses*, vol. iv, p. 213 and appendix pp. 260-63; Sarti, *De claris archigymnasii Bononiensis professoribus*, vol. ii, p. 287. Professor Kuttner holds that this Magister Robertus was a Magister Rodulphus Anglicus, see art. cit., p. 326, note 32. But in the above-mentioned annals of the Camaldunensian monks he was always referred to as "Magister Robertus de Anglia". This Robertus does not seem to be identical with the one mentioned by J. C. Russel, *Dictionary of Writers of thirteenth century England*, p. 129. Is there any identity between this Robert and the Robert de Clipstone mentioned by Thomas of Marlborough, *Chronicon Abbatiae de Evesham*, p. 151? Robertus de Clipstone was counsel for the Bishop of Worcester and although he was "facundissimus in utroque jure, civili videlicet et canonico" he nevertheless did not know the "modum curiae" when he opened his plea, "with a long speech and equally long and involved sentences", whereupon Innocent III cut him short with a forbidding: "Nolumus tantum proemium; ad ea, quae res desiderat, accede," ibid., p. 152. There does not seem to be any identity between the Robertus Anglicus and the one mentioned in the Bolognese necrology as having died in 1254, see A. Allaria, "English scholars at Bologna during the Middle Ages" in *Dublin Review*, vol. cxii, p. 78.

[2] See R. Saltet, *Les réordinations*, p. 355, J. de Ghellinck, *Le mouvement théologique du XIIème siècle*, p. 224; cf. also Schulte, "Die Summa Decreti Lipsiensis" in *SB d. kais. Ak. d. Wiss.*, vol. lxvi, p. 53, and Kuttner, *Repertorium*, p. 26. The communications of Alexander III to Magister Gerardus Pucella are in Denifle, *Chartularium Universitatis Parisiensis*, tom. i, p. 9, Nos. 10 and 11. Gérard died as Bishop of Coventry in 1184. According to Dom A. Morey, *Bartholomew of Exeter*, p. 53, he was Bishop of Lichfield.

[3] Written in 1254, see M. Gibbs and J. Lang, *Bishops and Reform, 1215-1272*, pp. 63 ff, where Miss Gibbs gives a helpful summary of the tract, supplemented by extracts from William de Mandegot's tract of the same title: MS. (hitherto unnoticed) in LC 151, fols. 1-20 (and not, as the catalogue has, to fol. 77).

Richard Wych.¹ And I do not hesitate to prophesy that a systematic investigation of the treasures in cathedral and college libraries, would bring to light a number of canonists hitherto totally forgotten.² This would perhaps go far towards meeting Maitland's complaint that "the schools of canon law at Oxford and Cambridge were singularly unproductive of anything that could be called original work",³ although Maitland would have been ably supported by Innocent III whose testimony we should not omit.⁴ During the famous trial between the bishop of Worcester and the abbey of Evesham, the pope himself was the presiding judge. After listening to the legal quibbles of the bishop's counsel who declared "My lord, we have been taught in our schools, and it is also the opinion of our masters that there is no prescription against episcopal rights", the pope remarked dryly: "Indeed, you and your masters had drunk too much of the English beer when you were taught this."⁵

A feature that is so typical of canonistic scholarship is its truly international character. Nearly every great civilized European nation contributed some outstanding figure. The Italians, for understandable reasons, were in the forefront: this was not only conditioned by the geographical position of the seat of the papacy, but also by that of the seats of learning. Though numerically far behind the Italians, the English nation contributed to canonistic scholarship to a degree quite disproportionate to its strength. There is hardly a tract, a

---

¹ See Gibbs and Lang, op. cit., p. 195; many other practical canonists, pp. 185 ff. Peter Quesvel and Simon de Boraston were theologians rather than canonists, cf. Schulte, *Quellen*, vol. ii, pp. 262, 237.

² One such product of the English school was the work *Quaestiones Londinenses*, Brit. Mus., Royal 9 E VII, fol. 191 to 198 verso, cf. Kuttner, *Repertorium*, p. 251. About the time of its composition and about the unidentifiable authors mentioned therein (Magister Simon or Symon, jo. de t., jct., Nicholas) see Appendix. The B.M. Codex Royal 9 E VIII contains the lectures of a considerable number of English canonists of the late fourteenth century.

³ Maitland, op. cit., pp. 97-98.

⁴ Maitland himself referred to it, see P. and M., vol. i, p. 116, although in a different context.

⁵ Thomas of Marlborough in his report of the proceedings, *Chron. Abb. Evesham*, (R.S.), p. 189: "Adversarius: 'Pater sancte, nos didicimus in scholis, et haec est opinio magistrorum nostrorum, quod non currit praescriptio contra jura episcopalia'. Et dominus papa: 'Certe et tu et magistri tui multum bibistis de cerevisia Anglicana, quando haec didicistis'." The whole of the proceedings makes delightful reading. Innocent III does not seem to have been without a good sense of humour, see pp. 153, 160.

commentary, or a gloss written in the thirteenth and fourteenth centuries that does not somewhere contain the names of Alanus or Richardus. But Alanus gained his reputation not only on account of his doctrines, but also as the compiler of a collection of decretals,[1] which, together with the collection of his fellow-countryman, Gilbertus,[2] formed the basis of the so-called *Compilatio Secunda*, composed by the Welshman, Johannes Galensis.[3] The Germans were worthily represented by a most remarkable man, Johannes Teutonicus (whose real name was Zemeke), who wrote not only the *glossa ordinaria* on Gratian's *Decretum*, but also glosses on the *Compilatio Tertia* and the *Apparatus* on the *Compilatio Quarta*, of which he himself was the author;[4] he also glossed the Constitutions of the Fourth Lateran Council. Hence, the three great civilized nations played their part in the making of the Gregorian collection (1234): the Italians contributed to the *Compilatio Prima* through Bernardus Papiensis, the English and Welsh to the *Secunda*, the Germans to the *Quarta*.[5] The Spaniards, too, sent

---

[1] Probably written in 1208, see J. F. v. Schulte, "Die Compilationen Gilberts und Alanus" in *SB d. kais. Akad. d. Wiss.*, vol. lxv, p. 619. Kuttner, art. cit., p. 289, note 52, says that it was published in 1206.

[2] Written between 1202 and 1204, see Schulte, loc. cit., p. 613. A MS. copy is in LB 105, fol. 220 verso—fol. 267 verso. Other copies (which I have not seen) are in Durham, C. III. 3, and BM, Harl. 3834, according to Kuttner, op. cit., p. 311.

[3] Although it was published after Innocent's *Compilatio Tertia* (1210) it still kept the name of "secunda" for chronological reasons: almost all the decretals belonged to the time before Innocent III, except seven (see A. Friedberg, *Quinque Compilationes Antiquae*, p. xxvii) some of which may be spurious, see Kuttner, op. cit., p. 345, note 1. There were numerous collections of decretals in England before the *Compilatio Prima*, that is to say, before 1192, see E. Seckel, "Ueber drei Canones-Sammlungen des ausgehenden 12. Jahrhunderts in englischen Handschriften" in *Neues Archiv d. Gesellschaft f. ältere deutsche Geschichtskunde*, vol. xxv (1900), pp. 521-37, and before him, K. Hampe, ibid., vol. xxii, pp. 387 ff., S. Kuttner, op. cit., pp. 23, 291, 294-95, 297, 298-99, and art. cit., p. 285, note 30. A collection of decretals preceding the *Comp. I* is in T R.9.17, fols. 72-129 verso (*Collectio Cantabrigiensis*). A collection of later date is the *Collectio Lambethana*, containing decretals of Clement III, Alexander III and Innocent III, LB 105, fols. 214-18.

[4] Composed between 1216 and 1218. On the authorship see H. Kantorowicz, "Das Principium des Johannes de Deo" in *Zeitschrift, kanon. Abt.*, vol. xii, p. 434. But see now Kuttner in *Miscellanea Mercati*, 1946, vol. v, p. 627.

[5] It has not yet been established who the author of the *Quinta* was, for a conspectus of opinion, see Kuttner, op. cit., p. 382, and *Misc. Mercati*, p. 633.

to the schools distinguished canonists, such as the two Bernardus Compostellanus, Laurentius, Vincentius, Johannes de Deo, Garsias, Alvarus, and a score of others, some of whom will evoke our interest. One of them, Melendus, seems to have been specially sought after by contemporary English personalities. He was not only the advocate selected by the bishop of Winchester for John when the important Canterbury election was pending in Rome (1205), but he was also counsel for Thomas of Marlborough in his quarrel with the Bishop of Worcester.[1] Rufinus, Stephen of Tournay,[2] Durandus,[3] Johannes Monachus[4] Petrus Bertrandi,[5] and many more[6] were of French origin. Even the Hungarians were represented, by Paulus Hungarus and Damasus, and the Bohemians by Petrus Boemus.[7] Held together as they were by a common bond and literally constituting a "world" of learning, this cosmo-

---

[1] Thomas's unmistakably great satisfaction at having obtained the Spaniard's services emerges plainly from his report, *Chron. Abb. Evesham*, pp. 152-53. At great length he paraded his legal advisers and said that he and his adversary had each four counsel, but "I have the better ones". He had selected them "from all parts of the world": Magister Melendus who is "second to no mortal in both laws"; as his civilian counsel he employed a certain Bertrandus "who is second only to Azo" (the monks of Canterbury had Bertrandus as their counsel in Rome); his third counsel was the later compiler of Innocent's collection, Petrus Beneventanus "who was held the first amongst curial counsellors"; and lastly Master William, a curialist in the service of the Roman chancellor. This was certainly a quite respectable collection of advisers, and the expenses were equally respectable. Melendus received 50 shillings for every day of the proceedings, Petrus and Bertrandus each 40 shillings, and the chancellor's servant only 20 p.d. When Thomas heard the favourable verdict on 24 December 1205, he fainted in court.

[2] About him see J. Warichez, *Etienne de Tournai et son temps*, and Kuttner, op. cit., pp. 12, 18, 133.

[3] For his attitude towards Thomism, see *infra* p. 86.

[4] About his political activities, see F. Lajard, *Histoire littéraire de la France*, vol. xxvii, pp. 201-24, also Hefele-Leclercq, *Histoire des Conciles*, vol vi, part i, pp. 431-34, and H. Finke, *Aus den Tagen Bonifaz' VIII*, pp. 177 ff. and O. Martin, *L'Assemblée de Vincennes de 1329 et ses consequences*, p. 125, note 3. On some of his canonistic opinions, see also *The Origins of the Great Schism*, pp. 204-7.

[5] See *infra* p. 85 n.4.

[6] Petrus de Sampsone, Guilelmus de Mandagoto (who took part in the compilation of the *Sextus*), Guilelmus de Monte Lauduno, Zenzelinus de Cassanis, and so forth.

[7] He was, however, quite unknown, see Kantorowicz, "Damasus" in *Zeitschrift, Kanon. Abt.*, vol. xvi, p. 339. Others who were known, were: Bohuslav of Prag, Laurentius de Polonia, and Stephanus Polonus, see Johannes Andreae, on *Sextus*, II.ii.14, and Schulte, *Quellen*, vol. ii, p. 170. The *Margarita Decreti* of Martinus Polonus are preserved in the B.M. MS. Royal 9 F I.

politan array of canonists stood far above national animosities.¹

The growth of canonistic doctrine may well be likened to an avalanche initiated by an insignificant snowball. And in the end popes, canonists and papalists found themselves caught in their own entanglements. When Alexander III issued a decree, canonistic interpretative skill exercised itself shortly in its explanation. The interpretation and the decree formed one inseparable whole which had to be taken as such by any lecturer on canon law, as was demanded by the statutes of medieval universities. The devoted pupil imbibed the teachings of his masters—and having become one of the canonistic guild himself he was only too eager to follow up and outdo his dominus by giving rein to his speculative imagination. The tendency continually to extend the pope's power is clearly noticeable in all canonists, especially those of the thirteenth and fourteenth centuries. And cardinals and popes emerged from their ranks—the latter appearing as God's vicars on earth. Surely one would not expect the decrees of these popes to differ fundamentally from their own canonistic teachings? The period which elapsed between the reign of Alexander III and that of Boniface VIII was the age of the canonists, and the difference between these two popes is measurable by the influence of the canonists. Papacy and scholarship complemented each other; though both starting from a different standpoint, both worked for the same end. This circulatory process—from the canonist to the pope and back to the canonist—is a feature that is of the utmost importance for the formation of canonistic political thought.² The continual encouragement, permanent incentive and logical insistence on the part of the canonists should be adequately assessed in any appropriate appraisal of medieval papal policy and influence. Indeed, the excessive glorification of the papal office at this period, both by the people and by the popes themselves, is an effect of canonistic doctrine. The pope as the vicar of God commanded the world, as if it were a tool in his

---

[1] The dissemination of canonistic doctrine was much furthered by the facility with which the professors changed the places of their academic activities. The following taught at two universities: Johannes Hispanus, Martinus Fanensis, Egidius Mandalbertus, Johannes Andreae, Bonincontrus, Paulus de Liazariis, etc., etc.; at three universities, Roffredus, Dynus Galvanus, Antonius de Rosellis, etc.; at four universities: Petrus Bertrandi, Antonius de Butrio, Alexander Tartagnus, Philippus Decius, etc., Baldus taught at six universities.

[2] This process is well described by F. Thaner, *Summa Rolandi*, preface, p. iv.

hands: the pope, supported by the canonists, considered the world as his property to be disposed of according to his own will.

In this context it appears advisable to say a word about the publicists. Although the views of the publicists gained considerable respect in our own day through the researches of Riezler, Finke, Scholz, Rivière, and McIlwain, their importance for the development and growth of papal power should not be overestimated. To begin with, we can see the emergence of the publicist literature only towards the end of the thirteenth century, that is to say, at a time when papal power was already firmly entrenched as a direct result of canonistic doctrine. Secondly, the publicists, though desirous to surpass the canonists in attributing still higher powers to the pope, relied on the canon law only to a negligible extent. We may take Egidius Romanus' tract *De Ecclesiastica Potestate* as a concrete example: in spite of its inordinate length references are only made to seven passages from the first part of the *Decretum*, and none to the second and longer part; only nine passages from the *Decretales* are quoted. And Egidius Romanus was a publicist whose thorough knowledge of canon law was beyond doubt. Others, like Henry of Cremona or James of Viterbo, referred to canon law no oftener than Egidius. Now the scanty reliance which the publicists placed on canon law (and the canonists) made them of course far less palatable to the curia and to the expounders of canon law. Apart from their emergence at a time when the ideological foundations of the all-embracing papal power were already laid, when, therefore, the publicists were able to come into the open and to sow the fertile ground freshly ploughed up by the canonists, their doctrines commanded comparatively little respect at a time that was soaked in legalism: the saying "nemo clericus nisi causidicus" epitomizes the trend of the age. The emperor based his powers on the law—and the power of the pope must have foundations of equal security. The law was surrounded with a halo of sanctity, whether imperialist or ecclesiastical, and not to have based papal power on the law would have been a most serious drawback. The publicists did not rely on the law, and therefore had far less influence than the canonists. It was all very well to derive the plentitude of papal power from extra-legal sources, mainly from "articles of faith" and other speculations, but all these taken together could not possibly command the same respect as one decretal of an Innocent III or one saying of an Hostiensis commanded. We do not wish to minimize the crafty efforts of the publicists, but their reputation should be seen in its proper perspective: they were, so to speak, a second echelon in the defence of papal claims: the front line was formed by the spearheads of Alanus, Tancred, Laurentius, Innocent IV, Hostiensis, the Archdeacon, and so forth. It is only too plain why neither the canonists nor the papalists amongst the legists nor the fiercest papal antagonists amongst the latter referred to the publicists. This, incidentally, may be a fitting occasion to remark, how frequently the emphasis is wrongly placed in contemporary political thought, according to the accessibility of modern editions of publicist tracts. Contemporaries, like Dante, quite correctly saw in the canonists, and not in the publicists, the ideological framers of the papalist system of government: the former, and not the latter, were made the target of imperialist attacks.[1]

The difficulties of the canonistic interpreter lay not so much in the inflexibility of the law that, as we shall see, purported to be the divine ordinance not only for spiritual exigencies, but also for the temporal affairs of Christians: the difficulties besetting the canonist lay rather in the irreconcilability of many of its own utterances, particularly in the *Decretum*. Nor is it difficult to explain the many contradictory passages in the *Decretum* which was, as its proper title *Concordia*[2] *discordantium canonum* suggests, intended by its author to be a concordance but never could be so: the letters, decrees, utterances of the Fathers of the Church, philosophers, popes, general councils, and so forth, were issued at times which bore little resemblance to the thirteenth and fourteenth centuries; moreover, in one and the

[1] cf. Dante, *Monarchia*, lib. III, cap. 3. See also *Paradiso*, canto IX, 133-136.

[2] And not "concordantia", see R. Köstler, "Zum Titel des Gratianischen Decrets" in *Zeitschrift, Kanon. Abt.*, vol. xxi, p. 370, and, following Köstler, Professor le Bras, "Les Écritures dans le Decret de Gratien", ibid., vol. xxvii, p. 47, note 2. The term "concordantia" belonged to the thirteenth century. Köstler maintains that it was coined in connexion with the Bible concordances, but it seems that it was also used, at least as far as England was concerned, for descriptions of other items, so, for instance, in the Stowe MS. 930 (BM), fol. 54-54 verso: "concordantia controversiarum inter regem et clerum". This MS. deals with the agenda discussed between Henry III and the bishops and archbishops in 1253, cf. Matthew Paris, *Chronica Majora*, vol. v, pp. 359-60, and *Annales Monastici* (Burton), vol. i, p. 305.

same *distinctio* we find a passage of, say, St. Augustine, immediately followed by a letter of a pope in the tenth century, issued upon an entirely different occasion. An attempt was made to overcome this incongruity by what we may style *Canonesharmonistik* which met with as little success as its modern counterpart, the *Pandectenharmonistik*. But the many divergences and inconsistencies gave an added stimulus to canonistic research which was, in many respects, livelier, more enthusiastic, more forceful, and also more aggressive than its legistic counterpart. Besides, the emergence of moderate and extreme parties amongst the canonists is directly attributable to the adherence to the more moderate or more extreme passages.

In attempting to show the importance of canon law and its study we must furthermore point to the authority with which canon law was invested. True, Roman law had the dignity of the imperial crown which reposed upon the laurels of the tradition and the glory that was Rome. But canon law, though younger and less voluminous, was in a sense more mature and of surpassing dignity. It was more mature because the canons were more easily adaptable to the conditions of the later Middle Ages than the many laws in Justinian's codification, some of which were incomprehensible to the civilians, as conditions in a feudal society were totally different from those prevalent in the second and third century A.D. Thirteenth and fourteenth-centuries Christianity was alleged to be essentially the same as Christianity of the second and third century. For this reason, then, the applicability of canon law to concrete cases met with fewer difficulties than that of Roman law. That the dignity and authority of canon law was infinitely greater than that of Roman law, is not difficult to perceive: the latter on its own admission, confined itself to the human and temporal aspect of social relations; the former was an ordinance that was primarily, though by no means exclusively, focused on the spiritual aspects of the individuals and his relations with his fellow creatures. Thus, the one deals with the earthly, the other with the divine. Who, then, can doubt the immense force and authority that medieval men attributed to canon law? That, in the eyes of the canonists, Roman law sank to the position of a merely secondary source of law, cannot cause surprise. Nor can it be wondered at that even the fiercest anti-papalists and staunchest imperialists amongst the civilians considered canon law as a worthy equal of Roman law, and never went so far as to declare the former a mere auxiliary source of legal knowledge and wisdom. Roman law was only able to appeal to a glorious past and could kindle no emotional enthusiasm; canon law was able to appeal, not to a dead past, but to a present and future life—to the *ecclesia triumphans* for which the *ecclesia militans* was supposed to be but a necessary preparation;[1] besides, the continuity of the rulers of the Church was preserved from the days of its Founder—a rather sore point with the empire that went East, then West, was "translated" to the Franks, and finally to the Germans who indeed cannot be said to have had much in common with imperial Rome. And was not the very translation of the empire alleged to have been effected by the pope? For this reason alone, if for no other, the empire ought to have been indebted to the papacy. Whenever driven into a corner, this was the last weapon in the legal armoury of the canonists—a legal weapon indeed, as the *translatio imperii* was dutifully incorporated in canon law.

The role should on no account be forgotten which canon law and above all canonistic scholarship played in the making of the constitution of these islands. In this respect the influence, though not so conspicuous as elsewhere, is nevertheless marked and real. It is especially in the field of representation in the late thirteenth-century England that we may detect the working of principles which were thoroughly canonical and through which canonistic thought penetrated deeply into the character and structure of the medieval English constitution. As a rule, the royal writ of summons to parliament stipulated that communities should despatch representatives with "full power" to consent to the ordinances of the king in court and council. Now, this "full power" with which the knights and burgesses were invested, was nothing but the canonical "plena potestas": this concept had been fully tried, elaborated, developed and applied by the canonists. The great canonist-pope Innocent III himself had acted upon this principle in his convocation of the Fourth Lateran Council in 1215.[2] The numerous provincial synods afterwards eloquently testify to the general acceptance

---

[1] The "ecclesia militans" was to be modelled on the "ecclesia triumphans". This idea was usually derived from Dionysius, *De coelesti hierarchia*.

[2] See Hefele-Leclercq, *Histoire des Conciles*, vol. v/2, pp. 1316-18, and Mansi, cols. 961-62. See also G. Post in *Speculum*, vol. xviii (1943), p. 229.

of this principle.¹ The contribution which this idea made to the constitutional structure of the English parliament should not be underestimated. The canonical concept of full power, however, is only one of the sources from which an important English constitutional principle is evolved.²

The other and complementary concept was "quod omnes tangit, ab omnibus approbetur", which also had been a stock phrase and a fundamental tenet in canon law and canonistic doctrine. The general principle was that wherever a matter of faith was disputed, laymen as well as clerics were to be consulted. "Ubi de causa fidei agitur, tam laici quam clerici debent interesse."³ But it was especially in the requirement for valid canonical elections and for representative assemblies that we meet the most subtle disquisitions.⁴ And, surely, if we

---

[1] For many examples, see Sir E. Barker, *The Dominican Order and Convocation*, pp. 32-36; the synod of Bourges furnishes a particularly good example, pp. 42-53 and *passim*. Speaking of the council summoned by Stephen Langton in 1226, Sir Maurice Powicke very pungently remarks: "If the principle of representation had become ... one of the marks of a united and universal Church, history might indeed have been changed," *Stephen Langton*, p. 159.

[2] See especially J. G. Edwards, "The Plena Potestas of English Parliamentary Representation" in *Oxford Essays in Medieval History presented to H. E. Salter*, pp. 141-54; above all, Gaines Post, "Plena Potestas and Consent in medieval assemblies" in *Traditio*, vol. i, pp. 355-408, with a wealth of material from the legists and canonists, especially at pp. 356-66, 386-94. For the Edwardian times cf. also R. S. Hoyt, "Royal Demesne, Parliamentary Taxation and the Realm" in *Speculum*, vol. xxiii (1948), pp. 58-69.

[3] Richardus Anglicus (Richard de Lacy) in his *Apparatus* on *Comp. I*, De haereticis, c. ad abolendam, s.v. "consilio", vol. 71 verso of W 122. The passage in LB 105, fol. 203 decr. cit., is in literal agreement and seems to belong to the second layer of glosses; on this *Apparatus* see Appendix.

[4] Since it is outside the scope of this enquiry, we can but briefly mention the theory of the early canonists. As far as I can see, the Alexandrian decretal "Si archiepiscopus" in De electione et electi potestate (*Compil. I*, c. 9) provoked enquiries relating to this topic. The first seems to have come from the compiler himself, Bernardus Papiensis. In his *Summa Decretalium* he said: "In his, quae a capitulo fieri vel ordinari debent, omnium consensus est requirendus, ut quod omnes tangit, ab omnibus comprobatur," quoted by Post in his most illuminating article "A Romano-Canonical Maxim 'Quod Omnes Tangit' in Bracton", in *Traditio*, vol iv (1946), p. 203. In a gloss which appears in the *Apparatus* of Richard de Lacy, (fol. 2 verso of W 122) Bernardus merely said that it would be "inhonestum", if the decision of a body were to be carried out when those whom it primarily concerned, had not approved of it. In a gloss which may be attributed to Richard and which is contained in the *Apparatus* on the *Comp. I*, De elect., c. si archiespisc. (c. 9), fol. 138 verso of LB 105 (about this

do not deliberately ignore the intellectual climate in which institutions grow and mature, it is no matter of surprise if we find this canonical maxim transformed into a constitutional principle in medieval England. This principle "was in the legal atmosphere and quite naturally it slipped into the style of the

---

MS. see Appendix) we read: "Honestum est omnes adesse, quos res tangit." Here fifteen specific cases are enumerated in which "consensus omnium" is required. When Richard composed his *Apparatus* on *Comp. I* (between 1193-1198) he also appended a whole series of cases and passages in which the principle of "quod omnes tangit" was legislatively laid down, fol. 2 verso of W 122.

This Alexandrian decretal was also glossed by Alanus, and this gloss came into the *Apparatus* of Tancred. Alanus, s.v. "ab omnibus" (*Compil. I*, fol. 4 of D 4) quoted the Roman passages and made the following distinction: a decision affecting individuals who in their aggregate failed to constitute "unum corpus" had to be approved by all: ". . . in pluribus vel privatis, qui non faciunt corpus unum, omnes tunc consentire, etiam usque ad ultimum debent, alias nihil agitur"; in making a decision affecting individuals who formed one corporate body, the majority principle was to prevail. Alanus vaguely touched on "cases of necessity" in which all the members had to accept the decision of the "sanior pars". This suggestion was taken up by Vincentius in his gloss on cap. cum omnes, tit. De electione, as embodied in Tancred's *Apparatus* (*Comp. III*, fol. 95 of D 4), s.v. "extremos". The Spaniard, glossing the collection shortly after its publication (1210), elaborated Alanus's view: a majority was sufficient if the "collegium" had to transact business "ex necessitate", as, for instance, in the case of elections (here then the "major pars" took the place of "omnes"); "in aliis, quae ex necessitate non geruntur, puta cum dividitur praebenda, nihil valet, nisi omnes consentiant". It surely is not difficult to see some connexion between prebends and taxes (art. 12 of Magna Carta) since both affect the income. The ground was well prepared by the time when Innocent III issued the forty-sixth Constitution in the Fourth Lateran Council which decree "encouraged the development of the system of representation by linking taxation with consent," Gibbs and Lang, op. cit., p. 98. In this context it is quite interesting to look at the reply which the legate of Innocent III, Nicholas, received from the bishops of Winchester, Lincoln and Hereford. During the negotiations of 1213 Nicholas conveyed to them a proposal of John, and the legate's report was as follows: "Quod cum proposui predictis episcopis responderunt, quod inde mihi respondere non poterant sine consensu et consilio aliorum, quod predictum negotium contingebat," see the report as transcribed by Cardinal Mercati, "La prima relazione del Cardinale Nicolo de Romanis sulla sua legazione in Inghilterra" in *Essays in History presented to R. L. Poole*, p. 286, cf. also p. 279. For another instance in the middle of the century, see Sir Maurice Powicke, *King Henry III and the Lord Edward*, vol. i, p. 360.

To these quotations we may add Innocent III's statement in a decretal of 2 August 1206 (Potthast, No. 2860): "Juris namque ratio postulat, ut in eorum praejudicium, quibus eaedem ecclesiae sunt subjectae, nihil ordinemus de ipsis cum nec citati sunt, nec convicti, nec per contumaciam se absentent," *Decretales I.* xxxiii, 8, see also ibid. I. xxiii, 7. Johannes Teutonicus in a gloss on *Comp. III*, De Appellat., c. significavit, s.v. "archiepiscopus", fol. 156 of D 4, remarked:

royal chancery".¹ Furthermore, the principle that what touches all should be approved by all, was by the year 1226 "a living principle both in secular and in ecclesiastical society: this doctrine was put into action, not only as regards taxation, but by the use of the principle of representation".² The influence of the theory cannot be better illustrated than by contrasting the ideas presented to us in the "Dialogue of the Exchequer" with those prevalent in the second decade of the following century. According to the former conceptions, no consent was required for any of the king's measures; on the contrary, the subjects were not even supposed to criticize the king's arbitrary decisions; according to the latter conceptions, embodied in art. 12 of Magna Carta, consent was explicitly demanded, at least as far as taxation (specified in this article) was concerned. Moreover, the Innocentian decretal—I.xxiii.7—and, we may well add, the canonistic doctrine based upon it, were "known and acted upon in England",³ as can be readily deduced from the

---

"Omnes enim sunt citandi, quos res tangit, LIV dist. c. I, LXVI archiepisc. (c.1) VIII q. I, licet (c. 15), III q. VI hoc quippe (c. 10), C. De aqua pluv., in concedendo, C. De auctor. praest., l. ult." The *gl. ord.* on III.xi.1 said: "Capitulum potest constitutionem facere, dum tamen intersint omnes, quos constitutio tangit." A very similar view was propounded by the advocate of the Canterbury monks in 1188, see *Epp. Cantuarienses*, p. 522.

Sir Ernest Barker's approach that the principle of representation and of "quod omnes tangit" came to England through the Dominicans, is too limited. These ideas were already well known, see also P. Vinogradoff, *Collected Papers*, vol. ii, p. 245. And it was certainly no coincidence that Vincentius contributed to the doctrine since, as Sir Ernest himself shows, op. cit., p. 26, the idea of representation was not unknown in twelfth-century Spain. The very fact that Bologna was the meeting place of the first chapter of the Dominicans (1220-21) throws significant light on the roots of the Dominican constitution.

¹ G. Post, *Traditio*, vol. iv, p. 249. Cf. also Stubbs' preface to the fourth volume of Hoveden's *Chronica*, pp. xcviii-xcix.

² M. V. Clarke, *Medieval Representation and Consent*, p. 266.

³ *Reg. of St. Osmund*, (R.S.), vol. ii, p. 20: "Rural deans shall be appointed and removed by the common consent of the lord bishop and the archdeacons;" and pp. 58-59 (1226): convocation of a full chapter to discuss proposed taxation of spiritualities, because this was a matter "that touched all the brethren" who should be consulted. "We may recognize here the maxim 'quod omnes tangit' thinly disguised and applied to the question at issue," Miss Clarke, p. 266. The decision of the Salisbury chapter which was composed of very able jurists, cannot therefore surprise, see the list of members collected by Miss Clarke, p. 265, note 5. cf. also the statutes of the English Benedictines of 1225, Dugdale, *Monasticon*, vol. i, l.; see also Matthew Paris, *Chronica Majora*, vol. iv, p. 37 (for 1240).

practices observed by the chapter of Salisbury (1222).¹ The principle of majority was merely a logical offshoot of the idea "quod omnes tangit", on the presupposition that what the "sanior" or "valentior pars" decided, had the same effects as if "omnes" had consented. This too was worked out by the canonists long before it was put into practice.² Did not Edward I expressly employ the very words "quod omnes tangit" in his writ to the Archbishop of Canterbury in 1295? Indeed, these few words were the core of Edward's writ and they sufficiently explain the king's purpose in summoning the unusually great number of lower ecclesiastics. Is it really too much to assume that Edward I tried to forestall Boniface's bull *Clericis laicos* issued barely a year afterwards, by hitting the adversary with his own weapons? The political idea that is enshrined in the maxim was turned into a constitutional principle. This idea together with its complement, the "plena potestas", goes a long way to account for the position of parliament in fourteenth-century England.³

To all seeming, the Statute of York (1322) was also a practical application of the ancient canonistic principle that "what touches all, should be approved by all". What other function, we may ask, should the communalty of the realm—the *communitas regni*—have?⁴ Such important legislative and con-

¹ Discussing the majority principle in Magna Carta (art. 61), Miss Clarke stated, p. 340: "In England party conflict brought the idea of the majority into prominence long before it was recognized by theorists," a statement which, I believe, cannot be upheld in view of the explicit theories of the canonists, see note at p. 22.

² Cf. also Professor G. O. Sayles, *The Medieval Foundations of England*, p. 445.

³ Canonistic influence is denied by G. Lapsley in his notes on Pasquet, *Origins of the House of Commons*, (trans. by R. G. D. Laffan), notes on pp. 241, 244; A. B. White, *Making of the English Constitution*, 2nd ed., pp. 371 f. Others maintain that these words were a mere embellishment esp. G. B. Adams, *Constitutional History of England*, p. 186, *id.*, *Origin of the English Constitution*, p. 335, note 16. But Stubbs, *Constitutional History of England*, 4th ed., pp. 133, 369, had already said that this principle was transformed "from a mere legal maxim into a great and constitutional principle". See also McIlwain, "Medieval institutions in the modern world" in *Speculum*, vol. xvi, (1941), p. 281, *id.*, *Constitutionalism and the Changing World*, pp. 145 ff., and his article in *C. Med. H.*, vol. vii, p. 679. See further G. Post, art. cit., pp. 197 ff., and B. Wilkinson, "The Coronation Oath of Edward II and the Statute of York" in *Speculum*, vol. xix (1944), pp. 445-69, at pp. 463-64.

⁴ See especially B. Wilkinson, art. cit., p. 463, though he does not refer to

stitutional principles are not born *ex nihilo* and it is possible to trace their filiation.

As far as private law comes into question, we need only refer to the canonical *actio spolii* which was contained in Anselm's collection in two different places and which formed the backbone of the assize of novel disseisin and reappeared in somewhat modified shape in the other two possessory assizes.[1] There is hardly any need to refer to the compendious system of canonical *exceptiones* which left their traces on the whole institution of trial by jury, even including the challenge to the jurors themselves. But I feel it would be presumptuous on my part to traverse this tract of English law which has been so well covered by Maitland himself. I may be allowed to quote one or two sentences of his: "It is by popish clergymen that our English common law is converted from a rude mass of customs into an articulate system, and when the popish clergymen yielding at length to the pope's commands, no longer sit as the principal justices of the king's court, the creative age of our medieval law is over." And: "English law, more especially the English law of civil procedure, was rationalized under the influence of canon law."[2]

But the very mentioning of Henry's judicial innovations recalls irresistibly a curious parallel between his practice and that of the pope. Both he and his contemporary mitred heads were unanimous in their attempts to centralize justice, the king's policy directed against feudal justice, the pope's against episcopal justice. Both invented the same means by which this

---

canonistic influence, and Gaines Post, *Traditio*, vol. i, p. 373, note 10. On the other hand, see J. R. Strayer, "Statute of York and the Communalty of the Realm" in *American Historical Rev.*, vol. xlvii, pp.1-23. This does not of course refer to the composition of "the communalty of the realm"; on this see W. A. Morris, "Magnates and Community of the Realm" in *Medievalia et Humanistica*, fasc. i, 1943, pp. 58-94, esp. at pp. 60-63, 79, 81-84, 88-91. If the imagination is stretched far enough, one might see a parallel between the "pars valentior" of Marsiglio of Padua and the "communalty of the realm".

[1] Against Richardson and Sayles, in Selden Soc., vol. lx, p. cxxviii f.
[2] For Bracton's dependence on Raymund's *Summa de Matrimonio* (which was in fact, Tancred's work) see H. G. Richardson, "Tancred, Raymund and Bracton" in *EHR*, vol. lix (1944), pp. 376-84, at pp. 379-83; for the influence of William of Drogheda on Bracton, at least in one point, see *idem*, ibid., pp. 22-48, at pp. 39 ff., against the unwarranted contention of Kantorowicz, *Bractonian Problems*, pp. 29-32; and for how much Bracton borrowed from Bernardus Papiensis, see Maitland, *Bracton and Azo*, (Selden Soc.), pp. 225-35.

policy of overriding the local judge was carried out: if the plaintiff had obtained an original writ, the king drew into his court the action; if the plaintiff was in the possession of a papal writ which had been "impetrated", the pope drew the action into the papal court. In both cases there was a "breve", issued by a central agency, "in the one case it comes from the English, in the other from the Roman chancery". It was not of course a mere accident that Bracton applied the term "impetration" of a writ to the initial stages of royal and papal jurisdiction.

II

Some knowledge of the canonists' views on their own branch of learning is well nigh essential to the understanding and proper evaluation of canonistic theories in the realm of politics. In what esteem, we may ask ourselves, did the canonists hold their own science?

It is a well-known phenomenon that each profession thinks highest of itself and that related professions are either tolerated as mere equals, or, in the majority of cases, relegated to an inferior position. Perhaps nowhere can this truism be shown in a clearer and, we venture to add, in a more glaring light than in canonistic scholarship. One might conceivably have entertained the opinion that canonists, the majority themselves clerics, would have conceded precedence of rank to theology. But nothing could be further from the truth. Canonistic scholarship was put on a pedestal, and it looked down on all other branches of learning and human knowledge, including theology, with that feeling of superiority that springs from the deep conviction of possessing inherent and intrinsic value.

In general, the canonists recognized three branches of knowledge—firstly, the so-called "civilis sapientia", then the "theologica scientia", and, thirdly, the "canonica scientia". Civil knowledge comprised the study of civil and natural law, and the "jus gentium". In typically medieval fashion civil knowledge sometimes branched off into an "iconomica" and a "politica scientia",[1] the first dealing with the study of the

[1] This seems to have been the generally accepted view, even before Aristotle's *Politics* was widely known. See, for instance, the Parisian doctor Nicholas de Parisiis, writing in the first half of the thirteenth century: "Politica dicitur a

administration of estates and other resources of society—the "regimen familiae" as it was rather loosely called—and the second with the administration of public matters arising in a State, kingdom or the universe.¹ Of these two, economics had the higher rank. According to the teachings of the canonists theology proper comprised the study of the laws pertaining to civil knowledge, and over and above them the study of Jewish law, the sayings of the prophets, the gospels and the apostolic parts of the New Testament. It is noteworthy that patristic literature and philosophy, for instance, were not apparently thought to lie within the province of theology. In fact, theological studies merely constituted a higher form of legal studies to be conducted on the well-known scholastic pattern. Thus the cardinal-bishop of Ostia, Hostiensis, whom we may choose as a particularly good example of thirteenth century canonistic scholarship, writes that "theologica scientia" is that science, "sub quae possunt comprehendi eaedem leges, scilicet lex naturalis, civilis et jus gentium, necnon Mosaica, lex prophetica, lex evangelica, lex apostolica".² This is indeed a remarkable statement at a time which is considered the heyday of theology. Or are we to assume that one of the foremost canonists of the century intentionally rendered theology an elevated branch of legal studies because he could conceive of no way of dealing with univeral problems in other than legal terms? Anyone having only the most superficial knowledge of canonistic scholarship is bound to answer the question in the affirmative. The characteristically medieval love for hierarchical order therefore puts civil knowledge on the lowest step of the ladder whose intermediate portion is taken up by theology, and whose august top is reached only by canonistic scholarship. To quote Hostiensis again: "Sed et haec omnia canonica, immo et

---

polis, quod est civitas . . . ultimae partes scilicet yconomica et politica, sicut quidam dicunt, traduntur in legibus et decretis. . . ." quoted by Mgr. Grabmann, "Die Politikkommentare des 13. Jahrhunderts" in *SB der Bayrischen Akad. d. Wissenschaften*, 1941, p. 9. A very similar view is expressed by the unknown glossator of the *Summa "Elegantius in jure divino"* of Vienna, National Bibliothek, MS. 2125, fol. 11. The text of this *Summa* is sometimes richly glossed.

¹ "Politica dicitur a polis, quod est civitas, quia est scientia de regimine civitatis, castri et villae seu regni vel orbis," Cardinal Zabarella in his *Com.* on the *Decretals* proemium, fol. 4, No. 21, ed. Coloniae, 1602.

² *Summa*, proemium, No. 11, fol. 6.

omne jus comprehendit, sive sit humanum sive divinum, publicum vel privatum." Hence, canonistic scholarship embraces every conceivable branch of law both in its divine and human aspects. It towers high above the humble civil knowledge and takes theology under its protective wings. Our science, the canonists declared, is neither pure theology nor civil knowledge, but absorbs both of them.[1]

In the conviction of the canonists, it is in the nature of an usurpation, for the science of the Roman law to call itself "ars artium", since Roman law not infrequently deals with the "vilest" matters and regulations. Consequently, every precedence must be conceded to the study and science of canon law. Convinced of his knowledge of the most intricate laws and mechanisms governing this universe, the canonist entertains not the slightest doubt about his superior wisdom, or about the importance of his task in shaping the course of history. For an intimate knowledge of the canon law gives one the assurance that on this firmest of all firm foundations every spiritual and temporal affair can be solved satisfactorily. It is worth while quoting the passage of Hostiensis: "For if this canon law is well known and understood, the mastery of all spiritual and temporal matters is assured."[2] The conclusion which is drawn from this somewhat astonishing, though by no means unique statement is merely this: namely that the canons must be accepted by all as the norm of human conduct: "Ideo debent ab omnibus recipi et teneri." If such all-embracing power is assigned to the canons, we surely cannot wonder at the sublime position to which canonistic studies were elevated.[3] Individual discretion and decision are banned and condemned: everything and everyone must be guided by the authority of the law and its science, and not by the possibly dangerous interpretation of the individual.

Forestalling opposition, the canonist would refer his secular

[1] ibid., No. 11: "Est igitur haec scientia nostra non pure theologica sive civilis, sed utrique participans nomen proprium sortita. . . ." Dante's denunciation of the canonists seems somewhat exaggerated, cf. *Epist.*, XI, 16: "Jacet Gregorius . . . jacet Augustinus . . . jacet Ambrosius . . . et Speculum, Innocentium et Hostiensem declamant. Cur non? Illi Deum querebant ut finem et optimum; isti census et beneficia consecuntur."

[2] "Nam si hoc bene sciatur et intelligatur, per eam tam spiritualia quam temporalia regi possunt."

[3] "Et ideo aliis scientiis praeponenda est."

opponent to a statement of Justinian himself, a statement which, however, was contained in a mere relative clause, a position indicative of the comparatively small importance which Justinian attributed to his utterance. Nor can we wholeheartedly agree with the somewhat artificial interpretation which the canonists were wont to give to this passage.[1] In one of the passages in the *Authenticum*[2] this emperor spoke of the advisability that so-called ecclesiastical crimes should not be tried by secular justices: their trial was the business of the ecclesiastical justice who should proceed on the basis of the "sacred and divine rules which our own laws hold worthy enough to follow".[3] What Justinian in all likelihood wished to say was that his own laws desired to implement and realize Christian ideas. That historical knowledge in the Middle Ages was not high, is certain, but men of Stephen of Tournay's and Hostiensis's standing and learning could not possibly have overlooked the historical fact that it would be idle to speak of canon law at the time of Justinian. It is of course true that Justinian employed the term "canon" rather frequently in his *Novellae*, though only once in the Digest—D.1.3.2 in the Greek original—but there is nothing to suggest that he employed the term in the very technical sense in which the medieval canonists interpreted it.[4]

Equally unacceptable to the canonist was the legistic retort restricting canon law to a law dealing with ecclesiastical matters only. Here again we are referred to a statement of Justinian in which he is reported to have said that he would follow in "everything" ("per omnia") the sacred rules and that the latter should be held as law. The employment of "omnia" by Justinian leads Hostiensis and the whole galaxy of canonists to the con-

---

[1] See, for instance, *Summa Stephani Tornacensis*, ad *Dist*. x, p. 19, of the edition by Schulte.

[2] *Collatio* VI, tit. xii, cap. 1. (*Novella* LXXXVIII, c. 1.)

[3] "Cum oporteat talia ecclesiastice examinari et emendari animas delinquentium per ecclesiasticam mulctam, secundum sacras et divinas regulas, quas etiam nostrae sequi non dedignantur leges." See also *Collatio* I, tit. v, cap. 9: "... ea, quae sacris regulis continentur, quas nostra sequitur lex."

[4] On the use of the term "canon" in the Roman sources, see now the penetrating study by L. Wenger, "Canon und Regula" in *Zeitschrift, kan. Abt*., vol. xxxii (1943), pp. 495-506, especially at pp. 497, 500. The same author's paper on a related subject in the Proceedings of the Vienna Academy (1942) was not accessible to me.

clusion that he who says "everything" does not admit any exceptions. Consequently, canon law embodies and embraces everything: "Immo quodlibet comprehendit."

It would have been remarkable had the canonist terminated his argument at this point without attempting to rest the superiority of canon law and its science on an extra-legal principle, in this case upon the always welcome but never defined idea of "natural reason". "I am also in a position to show by natural reason," said one of them, "that our science is well above any other, is worthier and that it must rank before any other department of human knowledge".[1] Natural reason shows the excellency and authority of canonistic scholarship which takes precedence over all other branches of learning. These contemplations lead us straight into medieval speculative thought, largely based as it was upon the philosophy of Realism. According to natural reason there are three aspects of man. These are the spiritual or angelic, the corporeal or earthly, and the human aspects. This last is a combination of the other two aspects, and consequently embodies all the features characteristic of both. As Hostiensis put it, man consists of mind (soul) ("spiritus") and of body ("corpus"). Man's humanity thus surpasses the moral value of his spiritual and corporeal component parts. That the combined spiritual and corporeal nature of man is "worthier" than either of them, is held to be demonstrated by St. Paul's words to the Corinthians: "Know ye not that we shall judge angels?" (I Cor. vi.3). Angels as purely spiritual beings are judged by man who consists not merely of one of two natures, but of two. When men sit in judgment over angels, how much more right have they to judge the purely corporeal things of life, that is to say, the things pertaining to the flesh?[2] And civil law and its science deals with the carnal things only—how inferior civil knowledge must appear compared with canonistic scholarship!

But this line of argument is not the only one open to the canonist who was bent on winning his cause. The nature of Christ Himself provides the canonist with additional support for his idea that the combined spiritual and corporeal elements are higher than either of them singly. For Christ was at once

---
[1] "Naturali etiam ratione ostendo hanc scientiam digniorem omnibus aliis et omnibus praeponendam."
[2] "Carnalia et temporalia," Hostiensis, loc. cit.

God and Man in one person, and therefore, in the words of Hostiensis, he "honoured" humanity by becoming man. Just as the humanity of man surpasses his spirituality and corporality, so also does canonistic scholarship stand above theology and civil knowledge. The former has exclusively the spiritual side of man as its object of study, whilst the latter deals with his merely corporeal exigencies; but canonistic scholarship, like the humanity of man himself, is concerned with both and, accordingly, commends itself "prae caeteris". Now if every combination is greater in value than its constituent parts, the mule might be considered a test case. We need not ask ourselves whether this particular example would have enriched Jhering's *Ernst und Scherz in der Jurisprudenz*, but Hostiensis puts the following question with all the zeal and fervour of which he is capable. Is the mule worthier than the horse and the donkey taken together? It is plain, he says, that theology is represented by the species horse, whilst civil knowledge must needs be compared to the donkey.

This line of argumentation is of course not peculiar to the cardinal-bishop of Ostia. From the writings of almost any of the great canonists proof could be drawn of the exalted contemporary view of canonistic scholarship. It is particularly the greater "dignitas" which is invariably assigned to the science of canon law. This "dignitas" was shown not only in the way in which Hostiensis chose to argue the matter, but also in the Aristotelian contrast between mind and matter. That the things pertaining to the mind, the "spiritualia", were on a higher level than those belonging to the body, the "temporalia", was a foregone conclusion for any medieval scholar who had perused the Stagirite's *Politics* and *Ethics* (book i). And since canon law dealt with both aspects of human life, the conclusion that the science of canon law had no rival amongst the humanities, was quickly reached. "Spiritualia" the statement usually ran, "sunt tanto digniora temporalibus quanto anima praefertur corpori".[1] We shall have occasion to demonstrate how pregnant and fruitful was this contrast between mind and matter. Since it dealt with every aspect of moral conduct, canonistic scholarship naturally excelled moral science as well as theology and civil knowledge. Moreover, canonistic scholarship treats of economic and political science. "Nam haec scientia non solum tractat

---

[1] Zabarella, op. cit., I, xxxiv. 6, No. 4. See also *infra* pp. 109 f.

de partibus ethicae, sed etiam iconomicae et politicae."¹ Canonistic scholarship is a true queen. Indeed, the solemn declaration of Julius II in the Fifth Lateran Council was simply a pontifical affirmation of the divine character of canon law. There this pope avowed the unalterable nature of the canons, because "these decrees were issued as it were by divine inspiration".[2] The decrees of the pope as a legislator were credited with greater authority than the sayings of the saints.[3] More weight was to be attached to a canonical enactment than to the *dicta* of St. Augustine or St. Jerome;[4] those who disregarded canon law were "ipso jure" condemned as heretics,[5] for they thereby denied their faith.[6]

However much we may be startled by these all-embracing claims of medieval canonistic scholarship, we must not attempt to graft upon the Middle Ages our own modern ideas about specialization. It was only in comparatively recent times that universities established special faculties of economics, political science, and so forth, and in many continental universities the study of political economy and related subjects still form part of the law curriculum. And, looking a little further afield, is not Kelsen's attempt to purify jurisprudence from its non-legal elements a step in the direction to cleanse the law from moral and political elements? On the other hand, the teachings of Roscoe Pound, Ehrlich, Cardozo and Gurvitch programmatically emphasize the importance of social psychology and ethics for the understanding of legal norms. We are on safe ground if we assume that the medieval canonists' exalted view of their own science sprang from some ulterior motives, particu-

[1] *Idem*, proemium, fol. 4: "et dicitur generaliter, quod scientia juris perfecte complectitur omnem scientiam moralem, et completior et perfectior est quam scientia moralis."

[2] See Raynaldus, *Annales Ecclesiastici*, ad 1512, No. 100.

[3] See Antonius de Butrio, *Com. in Decretales*, I.iv.17, No. 49: "Dicunt doctores, quod in opinione magis esset credendum papae quam dictis sanctorum."

[4] See Huguccio who was usually rather moderate: "In negotiis definiendis major est auctoritas canonis sive apostolici quam auctoritas Augustini vel Hieronymi," *Summa Decretorum*, *Dist.* xx, ante cap. 1, s.v. "secundum post", fol. 129 of p. 72.

[5] Huguccio, loc. cit., c. i, s.v. "indifferenter", fol. 129 verso: "Ipso jure sunt dampnati tamquam haeretici." He referred to *Dist.* xix, c. 5, *Dist.* xxii, cap. 1 and C. XXV, q. i, c. 5 and 6.

[6] *Id.*, ibid., "qui statuta conciliorum et apostolicorum contemnit contra sedem apostolicam."

larly from the motive of making the papacy the central institution of a world government and thereby lowering the legal position of the great rival of the pope, the emperor, whom, after all, the venerable Roman laws called the "dominus mundi". Everything was subordinated to the one aim: to prove the inferiority of the emperor by the sacred authority of the law. The exaltation of canonistic scholarship was but a symptom of this overwhelming desire and should not be taken merely at its face value. It is quite obvious that the authority of the civil laws, with their great backing of tradition, presented a formidable obstacle to the canonists. Moreover, who can doubt that in the Middle Ages the written, impersonal and seemingly detached word constituting the law, was held sacrosanct? Is it then not natural that the canonists tried to reverse the position, and in doing so gave free rein to speculative thought?

But we should guard ourselves against the facile assumption that the canonists were "mere" lawyers, exclusively occupied in the interpretation of papal decrees. This conception of the medieval canonists would be as wrong as the opinion which received such a characteristic rebuff from Dr. Johnson when he replied to the commonplace statement that no great lawyer had known anything besides law: "No, sir, Judge Hale was a great lawyer and yet he knew many other things and has written upon other things; Selden too; Lord Coke would have taken it very ill if you had told him he was a mere lawyer; he would have prosecuted you for libel." Nor was Mansfield a mere lawyer in the opinion of the venerable sage. Almost the same words could be used in the defence of the medieval canonists. However much we are bound to consider their claims extravagant, they themselves felt superior to their civilian counterparts: the civilian, though possessing a good deal more knowledge of philosophy, ethics and metaphysics than his twentieth-century brethren, was after all first and foremost a trained lawyer. The canonists, on the other hand, belonged to a considerable extent to the priesthood and were to some extent schooled in theology and philosophy. They usually entered the legal arena later than their civilian colleagues. Amongst the canonists, we find therefore a greater number of writers on non-legal subjects than amongst the civilians. To select only a few outstanding examples of canonistic versatility: Bartholomaeus Brixiensis who gave the *glossa ordinaria* of the *Decretum* its final shape, was a theologian and historian of some repute; Magister Gandulphus was reputed for his great theological work, the *Sententiae*;[1] As well as his *Stroma* Rolandus also composed *Sententiae* which shows that he mastered theology as well as canon law; Huguccio earned fame throughout the Middle Ages as a lexicographer and grammarian;[2] Guido Brito appears to have composed a *Vocabularium Biblicum*;[3] and Sicardus was a chronicler[4] as well as the author of a liturgical work[5] and of a *Liber Mythologiarum*.[6] Johannes de Lignano's versatility was astounding: he wrote on medical subjects and problems of natural philosophy before expounding the canon law; Cardinal Zabarella's tract on natural philosophy and theology attracted much attention at the time; and Johannes de Turrecremata's

---

[1] See J. de Ghellinck, "La diffusion des 'Sententiae' de Gandulphe de Bologne" in *Recherches des sciences religieuses*, vol. xiv (1924), pp. 293-95, and *Magistri Gandulphi Bononiensis Sententiarum Libri Quatuor*, ed. Johannes de Walter, Vienna, 1924. Gandulph was the master of Bernard of Pavia, the compiler of the *Compilatio Prima*, see the passage transcribed by Walter, pp. xxxix f., xcii.

[2] See M. Manitius, *Geschichte der lateinischen Literatur des Mittelalters*, vol. iii (1931), pp. 191 f. A MS. of Huguccio's *Summa super derivationibus, compositionibus, significationibus et interpretationibus*, is in the library of York Minster (xvi.Q.13). This copy was made by order of Magister John Le Gras, a canon of York in 1266, see the Explicit: "*Summa* ... quam fecit scribi ex propriis expensis Magister Johannes Lecras, canonicus ecclesiae beati Petri Eboracensis, pro commodo et utilitate sacerdotum et clericorum." On John Le Cras (or Le Gras) see *Annales Dunelmenses* (Surtees Soc. Publ.), ed. F. Barlow, p. 206. The scribe was a John de Gretham, whilst the "kalendare" was written by Master William of Thornton, see colophon. Huguccio stated in his preface the reason for writing this dictionary: the prevailing "ignorantia latinitatis", fol. 24. Another copy is in Lincoln, LC 162. Huguccio's work was one of the principal authorities of Ranulph Higden's *Polychronicon*, (R.S.), see vol. i, pp. 10, 114, 128, 168, 238, vol. ii, pp. 234, 306, 432, vol. iii, p. 194, vol. iv, pp. 198, 224, vol. v, p. 358, etc.

[3] MS. in Dulwich College, London, No. xxiii: "Guilelmi Britonis Vocabularium Biblicum". The incipit runs: "Difficiles studio partes quas Biblia gestat...." I am indebted to the librarian of Dulwich College for this information.

[4] His *Chronicon* is edited by Migne, *Patr. Lat.*, vol. ccxiii, cols. 441-538, and by Holder-Egger, in *Mon. Germ. Hist.*, *Scriptores*, vol. xxxi, pp. 78-182. He was bishop of Cremona and died in 1215, see p. 182, and col. 539 in *Patr. Lat.* For biographical material see Holder-Egger, loc. cit., pp. 22-78, Schulte in *SB der kais. Akad. d. Wiss.*, vol. lxiii, pp. 336-55, at p. 342, and Kuttner, "Zur Biographie des Sicardus" in *Zeitschrift, kanon. Abt.*, vol. xxv (1936), pp. 476 ff.

[5] The title is: "Mitrale seu de officiis ecclesiasticis summa", in Migne, *Patr. Lat.*, loc. cit., cols. 13-434.

[6] Cf. Holder-Egger, loc. cit., p. 24, and Kuttner, *Repertorium*, p. 151.

reputation as a theologian was no less than his fame as a canonist. That some canonists, such as Rufinus, Johannes de Deo, Guilelmus de Monte Lauduno also wrote pastoral treatises, need hardly be mentioned.[1] Careful study of the medieval canonistic literature conveys the impression that, as a rule, they worked on broader foundations than the civilians. However wildly exaggerated their political claims, they certainly attempted to view the universe from a universal standpoint, and were not satisfied with the strict boundaries of their province. But—and this is important to keep in mind—they came so much under the spell of their legalistic modes of thinking that whatever subject they treated, the lawyer was always preponderant; and whatever statement they made, some passage in one of the collections had to support it. "Your professional canonist would hardly have admitted that the sun shone at noonday without sending you to Gratian for the proof."[2] Every religious, theological, ethical, political question was seen through the eyes of the lawyer. Their writings abundantly prove that they translated into practice their ideas about their own branch of learning.

A noteworthy feature of canonistic writings is not only the already mentioned liveliness and forcefulness of argumentation, but also the astonishing variety of opinions, especially amongst the older generation writing at the end of the twelfth century and in the first two decades of the thirteenth century. The independence of judgment on the part of those canonists also appeals to the modern reader. This is shown, for instance, when Huguccio declared in one of his glosses that in a particular decretal Alexander III spoke not as pope, but as a mere teacher of canon law,[3] or when in other passages he said that Alexander III had badly stated his case[4] or that he refused to accept this pope's decretals as part of the law;[5] or when Tancred comment-

[1] On Rufinus see G. Morin, "Le discours d'ouverture du concile générale de Lateran (1179) et l'oeuvre littéraire de Maître Rufin, évêque d'Assise" in *Atti della Pontif. Accadem. Romana di Archaeologia*, Memorie, vol. ii, pp. 113 ff.

[2] Maitland, *The Mirror of Justices* (Selden Soc.), p. xxxii.

[3] See *infra*, ch. III, p. 60 n.3.

[4] "Ideo Alexander videtur male dicere. . . ." on C. II, q. vi, c. 5.

[5] "Decretales tamen Alexandri et ante litem contestatam admittunt appellationem . . . sed plus credo antiquo decreto et novo concilio quam decretalibus," on C. II, q. vi, proemium. In one place, C. II, q. vi, c. 39, he doubted the genuineness of some Alexandrian decretals: "Sed non adhibeo fidem illis decretalibus nec credo eas fuisse Alexandri."

D

ing upon another Alexandrian decretal said that he could approve of only two of the cases mentioned therein;[1] or when Richard de Lacy (Richardus Anglicus) blamed the compiler of the *Compilatio Prima*, Bernardus Papiensis, for corrupting and mutilating the text;[2] or when the compiler himself bluntly declared that Alexander III must have been asleep when he issued a particular decretal.[3]

Despite the dignified sombreness and the solemnity which we meet in the works of the expounders of this august branch of knowledge we shall not nevertheless be surprised to find canonistic writings oddly larded with anecdotes and cases. Questions like these were discussed: the case of a prisoner who swears solemnly that he will return to jail, if only he is allowed to go to mass on a certain feast day and who, once in the church, claims the right of asylum; the case of a woman who, at the bidding of the husband makes love to the physician who otherwise would not cure the husband: can the husband divorce her? The case of a youth who, disguised as a girl, makes profession as a nun and then seduces the abbess—juristic problem: can the bishop compel him to be a monk?[4]

Let us now briefly contrast with this exalted view on canonistic scholarship the view of the legist on "civil knowledge". Had the civilian the same high opinion of his own science, and did he take a correspondingly low view of canonistic scholarship? We may refer to Bartolus as a particularly good example. He too has a rather high opinion of his own branch of learning when he says that civil knowledge deals with the divine, the human

---

[1] Tancred in his *Apparatus* on *Compilatio Prima*, De officio vicar., c. clericos (c. 5), fol. 9 of D 4: "Licet plures casus in hac decretali ponantur, hos duos tantum approbo."

[2] Richard's *Apparatus* on *Compilatio Prima*, De judeis et sarac., c. pro auctoritate (c. 1), fol. 70 of W 122: "Circa finem totaliter mutilavit et corrumpit papiensis."

[3] See *Glossa Palatina*, C. XVII, q. i, c. 4 (§ Si ergo), fol. 99 verso of D 8: "Alexander contradicit extra. qui cler. vel vovo., c. ult., ..., b. vero pap. dicit ibi Alexandrum dormitasse."

[4] These cases are to be found in the *Collectio Quaestionum*, Vienna, National Bibliothek, MS. 2163. The first is on fol. 83, the second on fols. 79 verso-80, and the case of the abbess (who in fact became pregnant) on fol. 81 verso ("Juvenis quidam ... habitu mulieri sumpto professionem velud femina in manu abatissae fecit. Illa gravidata recessit, vult eum episcopus compellere, ut sit monachus. Quaeritur an possit?") Other cases from the same source are given by Kuttner, *Traditio*, vol. i, p. 324. On this MS. see Appendix.

and the universal. "I sit a queen and am no widow and shall see no sorrow," in these words Bartolus characterizes civil knowledge. It is independent of canon law and of other branches of learning; it stands on its own feet and is perfect in itself. On the other hand, the perfect canonist, says Bartolus, must have a complete mastery of civil knowledge; canon law without civil law appears to him a mere shell and an "imperfecta scientia". Roger Bacon's bitter complaint immediately comes to one's mind.[1] But there emerges one illuminating difference between the canonist and the civilian. In ironic contrast to the canonist the civilian thinks that theology stands on a level higher than that of his civil knowledge. The civilian modestly looks up to theology—the canonist looks down on it.

[1] The canonists ("juristae sacri canonis"), he declared, had no chance of earning their living, unless they had first devoted themselves to the study of civil law. The individuals best fitted to pursue theological and philosophical studies were so much attracted by civil law, because it was so highly respected by all the ecclesiastical and secular princes: "Compendium Studii" in *Opera Inedita*, ed. J. S. Brewer (R.S.), p. 419.

CHAPTER II

THE CANONISTS AND NATURAL LAW

THE canonists' conception of their own calling has been presented in order to promote the better understanding of their theory of law. This presentation may also have conveyed something of the mental atmosphere in which the theories of the canonists were evolved, and in which the claim to papal plenitude of power developed. Hardly any other idea played a greater part in investing the pope with the fullness of power than the idea of natural law. We may, therefore, profitably review the fundamental conceptions which the canonists held about natural law. It will be seen that their ideas do not always harmonize with those set forth in canon law itself.

In spite of Gratian's obvious intention to compile a system of law which should be, at all events outwardly, uninfluenced by Roman law and independent of it, the canonists, trained as they were in the spirit and the letter of the Roman law, quite openly borrowed some of the most important Roman ideas. In the matter of ethical conceptions it is perhaps significant that the canonists wholeheartedly accepted the chief moral tenet of law as it was shaped by Ulpian, that is, to live honestly, not to injure one's neighbour, and to give everyoneh is due (D.1.1.10.1). In the opinion of the canonists the moral import of the law could nowhere be more fully comprehended than in natural law. It was this law that most conspicuously realized the moral end of all law. Although everyone was agreed on this point, the older doctrine did not entirely follow the Isidorian conceptions as embodied in Gratian's collection; in particular the fundamental difference between Roman law and canon law was not always clearly grasped. Thus the unknown glossator of the Innsbruck *Codex*[1] distinguished between a natural law that was fundamentally the expression of a moral idea and one which was devoid of any ethical contents. The former kind the

---

[1] See J. F. v. Schulte, "Die Glosse zum Decret Gratian von ihren Anfängen bis auf die jüngsten Ausgaben" in *Denkschriften der kaiserl. Akademie der Wissenschaften*, vol. xxi, ii, p. 7.

glossator defined as "a force that is naturally implanted in man to do good and prevent evil".[1] A very similar conception was propounded by Huguccio who declared that natural law was to be identified with "natural reason", the faculty that enabled man to distinguish between the good and the evil and which, moreover, prompted him to select the good as the basis of his action.[2] The identification of law and reason was justified, Huguccio believed, because both were characterized by their binding force upon human actions.[3] This, he thought, was proved by an observation of the behaviour of primitive peoples who had no laws: they "naturally" acted, as if they had laws—"gentes, quae legem non habent, naturaliter ea, quae legis sunt, faciunt ipsi sibi".[4] Occasionally we find that this kind of "natural law" was identified with the *liberum arbitrium*. Thus the *Summa Oxoniensis*[5] declared (in terms very similar to the *Summa Lipsiensis*[6]) that natural law was the "facultas discernendi bonum a malo cum approbatione unius et detestatione alterius. Hoc est liberum arbitrium."

The second species of natural law was "everything that nature taught all animalic creatures"[7] which definition was of course in literal agreement with Roman law[8]. The fundamental

---

[1] "Jus naturale est quaedam vis humanae creaturae naturaliter insita ad bonum faciendum cavendumque malum," gloss, proem. In the same sense, Rufinus, ad *Dist.* i, p. 7 of the edition by Schulte.

[2] See Huguccio in his *Summa*, proem., fol. 116 of P 72: "Jus ergo naturale dicitur ratio scil. naturalis, jus ex quo homo discernit recte bonum et malum eligendo bonum et detestando malum."

[3] He continued: "Et dicitur ratio jus, quia lex ligat vel quia legitime agere compellat: naturale vel natura, quia ratio."

[4] Loc. cit.

[5] Oriel College, 53, Kuttner, *Repertorium*, p. 199. According to the *Summa Oxoniensis* this is the fourth kind of natural law; its author enumerates seven kinds.

[6] Kuttner, op. cit., p. 203.

[7] Also set forth by Huguccio, loc. cit.; "Jus naturale est, quod natura omnia animalia docuit: hoc jus commune est omnibus animalibus."

[8] The publicist, Egidius Romanus, not bound by the traditional legal terminology, invented a new category of law: he juxtaposed the "jus naturale" and the "jus animalium", see his *De Regimine Principum*, lib. iii, pars ii, cap. 24. In this way he was able to escape many of the difficulties which of necessity faced the canonist bound in as he was by the accepted legal terminology. A MS. copy of this tract (hitherto unnoticed) is in York Minster, xvi, D. 5. On Gratian and the Roman law see Vetulani in *Revue historique de droit français et étranger*, 1947, pp. 11-48.

difference between the Roman and the canonical versions was shown by Johannes Faventinus in his gloss on the *Decretum*.[1] The legists, this glossator said, interpreted the term "natural law" in a far wider sense. According to their usage the term covered the whole animalic creation, whilst the canonists conceived of a natural law that was applicable to human creatures only.[2] And this canonist clearly perceived a practical consequence of this difference: the Romans and the legists, he declared, had to count self-defence as an item of the "jus gentium", whilst the canonists saw in it an issue of the natural law. The Roman conception of natural law, the glossators correctly pointed out, would not have allowed the conception of self-defence to be an effluence of natural law.[3]

The identification of natural law with divine law was always strongly insisted upon by the canonists. This identification was so generally known and understood that we find no very lengthy discussions on this topic. The usual statement simply ran: "Jus naturale, id est, jus divinum."[4] The set of rules contained in the Old and New Testaments was conceived as natural law: "Jus naturale in libris Novi et Veteris Testamenti continetur."[5] This agreement between natural and divine law was explained by the Stoic and pantheistic idea that "nature is God".[6] Through the medium of the Old and New Testaments this law

[1] This gloss was finished in 1171, see Schulte, loc. cit., p. 43.

[2] The reasoning of Rufinus was similar, and it may be that Johannes Faventinus adopted Rufinus's argumentation. The latter said: "Hoc autem jus (scil. naturale) legistica traditio generalissime definit dicens: jus naturale est, quod natura omnia animalia docuit. Nos vero istam generalitatem, quae omnia concludit animalia, non curantes, de eo juxta, quod humano generi ascribitur," see *Summa Rufini*, ad *Dist*., i, p. 4, ed. cit.

[3] *Glossa ordinaria* on *Dist*. i, c. 7, s.v. "repulsio": "Hic etiam de repulsione violentiae agitur cum propulsatione injuriae. Sed legistae, cum generalius accipiant jus naturale, communitive ascribant illud omnibus animalibus; nosque specialius, ut attribuatur solis hominibus ideoque, cum sciant, talem violentiae et injuriae propulsationem brutis animalibus, quae injuriam pati non possunt, non esse communem, non dicunt eam de jure naturali debere esse, sed gentium."

[4] See the Archdeacon (Guido de Baysio) in his *Com.* on *Dist.* i.

[5] Rufinus in his *Summa*, on *Dist*. ix, p. 19 ed. cit.

[6] Cf. the Archdeacon, loc. cit.: "Et dicitur jus naturale, quia summa natura, id est Deus." See also the *Summa Oxoniensis*, Kuttner, p. 202: "Hoc autem jus naturale appellatur, vel quia a summa natura proditum est, a Deo scilicet, vel quia naturalem sive innatam equitatem imitatur. Illud idem jus divinum appellatur, quia a Deo sub miraculorum ostensione proditum est, praeter hominum ministerium. . . ."

taught men to do what was just and equitable. Moreover, the actions which were prescribed in divine law were identical with those dictated by natural reason: man was impelled to these actions by natural reason without the help of external promptings. Divine law was intrinsically based upon natural reason and hence medieval canonistic doctrine thought permissible the complete identification of divine and natural law.[1] Huguccio was perhaps clearest in his exposition. He maintained that natural law was identical with divine law, that is, the Mosaic law and the gospels, because "summa natura", that is God, had furnished us with that law: "Dicitur jus naturale jus divinum, quod continet lex Mosaica et evangelica; sic accipitur in principio et dicitur hoc jus naturale, quoniam summa natura, id est, Deus nobis illud tradidit et docuit per leges et prophetas et evangelium ... naturalis ratio, etiam since extrinseca eruditione ducit et impellit."[2]

It should be understood, however, that a minority of canonists conceived of natural law as a mere species of the divine law which latter thus became a generic concept. The unknown glossator of Stephen of Tournay's *Summa* considered as amongst the four species of divine law the "lex naturalis" which is implanted in man's mind by God Himself.[3] But this view was taken only by a minority of canonists, all of of whom belonged to the earlier generation.

The concord between natural and divine law made it comparatively easy to trace their origin to the same source, that is, to the creation of man. In the opinion of the canonists, there could have been no natural law before man was made, because it was only applicable to creatures endowed with reason. The divine creation of man and the birth of natural law occurred simultaneously. A typical representative of thirteenth-century canonistic scholarship, Goffredus de Trano, said: "Postquam Deus formavit hominem ad imaginem et similitudinem suam,

---

[1] The Archdeacon said that the identity was true, "quia ad ea, quae jure divino continentur, naturalis ratio etiam sine extrinseca excitatione ducit et impellit".

[2] See Huguccio, loc. cit., fol. 116. On a practical application, see *infra* p. 142, notes.

[3] "Jus divinum est a Deo insitum menti, ut lex naturalis," quoted after F. Thaner, "Zwei anonyme Glossen zur Summa Stephani Tornacensis" in *SB d. kaiserl. Akad. d. Wiss.*, vol. lxxix, p. 215.

prodiit cum eo jus naturale."¹ This idea remained, of course, unchanged in the fourteenth century. Johannes Andreae, writing nearly a century after Goffredus, said that natural law was all non-human law which was created by the founder of human nature itself, that is, by God.² But we shall search in vain for any sharp definition of the contents of the natural law with which the canonists operated, although they were all eager to outline its development. In the same passage Goffredus declared, for instance, that to this primeval natural law Moses and the prophets added the Old Testament, the "lex vetus", and, "after the translation of the priesthood", the New Testament must be considered as another addition. According to the same canonist, human law came into being at a far later date, after it had become evident that human wickedness and malevolence disturbed the divinely ordained peace on earth. This, incidentally, was also the leitmotif in Gregory's bull of promulgation. It was to promote peace amongst mankind that the Fathers and pontiffs promulgated their decrees and constitutions. There is no definition of the function of the secular law within this conceptual framework—we may perhaps assume that the omission was intentional.

Whilst Goffredus refused to recognize humanly devised laws as belonging to natural law, his great colleague, the Archdeacon, assigned not only the above-mentioned laws, but also canon law itself to the province of natural law, which he had identified with divine law according to the current fashion. Of course, this was not a novel idea. When explaining the term divine law, the previously mentioned anonymous glossator of Stephen of Tournay's *Summa* expressed his conviction that canon law, next to natural law, was a species of divine law. Canon law was made, he said, for the sake of God.³ The Archdeacon bluntly stated that "hoc nomine (scilicet jure naturali) etiam comprehenditur jus canonicum sive ecclesiasticum". And long before his time Huguccio had avowed that canon law or ecclesiastical law was divine law.⁴

¹ Rubrica "De Constitutionibus", fol. 2 verso of the edition, Venetiis, 1586, referring to C. XXIII, q.v., c. haec imago.
² Gloss on *Clem*. II.xi.2.
³ The whole passage runs thus: "(Jus divinum est) a Deo insitum menti, ut lex naturalis; a Deo traditum: lex Mosaica; a Deo editum: evangelicum; pro Deo conditum: canones," quoted after Thaner, loc. cit., p. 215.
⁴ See Huguccio's comments on "humanum genus", fol. 116: "Dicitur etiam

To understand these remarkable pronouncements we must realize that one of the most frequently quoted items of natural law was sexual union. The canonists argued that this natural urge to a union between man and woman—an issue of the natural (divine) law—was taken into account by canon law in the regulations of marital relations. Only in order to avoid graver things—"ut gravius vitetur"—the "coitus conjugalis" which in fact sprang from incontinency, was permitted. This was an instance in which canons were made on the basis of "indulgentia".[1] This was of course only one typical example which the canonists employed in their attempt to show that the manifold regulations of canon law could be traced back to natural law—and this kinship led a canonist of the Archdeacon's standing to maintain that the canon law or ecclesiastical law was divine (natural) law. But as previously mentioned, it would be inaccurate to ascribe to the Archdeacon the original idea that canon law was natural (divine) law.[2] Apart from the glossator on Stephen's *Summa*, the Innsbruck *Codex* as well as Stephen

---

jus divinum jus canonicum sive ecclesiasticum." He believed he found some support in C. XXIII, q. vii, c. 1. Only very occasionally do we find the opposite opinion which makes canon law a species of positive (human) law, so, for instance, with Damasus who said in his *Summa Decretalium* (written between 1210 and 1215) that "juris autem species sunt duae. Est enim jus naturale, quod natura omnia animalia docuit ... est autem jus positivum sive expositum (positum?) ab homine, ut sunt leges saeculares et constitutiones ecclesiasticae," quoted after Kantorowicz, "Das Principium des Johannes de Deo" in *Zeitschrift, kanon. Abt.*, vol. xii, pp. 440-41. On some consequences of this distinction, see *idem*, "Damasus", ibid., vol. xvi, p. 333. Another example can be cited from a gloss which may have been written by Simon de Bisignano: "Sed jus humanum dicitur omne jus ab homine inventum, unde et canonicum concluditur," quoted after J. Juncker, "Summen und Glossen", in *Zeitschrift, kanon. Abt.*, vol. xiv, p. 442.

[1] See also the passages of Gratian and Huguccio transcribed *infra*, ch. III.

[2] On the historical background and especially on the way in which the Bible became incorporated in canon law, see Fournier-Le Bras, *Histoire des Collections canoniques en occident depuis les fausses décretales justqu'au décret de Gratien*, vol. i, pp. 91 ff., and G. Le Bras "Les Ecritures dans le décret Gratien", in *Zeitschrift, kanon. Abt.*, vol. xxvii, pp. 50-52. Professor Le Bras succinctly points out (pp. 52-53) that Gratian in his collection "ne produit jamais un fragment scripturaire parmi ses *auctoritates:* il n'invoque la Bible que dans ses *dicta*." On Gratian and the Fathers see J. de Ghellinck, *Patristique en Moyen Age*, vol. ii p. 7.

himself[1] declared that the term "canon" might refer either to the whole of Holy Writ, or to the Old and New Testaments alone, or to the statutes of the Roman pontiffs and of the general councils.[2] When, therefore, on the one hand, scripture was natural law, and when, on the other hand, the term "canon" also referred to scripture, it was only a small step for the imaginative and speculatively inclined canonists to describe the whole ecclesiastical law as divine (natural) law. Some canonists, such as Stephen himself, even maintained that the reason for Gratian's collection was the growing ignorance of the divine law: Gratian's aim was, the canonist said, to prevent the divine law from becoming obsolete.[3]

But it was not only this loose terminology which induced canonists to identify the canon law with divine law. An influential section amongst the canonists can be made responsible for this widening of the scope of natural law. This section did not explain the origin of divine law in the manner which we have described above. They maintained that it would be inappropriate to speak of a divine law before the birth of Christ: according to this view, divine law did not exist before the establishment of the primitive Church. For it was only after the martyrdom of the early Christians had ceased under Constantine the Great, that the Fathers were able to hold their councils in safety and to issue binding rules for the whole of Christendom.[4]

---

[1] Schulte, *Denkschriften*, loc. cit., p. 6, and *Summa Stephani Tornacensis*, on *Dist.* viii, p. 17 ed. cit.: "Jure divino vel jure etiam canonum, quod divinum est . . . unde potest dici jure divino, id est, jure naturali nihil proprium est."

[2] A similarly wide terminology was also employed by some theologians, for instance, by Hugh of St. Victor, see Paré-Brunet-Tremblay, *La renaissance du XII siècle: Les écoles et l'enseignement*, 1933, p. 220, and J. de Ghellinck, *Le mouvement théologique du XII siècle*, pp. 16, 18, 46, 320-22. On the concept of natural law in the modern canon law, see Ulrich Stutz, *Der Geist des Codex Juris Canonici*, 1918, pp. 181 ff.

[3] See his *Summa*, proem., p. 5: "Causa operis (scil. Gratiani) haec est: cum per ignorantiam jus divinum in desuetudinem deveniret et singulae ecclesiae consuetudinibus potius quam canonibus regerentur, periculosum reputans id Gratianus diversos codices conciliorum et patrum capitula continentes collegit..."

[4] Cf. the Archdeacon, proem., fol. 1 verso, No. 4: "Alii compendiosius ordientes divini juris originem a primitiva sumunt ecclesia. Cum enim cessante martyrium persecutione ecclesia respirare coepisset sub Constantino imperatore coeperunt patres secure convenire concilia celebrare et in eis pro diversitate

It is plain that a terminology as vague, amorphous and flexible as the canonistic terminology was not apt to stimulate sharply definable concepts: it seems that a great many divergent streams of thought, irreconcilable in themselves, because antagonistic to each other, had been combined eclectically to form an idea appropriate for the furtherance of the ultimate aim of all canonistic doctrine, the aim of proving the superiority of the pope over the emperor. Platonic, Aristotelian, Ciceronian, Augustinian ideas were melted into one whole. The enquiries of the canonists into natural law appeared to be focused on the presentation of Christian moral principles as a set of fixed rules: these rules were epitomized in the notion of natural law which, for understandable reasons, was easily identifiable with divine law. Law was substituted for an ideology. The immensely equitable character of this law was pointed out again and again: its gist could be summarized in the formula: "Whatsoever ye would that men should do to you, do ye even so to them" (Matt. vii.12). The injunctions contained in Holy Writ were of a "natural" character, as, for instance, "thou shalt not commit adultery".[1] And some canonists, such as Johannes Faventinus and Huguccio, merely seem to have treated natural law as a category of morals: it consisted, they said, of injunctions, prohibitions, and admonitions: natural law ordered that which was useful, it prohibited that which was harmful, and it demonstrated that which was fitting.[2] The idea of natural law as it was shaped by the canonists, was merely a set of certain generally accepted rules emanating eventually from the principles of Christianity.[3] The gospels could therefore be interpreted as

---

negotiorum ecclesiasticorum diversos canones ediderunt et scripserunt." A similar view was expressed by Stephanus Tornacensis in the introduction to his *Summa*, p. 2 ed. cit.

[1] See, e.g. Johannes Andreae in his gloss on *Clem.* II.xi.2: "Item jus naturale dicitur aequissimum veluti, Quod tibi non vis irrogari, aliis non irroges . . . inde dicuntur praecepta naturalia, quae in lege et in evangelio continentur, ut non moechaberis."

[2] "Jus naturale in tribus consistit, scil. in necessariis, impossibilibus et mediis, id est, in mandatis, interdictis, et demonstrationibus. Mandat enim quod prosit, interdicit, quod laedit, demonstrat, quod convenit," gloss of Johannes Faventinus, proem., and Huguccio in similar terms, loc. cit., fol. 116 of P 72.

[3] The resort to supra-natural principles was not particularly favoured: miracles especially should not be the prototype of human actions, see Gratian, C. II,

constituting natural law; and since the Old Testament was an integral part of the Christian faith, the notion of natural (divine) law was extended to this part of Holy Writ; canon law itself was taken as a conspicuous and classical example of the practical realization of Christian ideas—natural law then could also embrace canon law without appreciable difficulty. We venture to maintain that it was a species of Christian pantheism which permeated the canonistic conception of the divine (natural) law. And this was explained and taught as a dogma at the very time, at which the Thomistic idea of natural law gained ground amongst philosophers and theologians. The saturation of this natural law with ethical elements and its practical identity with a "moral" law is shown in Huguccio's statements. For according to him, and all the canonists of the time,[1] "on the basis of natural law everything is held in common": "jure naturali omnia sunt communia". The terms "mine" and "thine" were inapplicable within the precincts of this "law"; Huguccio added, however, the rider that theology employed this terminology.[2] The idea of common property entailed that in times of necessity everything should be shared by all: "Omnia sunt communia, id est, tempore necessitatis indigentibus communicata." "For guided as we are by reason we deem it fit that we keep only those things which are indispensable to us, whilst we should distribute the rest to our neighbour."[3]

The natural (divine) law was throughout conceived as unalterable and immutable: derived as it was from the Supreme Being it was necessarily beyond the power of human individuals

---

q. vii, post cap. 41: "Miracula (et maxime veteris testamenti) sunt admiranda, non in exemplum nostrae actionis trahenda. Multa enim concedebantur tunc, quae nunc penitus prohibentur." With all due respect I think that Professor Le Bras goes too far when he says that Gratian denied the validity of miracles: loc. cit., p. 53, note 2. See also Gratian post cap. 18, C. XXII, q. ii, and ante cap. 1, C. XV, q. iii.

[1] Cf., for instance, the gloss cited by J. Juncker, art. cit., p. 442: "Omnia Dei sunt. Jure divino nihil meum, nihil tuum ... aliter enim dicitur jus de divino jure, aliter de humano."

[2] "Consimilibus modis loquendi invenitur in theologia." See also his remarks on *Dist*. viii, c. 1, fol. 121 of P 72.

[3] "Naturali enim ductu natura rationis approbamus tantum necessaria nobis retinere, reliqua proximis indigentibus debere distribuere ... tempore necessitatis aliis est communicandum," fol. 116 of P 72.

to change it. And yet, in spite of the solemn and emphatic insistence on the unalterable character of natural law, a great many instances can be adduced to show that, by his fullness of power, the pope was deemed to have the faculty of changing even this law. Natural (divine) law was a set of rules vaguely resting upon the principles of Christianity. And since the pope was, if no more, the vicar of Christ, it was consequently in his power to change this law, like any other. The Roman idea that the pope as a prince was not bound by the laws, was made to apply not only to human, but also to divine laws. And this particular instance of natural (divine) law provides a fitting occasion to observe, firstly, how little canonistic scholarship was influenced by contemporary scholastic theology and philosophy, and, secondly, that the Thomistic system of law in particular made no impression upon contemporary or later canonists. On the other hand, the Stagirite's Christian interpreter[1] was frequently at loggerheads with his brethren in the canonistic camp. In one place he charged them with following the human rather than the divine law, whilst in another he complained of the professors of sacred theology who referred to the "glossulas juristarum" as an authority.[2] On the whole, the mutual relations between St. Thomas Aquinas and the canonists were somewhat strained, and the mutual influence negligible.

That this conception of natural (divine) law as a set of Christian principles was in fact the chief tenet of the canonists, may also be deduced from the continually emerging question,

---

[1] On St. Thomas Aquinas's desire to "baptize" Aristotle, see Professor M. D. Knowles, "Some recent advance in the history of medieval thought" in *Cambridge Historical Journal*, vol. ix (1947), p. 36, and on Thomas's eclecticism, pp. 38-39. See also Mgr. M. Grabmann, "Studien über den Einfluss der aristotelischen Philosophie auf die mittelalterlichen Theorien über das Verhältnis von Kirche und Staat" in *SB d. Bayrischen Akademie der Wiss.*, (phil. hist. Abt.), 1934, pp. 6-18.

[2] Cf. *Quaestiones Quodlibetales*, XI, art. 9: "Opinio decretistarum non est vera, quia ipsi plus assentiunt in his et sequuntur jus humanum quam divinum, cum plus sit assentiendum divino quam humano ... inconsonum et derisibile videtur quod sacrae doctrinae professores juristarum glossulas(!) in auctoritatem inducunt, vel de eis disceptent, cum sit plus assentiendum divino judicio quam humano." As we remarked somewhere else, St. Thomas's reflections seem to have been dictated by too great an emphasis on the divine law, a defect which the canonists clearly perceived, see *The Medieval Idea of Law*, p. 50, note 6. On St. Thomas's conception of natural law, see also O. Lottin, *Le droit natural chez saint Thomas d'Aquin et ses prédécesseurs*, 2nd ed., *passim*.

Was the natural (divine) law of every nation identical? The very question indicated that the idea of natural law as originally conceived by the Romans, had undergone a considerable modification. Since natural (divine) law was all which was contained in the Scriptures, and since, on the other hand, not every nation was Christian, how could one maintain that the natural (divine) law of all nations was identical? Here again the Archdeacon was quite outspoken. "Quidam," he said, "voluerunt, quod lex naturae non est una apud omnes, nam cum hic dicit, quod jus naturale est, quod in evangelio et lege continetur, et hoc non est commune omnibus."[1] But the "natural" law itself was clear on this point. St. Paul in his epistle to the Romans declared that the Jews and Greeks were ignorant of the laws of Christ—and therefore natural law itself admitted that it did not apply to every nation.[2]

The idea of natural (divine) law, as we have reconstructed it, should not lead to the assumption that another kind of natural

[1] The Archdeacon, loc. sit., Gratian himself had clearly recognized that the Old Testament concerned one race only, the Jews, whilst the New Testament applied to the whole world, see his *dictum*, C. XXXII, q. iv, post cap. 2: contrast between "domus Judae et domus Israel" and "omnes gentes". For other distinguishing marks between the Old and New Testaments see Gratian's *dicta* in the tract "De poenitentia" post cap. 14, *dist.* ii, and C. XXIII, q. iv, post cap. 15 ("timor" and compulsion in Old Testament, liberty, love and voluntariness in New Testament). Gratian also often referred to the prohibition of actions in the New Testament, which were permitted in the Old Testament, see, e.g. C. XV, q. iii, ante cap. 1, C. XXVI, q. ii, post c. 1, C. XXXI, q. i, post cap. 7, etc. Priestly marriages, or marriages between certain relatives were not prohibited "legali, nec evangelica, vel apostolica auctoritate" but only by "ecclesiastica lege", C. XXVI, q. ii, post cap. 1. Hence, the Church alone was to declare what was licit and illicit: "L'eglise détient le magistère suprême, et d'une certaine façon, la maîtrise des écritures. C'est elle, qui a fixé le canon des deux testaments, defini leur autorité. C'est elle qui fait reluire la verité divine encore violée dans les écritures. Quand il le faut, elle la compléte et en tous cas elle la sanctionne avec une autorité souveraine," Professor Le Bras, loc. cit., p. 77, also referring to Gratian's *dicta* in C. XXXV, q. i, post cap. 1, C. XI, q. iii, post cap. 21 and post s. 24. *Roma locuta, causa finita* was the keynote of Gratian's *dictum, Dist.* xxi, ante cap. 1: "Decretis ergo Romanorum pontificum et sacris canonibus conciliorum ecclesiastica negotia, ut supra monstratum est, terminantur." Quite naturally, the Roman (and no other) Church was above the canons: Gratian in C. XXV, q. i, post c. 16: "Habet (scil. Romana ecclesia) jus condendi canones, utpote quia caput est et cardo omnium ecclesiarum, a cuius regula nemini dissentire licet. Ita ergo canonibus auctoritatem praestat, ut seipsam non subjiciat eis."

[2] Rom. x. 3, 14, 19.

law was unknown to the canonists. The Archdeacon made a typical declaration to the effect that there was one natural law which was "something concrete", and one which was "inspired", and it was this latter with which a canonist had to deal. The former was a kind of natural law that could be found amongst all animalic creatures through the presence of natural appetites; within the compass of this natural law there was nothing common or private.[1] But a natural law of this kind was not thought to fall within the framework of the law proper: "De hoc non agitur hic." The "inspired" natural law was the one which was the proper object of canonistic studies and which was identical with divine law. Its gist was "natural equity", according to which, if there were any sinless State, men would be able to rule themselves. Perhaps the clearest exposition of the "concrete" kind of natural law we find in an anonymous *Summa* of the early thirteenth century which shows a strong Romanistic influence on the formation of the notion of natural law. Canonists found great difficulty in freeing themselves from the Roman ideas. The author of the *Summa* "*Animal est Substantia*"[2] saw the concept of sensuality as an element common to both mankind and the animalic world. "Homo habet communem naturam cum quolibet animali, scilicet sensualitatem."[3] Man derived a "natural right" from this sensuality, just as animals did, and this right again was common to both man and animal. "Unde homo a sensualitate quoddam jus habet, quod etiam commune est omnibus animalibus, scilicet jus naturale, quod natura omnia animalia docuit." And because this kind of natural law entailed no moral obligations, actions taken within its compass could not be classed as just or unjust. This natural law was merely the manifestation of the animalic instinct in man and animal: "Secundum hoc jus nihil est justum vel injustum, quia istud jus nihil jubet, sed tantum impellit hominem ex vi naturae."

---

[1] "Nam est quoddam concretum, quod est in quolibet animali, quo aliquid appetit, secundum quod nihil est proprium, nulla discernuntur secundum illud nec etiam aliquid est commune," Archdeacon, *Dist.* 1, omnes, fol. 3 verso. See also Egidius Romanus, *supra* p. 39, n.8.

[2] On the *Summa* itself, see Kuttner, *Repertorium*, p. 207.

[3] Quoted after Schulte, "Dritter Beitrag zur Geschichte der Literatur über das Dekret Gratians" in *SB d. kais. Akad. d. Wiss.*, vol. lxv, p. 60.

CHAPTER III

THE POPE AND NATURAL LAW

THE immutability of natural law was presented in Gratian's *Decretum* as a fundamental and unimpeachable principle. The same solemn pronouncement was given by all the canonists: the immutability of natural law was affirmed with a reverence almost as profound as that accorded to a dogma. But despite all this, the principle suffered more than one substantial inroad. It is evident that the conception of natural law whose frontiers were so widely and liberally drawn as to include even canon law itself, entailed a number of problems. Of these perhaps the most important concerned the position of the pope in regard to natural law. As soon as the principle of the immutability of natural law was put to the test, it became no more than a pious assertion—a device that declared something sacrosanct so long as it was convenient to do so: expediency and other utilitarian considerations played an important part in bringing about a relationship between natural law and the pope in which the immutability of natural law was but a hollow name.

For, resting on the fullness of his power, the pope was to be beyond the reach of any mortal. The idea of a papal responsibility was unanimously rejected. There was nobody on earth who could say to the pope: "Cur ita facies?" as the standing phrase in canonistic writings ran. The pope could do and say whatever he pleased to do and say, in all and everything. "In omnibus et per omnia potest facere et dicere, quicquid placet."[1] He disposed of kingdoms and judged them as he pleased— "prout sibi placet". "The pope can do whatever God can do" —"papa potest facere, quicquid Deus potest".[2] He was a true vicar of God, for, according to Tancred, "whatever is done by the authority of the lord pope, is done by the authority of

---

[1] *Speculum Judiciale*, Lib. 1, partit. i, De Legato, § Nunc, fol. 51 of the edition Basileae, 1574.

[2] Panormitanus, *Com. in Decretales*, I.vi.34, fol. 115 verso, No. 18. On this point see also *infra* ch. VI.

God".[1] All this was no pious assertion or declaration on the part of the canonists. It was a formal pronouncement of a principle. The pope was above the law whether natural (divine), or humanly devised. The Roman and medieval principle that the prince was above the human law was thus transferred to the ecclesiastical prince and extended to the natural (divine) law. Whilst attacking the imperialists for their temerity in declaring that the emperor possessed the "coeleste arbitrium", the canonists quite openly borrowed this idea and invested the pope with this "coeleste arbitrium". Whatever pleases the pope, has the force of law: "Quicquid ei placet, legis habet vigorem." All human and divine law has been entrusted to him alone.

Dispensation from an obligation imposed by the law was the prerogative of the pope: if he saw fit, he was empowered by canonistic doctrine to give dispensations also from obligations imposed by natural law.[2] For he of all the earthly powers could change the nature of a thing—"de aliquo facit nihil, mutando etiam rei naturam,"[3] and he was the only individual who, like God Himself, created something out of nothing: "De nihilo

---

[1] See his *Apparatus* on the *Compilatio Tertia*, tit. De translatione episcopi, c. inter corporalia (c. 2), fol. 102 verso of D 4, s.v. "divina". He adds however that the Pope should have a "justa causa". In order to corroborate his statement, Tancred refers to C. XXIV, q. i, c. 6, and q. iii, c. 4. A bishop was held to be a vicar of Christ, see, for instance, Laurentius, ibid., s.v. "vicarius": "similiter quilibet episcopus est vicarius Christi". Master Ugolino (the later Gregory IX) as a judge of appeal in the curia held that Innocent III was the vicar of God: "Deus judex justus est et fortis, per vicarium suum et patrem nostrum papam Innocentium, quem constituit super gentes et regna...." *Epp. Cantuarienses*, p. 472.

[2] It is perhaps significant that Rufinus's *Summa* starts with these words: "Sacrosanctae ecclesiae regularis institutio omnibus communiter, sed non aequaliter singulis dispensat," p. 1 ed. cit. The work was finished in 1156, see p. xl. Rufinus was a pupil of Gratian, p. xlii. This canonist sees the "majestas" of the Pope epitomized in his power to loosen and to bind, and secondly in his dispensatory authority, see *Summa* on *Dist.* xxv, proem. Gratian appeared to have laid stress on the "Romana ecclesia" rather than on the Pope, see his *dictum* in C. XXV, q. i, post cap. 16: "Nisi auctoritas Romanae ecclesiae aliter fieri mandaverit vel permiserit ... valet ergo sancta Romana ecclesia suis privilegiis quoslibet munire et extra generalia decreta, quaedam speciali beneficio indulgere...." But Huguccio gave preference to St. Jerome in *Dist.* xciii, Legimus: "Ergo cum sit orbis major quam Roma, major est auctoritas orbis quam Romae", LC 2, fol. 165 verso.

[3] *Spec.*, loc. cit., No. 41, fol. 49; he continues: "Immutat ergo substantialem rei naturam."

aliquid facit."[1] It is understandable that a pope who was endowed with such powers, was also enabled to give dispensations from the obligations imposed by natural law. "Dispensare potest prout sibi placet" was the general verdict. And it is significant that in one of his bulls Clement V restricted the immutability of natural law to the emperor: the emperor was not allowed to change the contents of natural law. The omission in this decree of any reference to the pope is not therefore without significance.[2]

Before we deal with any concrete instances it will be advisable to review the teachings of the canonists concerning the pope's position with regard to some important items of the "natural" law so-called. We have seen that, in canonistic doctrine, the gospels formed an essential part of natural law. How did the pope stand with regard to this part of the "natural" law? Could he give dispensations from any of the obligations imposed by the gospels? In his usual curt manner, Innocent IV stated that the pope could do this, though only as regards the letter and not as regards the spirit of the gospel teachings. "Et dispensat contra verba evangelii, licet non contra mentem."[3] Apparently following Laurentius Hispanus, the Archdeacon declared that the pope must be enabled to grant dispensations from the obligations imposed by the gospels, although not from actual evangelical injunctions and prohibitions: evangelical counsel, however, and the teachings of Christ contained in parables, were considered to fall within the papal power of dispensation. "Nam in his," said the Archdeacon, "quae sunt consilii, non praecepti et quae parabolica dicta sunt et non consistunt in praeceptis vel prohibitionibus, dispensari potest."[4] The only stipulation which the canonists considered necessary was that the pope should have sufficient reason ("justa causa") to give dispensations from these parts of the gospels: he would commit a sin and the dispensation would lack validity, if he could not adduce some adequate reason for his dispensation. This "justa causa",

[1] Tancred's *Apparatus* on *Comp. III*, tit. De trans. episc., c. quanta persona (c. 3), fol. 103 verso of D 4, s.v. "vicem": "Gerit vicem Dei ... item de nihilo facit aliquid ut Deus ... quia dispensare potest supra jus." Hostiensis, *Summa*, tit. De officio legati, col 284: "Ens non esse facit, id est, de aliquo facit nihil, mutando etiam naturam rei; non ens fore, id est, de nihilo aliquid facit."

[2] *Clem.* II.xi.2.

[3] In his *Com.* on *Decretales*, I.ix.11, fol. 95.

[4] *Com.* on C. XXV, q. i, Sunt quidam.

incidentally, was only required for the grant of dispensations from natural law: no reason was demanded from him when he gave dispensation from human law.¹

The same line of argument was pursued with regard to the relationship of the pope to the epistles of St. Paul. Although an extreme section of the canonists wished to set the pope entirely above the epistles and to give him the power to grant dispensations from any of the injunctions and prohibitions contained therein, the more moderate view prevailed, viz. that his position as the successor of St. Peter would not by itself entitle him to do away with all the apostle's *dicta*. The general opinion was that he could grant dispensations from apostolic ordinances, so long as they were not defined as articles of faith. "Bene potest dispensare contra apostolum, non tamen in his, quae pertinent ad articulum fidei."² But—and this is important to keep in mind when assessing the true worth of papal dispensatory power—it was left to the pope himself to decide what constituted an article of faith, since in all spiritual matters he was the highest tribunal.³ The reason why articles of faith were exempted from papal dispensation was that without them eternal salvation was impossible to achieve. This was also the reason for exempting the decalogue from papal dispensation, because, as Johannes de Deo had already taught, the ten commandments were not articles of faith in the strict meaning of the term, but only so-called "annexes" to the articles, they therefore withstood encroachment by the pope. "Quia etsi non sunt articuli fidei, sunt tamen articularia fidei, id est, annexa articulis fidei."⁴ A very similar problem was constituted by the ordinances contained in the decrees of the four councils. By the incorporation of Pope Gelasius's *dictum* in the *Decretum*,

---

¹ *Spec.*, Lib. I, partic. 1, De dispensationibus, § Nunc, fol. 84, No. 2: "Nota, quod nisi papa ex justa causa dispensat, peccet; nec dispensatio prodest. Quod verum est, quando dispensat contra votum tacitum vel expressum, vel contra evangelium vel contra generalem statum ecclesiae: secus in dispensationibus, quae fiunt contra jus positivum, quia in his sufficit sola voluntas dispensatoris, etiam sine causa, quia de jure potest supra jus dispensare."

² *Spec.*, loc. cit. Bartholomaeus Brixiensis went a little further, see *gl. ord.* on C. XV, q. vi, c 2: "Dico enim, quod contra jus naturale potest dispensare, dum tamen non contra evangelium, vel contra articulos fidei, tamen contra apostolos XXXIV lector, LXXXII presbyter."

³ *Decretum*, C. XXIV, q. i, c. 12.

⁴ *Spec.*, loc. cit. quoting Johannes de Deo's *De dispensatione papali*.

these decrees were made an essential part of the dogma. They were: the Niceaen, the Constantinopolitean, the Ephesian and the Chalcedonian councils. That they escaped papal dispensation was not because these were part of the natural law, but because they contained some articles of faith. However, it would be inaccurate to say that all the canonists adopted this point of view. A minority would have supported the pope, if he had tried to set aside the decrees of these councils. But the prevailing opinion was that he could not grant dispensation from them by simply suspending or annulling them.

In general, the *raison d'être* of the dispensatory power of the pope was found in the "necessitas vel utilitas": it was in these words that the *glossa ordinaria* on the *Decretales* epitomized the whole foundation of papal dispensation.[1] A materialistic basis of dispensation was thus furnished by considerations of expediency and usefulness. Turning to the functional side of the question we shall find that the pope's dispensation was considered merely an act of administration, within the scope of which he could indeed act as he pleased. Moreover, as far as pure administration was concerned, the pope wielded greater powers than St. Paul. For the pope as the successor of St. Peter was invested with the same powers as the apostle whose authority according to canon law exceeded that of St. Paul.[2] Consequently, the pope's powers too exceeded those of St. Paul whose ordinances fell therefore within the orbit of papal dispensation. And since dispensations came within the administrative sphere of papal activity, it was a "negotium", and here too, as in every essential point of canonistic doctrine dealing with papal power, Christ's words to St. Peter "Whatsoever thou shalt bind on earth, shall be bound in heaven; and whatsoever thou shalt loose on earth shall be loosed in heaven" were given their full application.[3]

But the pope was made out to be not only the successor of St.

---

[1] See *glossa ordinaria ad* III.v.33, s.v. "necessitas vel utilitas": "Ista duo frequenter inducunt dispensationem."

[2] *Dist.* lxxx, c. 2; here the argument usually rested on the last words of this pseudo-Isidorian passage: "Quoniam nec inter ipsos apostolos par institutio fuit, sed unus omnibus praefuit."

[3] See Goffredus de Trano, *Summa*, De Rescriptis, fol. 4, No. 7, referring to Gratian, *Dist.* xx, § 1, where he said: "In negotiis definiendis non solum est necessaria scientia, sed etiam potestas. Unde Christus dicturus Petro: 'Quodcumque ligaveris'...."

Peter and the vicar of Christ—as Innocent III at one time modestly stated[1]—but also the vicar of God, as Gregory VII had dogmatically asserted in a less moderate tone.[2] The pope resembles God in his power.[3] It is then not surprising to find that Bernardus Parmensis, following Tancred, declared "Whatever is done on the authority of the pope, is done on the authority of God Himself", provided that there exists a just cause.[4] Any remaining doubt was dispelled by adducing the legal maxim that "par in parem imperium non habet", that is to say, that equals have no power over each other.[5] Upon God's vicar was bestowed a greater authority than upon St. Peter. Who then could put the embarrassing question to a pope possessing the plenitude of power, Why do you do this? Lastly, Christ Himself came to earth, not to destroy, but to fulfil the law (Matt. v.17), and, accordingly, papal dispensations should not be regarded in any other sense or spirit than as a fulfilment of the law. Mercy was a Christian virtue, and should not the pope be imbued with this virtue when he gave dispensations from "natural" law?[6] The canonists knew how to put their case into persuasive words. We may now select some of the most important examples to show the practical implications of this far-reaching doctrine.

In the first place the papal powers of deprivation of the individual's liberty must be mentioned. Liberty, the canonists declared in conformity with Roman law, was founded upon natural law, and seemed therefore to be inaccessible to human restrictions. "Jure naturali omnes homines sunt liberi."[7] The

---

[1] *Decretales*, I.vii.2.

[2] See Jaffé, *Monumenta Gregoriana*, vol. ii, p. 465.

[3] Guilelmus de Amidanis, *Reprobatio Errorum*: "Papa assimilatur Deo", Scholz, *Unbekannte kirchenpolitische Streitschriften*, vol. ii, p. 24. Very properly says Professor Le Bras, "Les écritures dans le décret de Gratien" in Festschrift für Ulrich Stutz, *Zeitschrift, kanon. Abt.*, vol. xxvii, p. 79: "Comme le Christ, le pape peut modifier la loi, accorder des privilèges. Il est le législateur et le judge sans recours."

[4] *Glossa ordinaria*, on I.vii.2: "Quod fit auctoritate papae dicitur fieri auctoritate Dei, et est verum, si justa causa hoc facit."

[5] The axiom itself was derived from Roman law.

[6] See the Archdeacon in his *Com.* on C. XXV, q. i, Sunt qui dam, No. 4, fol. 326, and Goffredus de Trano, loc. cit., No. 10.

[7] It was usually contended that the loss of "natural" freedom came about through custom. This was seen in the institution of slavery which rested upon the custom of making slaves of those who were captured in battle.

permanent deprivation of liberty would be against natural law and consequently beyond the power of a human legislator. The great glossator of John XXII's collection, Zenzelinus de Cassanis, was perhaps clearest and most outspoken on this point. In his gloss[1] he treated of the right "of the prince of the Church" ("princeps ecclesiae") to deprive any individual, whether clerical or layman, of his ecclesiastical, temporal and "mundane" benefits. Liberty was one of these benefits which an individual might enjoy. "Et libertate, quae est de jure naturali, privat eum quandoque." To prove this assertion, the canonist refers us to a decree of Alexander III promulgated in the Lateran Council.[2] In this decree the pope spoke of the sanctions to be taken against all those Christians who disregarded the embargo enforced against the Saracens or who sailed in their ships; one of the punishments was to be servitude of the Christians in the hands of their captors. According to this glossator, this was one instance in which by the authority of a pope an individual was to be deprived of his liberty for the rest of his life.[3] Now it is interesting to note that the glossator Vincentius Hispanus, in his gloss on this decree of Alexander III in the *Compilatio Prima*[4] stated in a rather abrupt manner that slavery was not only compatible with natural (divine) law, but was also permitted by canon law itself. As to natural law, Vincentius adduced a saying of St. Ambrose that "there would be no slavery to-day, if there had been no drunkenness on the part of man";[5] on the basis of this utterance the saint can hardly be reproached for approving of slavery or of having stated its connexion with natural law. In default of any other reference the canonist cannot be considered to have proved his assertion, viz. that the view was expressed in canon law that slavery was

---

[1] *Glossa ordinaria* on *Extravagantes Johannis*, xii, 1, s.v. "mundanus".

[2] *Decretales*, V.vi.6.

[3] Innocent III dealing with the same subject, ibid., cap. 17, laid down that Christians who supplied the Saracens with arms, etc., were to be excommunicated and made the slaves of their captors.

[4] See Vincentius, *Compil. I*, tit. De judeis sive saracenis, c. 5, s.v. "servos", fol. 51 of D 4. This gloss bears the usual siglum of Vincentius, but it appears that there is some doubt about the authorship: the same gloss is signed in other MSS. by Alanus, in others again by Tancred, see Schulte, "Literaturgeschichte der Compilationes Antiquae" in *SB d. kais. Akad. der Wiss.*, vol. lxvi, p. 84. But the *glossa ordinaria* also attributes this statement to the Spaniard.

[5] "Non est hodie servitus, si ebrietas non fuisset," referring to *Dist.* xxxv, c. 8.

an institution of natural law: as far as the available evidence goes, neither the *Decretum* nor later collections explicitly maintained that slavery belonged to natural law. But the Spaniard's second point, namely, that slavery was recognized as a legal institution by canon law itself, has more to commend it. In a decree issued at the Council of Toledo in the year 655 it was laid down that the children of clerics should become the slaves of the church to which the cleric-father belonged.[1] Moreover, in his dispute with the Florentines in 1376, Gregory XI decreed that any Florentine, wherever he might be found, should belong to his captor and be made a slave.[2]

We find, then, two notions current in canonistic doctrine—the one that human liberty was founded in natural law, and the other that slavery was recognized by canon law. This conflict touching a most fundamental conception, was solved by a "compromise": the pope was not entitled to deprive a Christian of his liberty, unless there existed a just cause. And the nature of the "just cause" was defined in the law itself, that is to say, in papal decrees. The canonists found the solution of the theoretical difficulty partly in Roman law and partly in canon law, both of which recognized slavery as a legitimate institution. Hence the pope could not be said to have gone beyond the frontiers of the law, when he deprived an individual of his liberty. Nevertheless, some canonists, such as the previously mentioned Zenzelinus, attempted a theoretical and legal justification of the papal right. How could one maintain, he asked, that the pope was able to deprive a man of his freedom, when a pope himself had laid down that the natural law was unalterable? It is true, Zenzelinus said, that "natural law in its totality and in itself is unalterable"—"jus naturale in se totale immutabile est"—but special cases were exempted from this rule. In these the pope was allowed to dispense with the stipulations of natural law. Consequently, liberty too could be suspended: "Unde libertas, licet de jure naturali sit, tolli potest." This is proved, the canonist declared, by the institution of a private treaty which an adult individual concludes, thereby "selling himself as a slave" to his creditor in case of non-payment of his debt. If this was conceded to a private individual, surely the pope must have the right to set aside human liberty "ex causa"? To sum up:

[1] See C. XV, q. viii, c. 3.
[2] See Raynaldus, *Annales Ecclesiastici*, vol. xvi, ad annum 1376, No. 5.

freedom of the individual, although an integral tenet of natural law, was subject to the pope's encroachments, provided that he could make out a just cause on the basis of the law. And the law was made by him who was supreme in every sphere, including that of legislation. Slavery for life was provided as a sanction by those laws issued by the supreme legislator on earth.

Closely allied to the papal deprivation of freedom was another aspect of the pope's powers in dealing with individuals. In the case of a quarrel between an abbot and one of his monks, according to the teachings of the canonists, the pope was entitled to expel the monk from his monastery, to "assign", that is, to hand him over to the bishop or to the secular prince and to detain him in Rome.[1] Now here we have a typical example of canonistic interpretation—and exaggeration. We are referred to two passages in the *Decretum* which were to prove the legal basis for the pope's action against a recalcitrant monk. The one —*Dist*. viii, c. 2—was an excerpt from St. Augustine's *Confessions* and, in very general terms, laid down that any part that did not harmonize with the whole, must be thought of as base and discreditable: everything amounting to scandalous behaviour must be shunned, because it disturbed the peace of the whole.[2] By some free interpretation it is of course possible to maintain that since a monk who quarrelled with his abbot was a shameful object and did not therefore conform to the general pattern of the monastery, he should be excluded. It is interesting to observe that the pope was supposed to take action against the monk without investigating the cause. The second passage which was cited to support the papal right—C. XI. q. iii, c. 21 —was a letter of Pope Nicholas I to Emperor Michael in the year 865. Here this pope merely said that, on the basis of his power derived from the apostles Peter and Paul, he had the right to "convoke", that is, to summon, any monk or cleric, to Rome.[3] Thus the canonistic interpretation is not fully borne out by the references adduced.

---

[1] See *Spec.*, fol. 50, No. 43, where this right of the Pope was the 49th of 89 papal prerogatives.
[2] "Quae contra mores hominum sunt flagitia ... vitanda sunt ... turpis enim omnis pars est suo universo non congruens."
[3] "Jus habemus non solum monachos, verum etiam quoslibet clericos de quacumque diocesi, cum necesse fuerit, ad nos convocare."

Within the compass of matrimonial legislation the pope's powers should also be considered in this context, and it is significant that in this particular field canonistic doctrine in part allowed the pope greater freedom, and in part subjected him to more restrictions, than canon law itself did.[1] Whether the "natural" law was expanded in favour of the pope or restricted in its application by the pope, its immutability remained but a formal title. The question of divorce was of course one that continually attracted the attention of the canonists. The prohibition against a divorce when the marriage was validly contracted between two Christians was based upon Christ's famous words, "What God hath joined together, let no man put asunder". This saying received two main modifications at the hands of the canonists. "Sic modificatur hoc verbum per summum pontificem", in these words Goffredus de Trano introduced his speculations on this point. The first modification by the pontiff of Christ's *dictum* was this. If a marriage was ratified,[2] but not consummated, it could be

[1] The purpose of marriage does not enter into this enquiry. I may refer to Gratian's *dictum*, C. XXXII, q. ii, post cap. 2, where he declared that the gratification of the sexual impulse was a legitimate end of marriage: "Qui ergo propter incontinentiam in naturalem redire usum moventur, patet, quod non propter filiorum procreationem tantum misceri jubentur. Non tamen ideo nuptiae male judicantur." In other respects, however, Gratian echoed the temper of his time; in C. XV, q. iii, ante cap. 1 he declared that the Old Testament rule that women and wives could be judges and accusers was abolished: the husband was to be the "head of the wife". Many things were permitted in the Old Testament, which "to-day" were forbidden.

Huguccio's conception of marriage was not entirely different from that of Gratian. In the proemium of his *Summa* he stated that "coitus conjugalis, qui fit causa incontinentiae (qui) permittitur," fol. 116, of P 72.

[2] It should be pointed out that, according to canonistic doctrine, the constituent element of matrimony was the consent of the two partners, not subsequent sexual union. The reason of why the consent alone mattered, can easily be understood, if the dogma of the virgin birth of Christ is taken into account. The marriage of Joseph and Mary was considered to be the prototype of everything belonging to the matrimonial sphere: their marriage, although valid, had never been consummated. See Rolandus in his *Summa*, on C. XXVII, q. ii, p. 128 ed. cit.: it is said "matrimonium inter Mariam et Joseph, inter quos nec fuerat nec futura erat ulla carnis commixtio" was nevertheless valid. See also Rufinus, *Summa*, ibid., p. 393 ed. cit.: "Cum ergo Joseph et Maria carnaliter commixti non fuerint, patet, quod in desponsatione absque carnis commixtione perficitur et firmatur matrimonium." Their marriage had sacramental character: "Quod vero dicitur inter eos fuisse sacramentum, intelligendum est propter effectum, scil. inseparabilitatem, quae illius sacramenti effectu est." In the same

dissolved by the entry of one partner into a monastery, provided that the other partner consented to it. The divorced spouse was free to marry again. Now this divorce was based upon a decision of Alexander III[1] who, it will be recalled, acquired great fame as Magister Rolandus. The canonistic training of Alexander III emerges plainly from his verdict on a practical case which Gregory IX considered important enough to include in his collection (III.xxxii.7). A very brief review of the case and the decision itself seems indicated.

An appeal was made to the pope against the decision of the Bishop of Verona in a case of matrimony. The wife who was anxious to enter a religious order, was commanded by episcopal sentence to return to her husband and to show him true marital affection: if she refused she would be excommunicated. The husband denied consummation of the marriage. According to the episcopal decision the marriage was valid and could not be dissolved. The pope took a different view. He ordered the bishop to rescind the sentence and to absolve her from the threat of excommunication: the wife was to be free to go into a nunnery within two months. Alexander hastened to add that this

---

sense was the doctrine set forth in the *Summa Lambethana*, LB 139, fol. 146 verso, on C. XXIX, q. ii: "Inter beatam virginem et Joseph fuisse matrimonium catholica ecclesia profitetur, licet carnalis non intervenerit copula." Hence, a dogma became part of the law. Since consent alone was the constituent element of matrimony, the enormous canonistic literature on the requirements for the validity of matrimonial consent can cause no surprise: the numerous reasons which might affect its validity gave rise to the many thorny problems concerning matrimony. One such problem was provided by the case of a man's jokingly putting the ring upon the finger of a girl and at the same time adding the words: "accipio te in meam", whilst she declared: "accipio te in meum". The case is treated at great length by the author of the *Quaestiones Londinenses*, BM, Royal 9 E VII, fol. 193: he concludes, for understandable reasons, that there is no valid consent in this case, but adds significantly enough that if the two had been sleeping together, the Church would presume a valid consent. "Si vero dormieret cum ea, presumeret ecclesia non esse jocum."

[1] The matrimonial innovations legislated by Alexander III did not seem to have found the unanimous approval of the canonists. Whilst Richardus Anglicus (Richard de Lacy) approved, for instance, of IV.xi.3, Petrus Hispanus was only lukewarm, and Huguccio maintained that was not a decretal at all, because the Pope could have spoken only as "magister", not as "legislator". "Huguccio autem dicit hanc non esse decretalem, vel si est, locutus est ut magister, non ut papa." See the long passage of Petrus transcribed by Schulte, "Literaturgeschichte der Compil. Ant." in *SB d. kais. Akad. d. Wiss.*, vol. lxvi, p. 94. On the authorship of Petrus, see Kuttner, *Repertorium*, p. 324.

decision was not contrary to a fundamental article of faith: the true meaning of Christ's *dictum* that the husband may not dismiss his wife, except in case of fornication, was that Christ spoke of consummated marriages. Let us quote this important passage of Alexander III in full:

> Sane, quod dominus in evangelio dicit, non licere viro, nisi ob causam fornicationis, uxorem suam dimittere, intelligendum est, secundum interpretationem sacri eloquii, de his, quorum matrimonium carnali copula est consummatum, sine qua consummari non potest.

The very same problem was treated by Innocent III[1] who showed himself less anxious to stress the point of a consummation. Marriage, Innocent declared, was indissoluble, as long as both spouses were alive, even if one of them should become a heretic or should be unwilling to live together with the other. The exception admitted by Innocent concerned "divine revelation" which superseded every other law "as was in fact shown by some saints". The form taken by the divine revelation was usually the discovery on the part of one spouse of a vocation to enter a religious order.[2] Nevertheless, Innocent declared that he would not like to deviate from the rules laid down by his predecessors, and he would adhere to their viewpoint, viz. that only non-consummated marriages could be dissolved by the profession of solemn vows.[3] Moreover, despite Innocent's explicit refusal in the above mentioned decretal to consider heresy of one spouse as reason for dissolving a marriage, Urban V in fact dissolved the marriage of the Duke Barnabo Visconte of Milan on this very ground (1363). The pope declared that by reason of the Duke's position as a condemned unbeliever and heretic, his Christian wife was to be absolved from the bonds of matrimony.[4]

---

[1] Loc. cit., cap. 14.

[2] "Illis viventibus in nullo casu possit dissolvi, ut vivente reliquo, alter ad secunda vota transmigret . . . nisi forte secus fieret ex revelatione divina, quae superat omnem legem, sicut a quibusdam sanctis legitur esse factum."

[3] "Nos tamen nolentes a praedecessoribus nostrorum vestigiis declinare, qui respondere consulti, antequam matrimonium sit per carnalem copulam consummatum, licere alteri conjugum, reliquo inconsulto ad religionem transire, ita quod reliquis ex tunc legitime poterit alteri copulari. . . ." *Decretales*, III.xxxii,14.

[2] Spondanus, *Ann. Eccles. Baronii continuatio*, Lyons, 1678, vol. i, p. 557, (ad annum 1363, No. 1): "uxorem . . . a vinculo matrimonii liberavit."

By the decree of Alexander III and also that of Innocent III non-consummated marriages were exempted from the rigor of the divine law, in the place of which more flexible papal decrees were substituted. As the English canonist Alanus put it, divine character was not attributed to this kind of marriage, because it receives its real character only by means of the ecclesiastical rules.[1] It is possible that Alanus merely echoed the general conviction of the time that "marriages are made by canon law" as was clearly stated by Johannes Faventinus: "cum hodie jure poli matrimonia fiant."[2] The pope, therefore, had the greatest latitude in his judgments on these marriages: "Ideo circa illud (scilicet matrimonium) latissime potest papae potestas."[3] And Vincentius even went a step further and declared that the pope by admitting a second marriage could invalidate a first marriage.[4] The consummated marriage, however, was still subject to divine law.[5] The ingenious distinction drawn by Alexander III and Innocent III is indeed difficult to reconcile with the relevant passages in the *Decretum* which were mainly based upon sayings of Augustine, Chrysostom, Ambrose and Gregory.[6]

The second modification concerned the dissolution of a validly contracted and consummated marriage. The meaning to be attached to the saying of Christ, "What God hath joined together. . . ." was that the dissolution of a marriage should not proceed in a rash and precipitated manner, but should be carried through according to the law and in harmony with reason. "Item modificatur et aliter illud verbum 'quod Deus conjunxit, homo non separet' scilicet *violenter, sine lege et absque ratione*."[7] These were in fact the words of Isidore, although he somewhat restricted their meaning by the addition of some specifying clauses.[8] But these clauses of Isidore were omitted

[1] "Matrimonium non consummatum sortitur naturam ex constitutione ecclesiae."

[2] Quoted after Schulte, "Die Rechtshandschriften der Stiftsbibliotheken, etc.", in *SB d. Kais Akad. d. Wiss.*, phil. hist. Cl., vol. lvii, p. 591: cf. also his observations in *Quellen*, vol. i, p. 97.

[3] Alanus ad III.xxxii.7, embodied in *glos. ord*.

[4] "Posset etiam statuere, quod secundum matrimonium rumperet primum."

[5] "Ab ipso domino naturam suam sortitur," Vincentius, embodied in *glos. ord.* on III.xxxii.7.

[6] See C. XXVII, q. 2, *passim*.

[7] Goffredus de Trano, *Summa*, De rescriptis, fol. 4, No. 7.

[8] C. XXXIII, q. ii, c. 18.

by the canonists who stated in general terms that Christ's words should be read, as if the specification "sine lege absque ratione" was implicit.¹

This may be a proper occasion to touch briefly on a kindred topic which also reveals that matrimonial legislation was not always in strict consonance with what the canonists considered "natural" law, that is, with the gospels. The case in question was the fate of a marriage when one partner had formerly been betrothed to somebody else. The custom prevailing in France as well as in other individual churches and dioceses was that the marriage, especially when consummated, superseded the foregoing betrothal. If, therefore, according to the custom observed in the churches of Bologna, Imola, Modena, Reggio and Parma, and in French dioceses,² one partner in the betrothal deserted the other and subsequently married somebody else,

---

¹ Alexander III before he became pope, was rather cautious when he maintained that "the judge does not seem to be permitted" to resort to any of the measures envisaged by Isidore: "Videtur judici non licere conjugatum criminibus irretitum perpetuo deportare vel ligare aut neci tradere, cuius auctoritas sensum Isidorus aperit dicens: quos Deus conjunxit, subaudi violenter, sine lege," *Summa Magistri Rolandi*, on C. XXXIII, q. ii, c. 18, p. 192, of the edition by F. Thaner. Rolandus's *Summa* was, next to Paucapalea's, the oldest treatment of the *Decretum*, see Thaner, p. xviii; Roland's *Summa* was written about 1150. cf. also E. Portalié, s.v. Alexander III in *Dictionnaire de théologie catholique*, and also F. Ehrle, *I piu antichi statuti della facoltà teologica dell' università di Bologna*, p. lxix.

The feudal character of the sacrament of marriage emerges clearly from the older canonistic doctrine. It maintained that no matrimony was contracted and no sacrament created, unless dowry was given: dowry signified the handing over of virtues and should be likened to the "dowry" given by Christ to His Church. See the anonymous gloss on C. III, q. iv, c. 4: "Nota, quod quidam dicunt non esse matrimonium sine dote innuentes decreto evaristi, XXX, V.V, c. I, et dicunt aliter non esse expressum Christi et ecclesiae conjunctionis sacramentum, nisi dotis celebritate matrimonium consumatur, quia dotis datio significat virtutum dationem, qua Christus ecclesiam dotavit," quoted after Thaner, "Zwei anonyme Glossen zur Summa Stephani Tornacensis" in *SB d. kaiserl. Akad. d. Wiss.*, vol. lxxix, p. 231. The passage referred to is pseudo-isidorian. On the English position, see P & M, vol. ii, pp. 372-73.

² See F. Maassen, "Paucapalea, Ein Beitrag zur Literaturgeschichte des Canonischen Rechts im Mittelalter" in *SB d. kaiserl. Akad. d. Wiss.*, vol. xxxi, p. 468, note 42, and *Summa Parisiensis*, see Schulte, "Zur Geschichte der Literatur über das Decret Gratians", ibid., vol. lxiv, pp. 23, 24; and *Summa Coloniensis*, ibid., p. 6, note 1. On the former *Summa* see also Kuttner, op. cit., pp. 170-72, and on the latter, pp. 177-78. Both *Summae* seem to be of French origin.

this marriage was considered indissoluble. That was, moreover, the point of view of Huguccio and of Pope Lucius III.[1] But the influence of the typically dialectical distinction between "sponsalia de praesenti" and those "de futuro", drawn by Peter Lombard in his *Sentences*, proved too strong a temptation for those who were loyal and devoted followers of the Lombard's classifications.[2] Alexander III,[3] Innocent III and Gregory IX succumbed to this influence and declared the prevailing custom invalid, that is to say, they dissolved the marriage, contracted after a breach of promise, provided that it was given in words "de praesenti". This doctrine was clearly developed in the *Summa Lambethana* which declared that words to the effect "accepio te in meum seu meam, volo te in meum vel meam" constituted indissolubility of the union.[4] After cautiously observing that it would be "safer"[5] to recognize the promise as binding than to dissolve the marriage, Alexander III later declared—explicitly opposing the decisions of his predecessors—that the woman (the man was not mentioned here) who had married after she was betrothed to another man, must be divorced and must return to her former fiancé, even if the marriage had been consummated.[6] The mere promise to marry given in words "de praesenti", then, was preferred to a con-

---

[1] Cf. Thaner, loc. cit., p. 214.

[2] See *Sententiae*, lib. IV, dist. xxvii (c), and also Innocent II in *Compilatio Prima*, iv.1.18.

[3] As a canonist, however, he knew nothing of this distinction, see *Summa Magistri Rolandi*, on C. XXVII, q. ii, pp. 129-33, ed. cit. On the contrary, Rolandus flatly rejected the matrimonial character of a betrothal: "Liquet ergo non esse conjugium inter sponsum et sponsam...." "credimus non esse matrimonium inter sponsum et sponsam", pp. 130, 132, ed. cit. The distinction was fully developed in the system of Rufinus, see *Summa Rufini*, on C. XXVII, q. ii, pp. 391 ff., ed. cit. Rolandus, however, considered that neither of the betrothed was allowed to desert the other: "In numeris auctoritatibus ostenditur non licere sponsae vel sponso utroque vivente ad secunda vota transire," loc. cit., although this was plainly against the "consuetudo ecclesiae", as he himself pointed out, and added: "Quae consuetudo tamen quibus auctoritatibus defendatur, me latere non denego," p. 133. The distinction in "verba de futuro" and those "de praesenti" was well developed in the *Summa Lambethana* on C. XXIX, q. ii, fol. 146 verso of LB 139. This distinction was also alluded to in the *Quaestiones Stuttgardienses*, written soon after Roland's *Summa*, see Schulte, "Dritter Beitrag zur Geschichte der Literatur über das Dekret Gratians" in *SB d. kais. Ak. d. W.*, vol. lxv, pp. 43-44.

[4] *Summa Lambethana*, loc. cit. [5] "Tutius": *Comp. I*, IV.iv.7.

[6] The fate of the children was not decided.

summated marriage.¹ The dissolution of the marriage was to be effected by the usual threat of ecclesiastical strictures. Moreover, Alexander III would not even allow a release from the promise, if the woman wished to enter a religious order.² In a strongly worded letter to the bishop of Modena³ Innocent III asserted his pontifical supremacy in order to break the bishop's resistance to the papal decision: the bishop should "humbly" recognize and follow what the occupant of St. Peter's throne considered right and just. This letter ended with the significant words: "Whatever was carried out by the authority of the law cannot be altered afterwards." The purely theological and scholastic invention of "verba de praesenti" was made a point of law—a deviation from which no mortal would dare to attempt. And a validly contracted and consummated marriage had to give place to a mere promise, unless the words used were those "de futuro".⁴

In another respect, however, canonistic doctrine restricted the pope's power as regards natural (divine) law. In Tim. iii.2 (and Titus i.6) St. Paul had declared that a bishop must be blameless and the husband of one wife. Finding support in a decree of Pope Martin I (649-654), in which he maintained that a so-called bigamist⁵ could reach no higher clerical order than that of the subdiaconate, Urban II ordered the expulsion of all "bigamists and widowers" who held any higher clerical orders.⁶ Innocent IV and with him all the canonists asserted

---

¹ See *Decretales*, IV.iv.3. The gloss of Richard de Lacy, s.v. "aliter" referred to the Bolognese custom: "ut boloniensis", fol. 57 verso of W 122. Incidentally, the wording of the decretal in the *Gregoriana* is not identical with that of the *Comp. I* which reads: "Quamvis quidam aliter sentiant et aliter etiam a quibusdam predecessoribus nostris sit aliter judicatum. . . ."

² Cf. his letter to the archbishop of Genoa, in *Decretales*, IV.iv.4.

³ ibid., IV.iv.5.

⁴ The hardly justifiable view on the sacrosanct character of the "sponsalia" emerges from a decretal of Gregory IX (IV.i.31) in which he even spoke of the (real) marriage as a "secundum matrimonium". So that no doubt can exist about the nature of a promise, we may refer to the definition of "sponsalia" as given in the *glossa ordinaria:* "Sunt futurarum nuptiarum promissio: per illa ad matrimonium pervenitur," I.vii.4. Needless to say, the modern canon law (can. 1017) does not adhere to the medieval viewpoint.

⁵ The term had a different meaning from that attached to it to-day: it merely meant that somebody was married consecutively, not simultaneously. On the whole question of canonical marriages see A. Esmein, *Le marriage en droit canonique*, vol. i (2nd ed.), *passim*.

⁶ *Bullarium Romanum*, vol. ii, bull 52, cap. vii, p. 199.

that the pope had no power to admit anybody to holy orders who had lawfully been married twice. Hence, St. Paul's term "bishop" was made to refer to "holy orders" in general.[1] In this instance, then, the canonists curtailed the dispensatory powers of the pope: "Videtur" said Innocent IV, "nec etiam papae liceat dispensare cum bigamo." The wording of St. Paul's injunction would surely have suggested the interpretation that any order including and above that of a bishop must be "monogamous", but that those below a bishop might conceivably therefore be "bigamous". Canonistic doctrine extended the apostle's words to all higher clerical orders.

The oath may be taken as the last concrete example of the dispensatory powers of the pope in regard to "natural" law. The presentation of the canonistic view may profitably be preceded by a brief sketch of the canonical justification of the taking of an oath. It will be recalled that one of the chief tenets of the Waldensian "heresy" was the refusal to swear, since Christ Himself had explicitly declared "Swear not at all ... let your communication by yea, yea; nay, nay" (Matt. v. 34–36). The fury with which the Roman curia attacked the Waldensians is too well known to be dwelt on here, but the tone of Innocent III's decree, embodied in the Gregorian *Decretales*, is noteworthy because of its outspokenly defensive character. But it should be borne in mind that Innocent III was not the first to treat of the permissibility of the taking of an oath, since Gratian himself had studiously collected those patristic passages which set forth that it was not sinful to swear.[2] And before Innocent III the *Summa Lambethana* also dealt with this problem, though it merely referred to Gratian's chapters and was content to declare that the Church had given its blessing to the custom of taking an oath.[3]

The decree of Innocent III puts the case for the legitimacy of the oath very neatly and succinctly and for this reason stands far higher than, say, the Thomistic justification of half a century later.[4] Although the wording of Christ's injunction would, at

[1] See Innocent IV in his *Com.* on I.xx.2, No. 1, fol. 112, and Goffredus de Trano, loc. cit.

[2] C. XXII, q. i, *passim*.

[3] LB 139, on C. XXII, q. i, fol. 144 verso: "Quibus (scil. capitulis) assentit consuetudo ab ecclesia approbata." This work was first described by Professor S. Kuttner, *Repertorium*, pp. 139-41.

[4] *Summa Theologica*, II.ii. qu. 89, art. 2 and 3.

THE POPE AND NATURAL LAW

least superficially, support the view that no oath at all should be taken and that therefore all oaths were forbidden by Christ, we cannot read anywhere, Innocent III argued, that He had forbidden swearing by God Himself: the proper interpretation of these words was that swearing by man, not by God, was forbidden. "Licet juramentum prohibuisse dominum videatur, nusquam tamen per creatorem, sed per creaturam jurare prohibuit."[1] The reason for the exclusion of man as an object of an oath lay in that thereby honours would be bestowed upon man which were solely due to God alone.[2] But Innocent hastened to add that if an oath was taken "per creaturam", it was nevertheless valid, provided that the contents of the oath were "licit".[1] As so often in connexion with this particular topic, the important point is the permissibility of the contents of the oath. We will return to this idea when we deal with the canonistic doctrine. The distinction between "creator" and "creature", typically scholastic, bears the stamp of ingenuity, though we are not called upon to pass judgment upon the correctness of this classification. That Christ had merely forbidden swearing by man followed according to Innocent III, from the preceding prohibitions of Christ: "Swear not by heaven, nor by earth, neither by the city of Jerusalem, neither by the head" (Matt. v.34—6). God was not mentioned and therefore man was allowed to swear by Him. Nor did James teach that no oath should be taken. It was true, Innocent remarked, that the apostle said: "Above all things, brethren, swear not" (James v.12). However, only a very superficial reading of these words could lead to the view that James forbade all oaths. He too merely said that man should not swear by man: the "nolite jurare" clearly pointed to a volitional act. This was the true interpretation and meaning of James's words, Innocent asserted, and all James desired to say was that no facile oath should be taken, but only one which was prompted by "urgent

---

[1] *Decretales*, II.xxiv.26. With this should be compared Gratian's *dictum* in C. XXII, q. i, c. 16: "Jurare per creaturam malum est, quia a Deo prohibitum est." Nevertheless Gratian says that "Joseph vir sanctus per creaturas juravit" (referring to Gen. xlii.15). A few lines later Gratian asks: "Sed quaeritur, quid gravius sit, an per creaturas, an per creatorem jurare fallaciter?"

[2] "Nec per huiusmodi juramentum transferretur ad creaturam honorificentia creatoris."

[3] "Et quamvis non sit per creaturam jurandum, si tamen juretur per creaturam, servandum est quidem, dummodo sit licitum, quod juratur."

F

necessity".[1] Innocent found a confirmation for his distinction between creator and creature in St. Paul's epistle to the Hebrews (vi.12), where the apostle said: "Men verily swear by the greater." This "greater", Innocent concluded, could only be God. Moreover, St. Paul himself swore when he said: "God is my witness" (Rom. i.9). In spite of its apparent prohibition by Christ the oath, then, was a fully legitimate means to end all strife (Heb. vi.16).

Innocent's argumentation was of course fully endorsed by contemporary canonistic scholarship. The oath, the canonists declared, belonged to natural (divine) law, as Innocent had shown in his decree. Here again, despite the solemn affirmation that the "juramentum est de jure naturali" and in spite of the usual solemn pronouncement that natural laws were immutable,[2] ways and means were found to make the pope the sole judge as to whether or not an oath should be kept. We need not dwell on the older minority opinions, some of which maintained that the pope could under no circumstances grant dispensations from the obligations incurred by an oath,[3] whilst others attributed to the pope powers to give dispensations from any obligations: these latter extremists asserted that in case of grave scandal or of bad example, the pope would be entitled to grant a dispensation from the oath altogether.[4] This older doctrine was effectively challenged by Huguccio who pointed out that an issue of natural law should not be made dispensable in such general and wide terms. He advocated the reference to a more juristic criterion, that is, to the permissible character of the obligation sworn to. According to Huguccio, then, the pope was allowed to grant dispensation from an oath, if its obligations were "illicit". Innocent, following in the footsteps of his master, stressed the importance of this criterion, but it was to be left to canonistic doctrine to decide which obligations could be termed "licit" or "illicit".[5] Yet, the canonistic writings left their

---

[1] *Decretales*, II.xxiv.26.

[2] See, e.g., *Spec.* fol. 48, No. 24: "Juramentum et votum sunt de jure naturali, extra etsi Christus (II.xxiv.26) et jura naturalia sunt immutabilia, et indispensabilia."

[3] Cf. *Summa Stephani Tornacensis*, on C. XV, q. 6, p. 221, ed. cit.: "Sunt, qui dicunt, quod apostolicus neminem potest absolvere a juramento."

[4] See the report of Innocent IV in his *Com.* on II.xxiv.18, fol. 285 verso.

[5] The contest between Philip of Swabia and Otto of Brunswick had of course furnished a test case. Whether the oaths of the dukes who had sworn loyalty to

readers in the dark: instead of furnishing fundamental principles whereby the illicit character of the obligation could be recognized and judged, they once again spoke in mere general terms—and left the judgment of the "licit" and "illicit" character and the subsequent decision whether an oath should be kept or not, to the pope. It is true that the canonists alone cannot be made responsible, because Innocent III had declared that every oath taken must be presumed to have been taken without the authority of the pope: in other words, it was left to the discretion of the pope to decide upon the validity of an oath.[1] This was of cource seized upon by the canonists, who were always eager to augment the power of the pope, and thus we read the general statement that "whenever there is any doubt whether an oath is licit and enforceable, the definition and decision belongs to the pope",[2] since "in every oath the authority of the pope is understood to be excepted".[3] And the canonists were able to refer to a decree of Honorius III[4] in which this pope applied the viewpoint of Innocent III in a concrete case.[5] The gloss of Bernardus Parmensis was equally outspoken on this point: the obligations sworn to were enforceable only so long as the pope did not grant a release from the oath: "Quando juravit quod debuit intelligi nisi dominus papa remittat et juramentum."[6]

Already Alexander III had introduced a criterion which proved a flexible instrument in the hands of the canonists. In a communication to the archbishop of Siena Alexander declared that an oath need not be kept if serious danger to eternal

---

Philip "tamquam imperatori" were licit or illicit, was a matter to be decided by the Pope, see, for instance, Panormitanus, I.vi.34, fol. 114 verso, No. 13: "Ad solum papam pertinet cognitio."

[1] *Decretales*, II.xxiv.19: in oaths "debet intelligi jus superioris exceptum."

[2] "Quando dubitatur utrum juramentum sit licitum vel servandum vel non servandum, ad papam pertinet diffinire et decernere," *Spec.*, loc. cit.

[3] "Cum in omni juramento intelligatur eius auctoritas excepta."

[4] In III.iv.15.

[5] The case is of some interest. The canons of Meaux had taken an oath to the effect that they would observe the "common" law which forbade the giving of any fruits of prebends to those canons who were absent, unless they were infirm or employed in papal service: Honorius III set the oath of the canons aside and ordered that those two canons who were absent on account of service with the bishop, must also receive the fruits of their prebends.

[6] *Glos. ord.* on II.xxiv.19.

salvation were thereby entailed.[1] This Alexandrian statement was inflated by a few extremists, who maintained that if the fulfilment of an oath would be injurious to the health of the body *and* of the soul, the pope was entitled to grant a dispensation from the oath.[2] To the papal solicitude for the soul these canonists added their own solicitude for the body. One more criterion was introduced by some canonists. If the oath was taken rashly and precipitately, the pope too was the proper authority to absolve individuals from its observance. The papal right of dispensation also extended to purely temporal affairs,[3] and if the pope saw fit, he could then grant a partial release from the obligations or suspend their enforcement for a time.[4] Apparently overjoyed by his accommodation with Philip IV, Clement V applied this canonistic teaching in a far-reaching manner. The king, the queen, as well as all their lawful successors enjoyed by papal decree the privilege of being released by any confessor from any obligation undertaken on oath—no difference was to be made between past and future oaths—provided that the royal penitents would change the sworn obligation into a work of charity.[5]

According to later reports, Johannes de Deo had suggested that even the bishop was empowered to give dispensations from "illicit" oaths or from ones which infringed upon the liberty of the Church; moreover, next to the pope, the bishop was the proper authority to judge whether perjury was committed, though the canonists were silent on the subject of the criteria by which the bishop was to be guided in his judgment.[6]

Oaths, like marriages, were issues of natural (divine) law, and the pope was necessarily considered the sole jurisdictional authority for dealing with any litigations connected with it. The practical and concrete application of this principle took

---

[1] II.xxiv.8. The advice that the oath need not be kept, if it may be accompanied "animarum periculo" was already expressed in a bull of Calixtus II, 30 June 1119, see *Bullarium Romanum*, vol. ii, p. 295.

[2] This doctrine goes back to Johannes de Deo's *De dispensationibus*, art. 6: "Quid servatum vergit in detrimentum utriusque salutis, id est, animae et corpus...." quoted after *Spec.*, loc. cit. See also *infra* p. 74 n.3.

[3] "Videtur, quod potest illum absolvere, qui juravit ... item in temporalibus."

[4] "Etsi non absolvat omnino, relaxat tamen sive suspendit ad tempus ex causa," *Spec.*, loc. cit.

[5] D'Archery, *Spicilegium*, tom. iii, p. 724.

[6] See *Spec.*, loc. cit.

place in the dispute between John and Philip Augustus in 1204, when Innocent III claimed his jurisdiction, not only by reason of a sin committed ("ratione peccati"), but also on the ground that the dispute centred in an oath. And who can deny, Innocent exclaimed, that we are the sole judge in matters concerning oaths?[1] It was not difficult to extend the basis of jurisdictional powers to everything that could be alleged to be a sin—"ratione peccati" the pope was the sole judge in every temporal affair. We will return to this point later.

Innocent's views on the nature of an oath may profitably be brought to bear on his annulment of Magna Carta. That he heartily disliked this instrument needs no explanation—in his eyes the Charter was a blemish on royal authority, the king having been forced by his barons to surrender vital and fundamental royal prerogatives. The idea of kingship as embodied in Magna Carta was utterly repugnant to Innocent's mind: to him a king was to be an absolute ruler, unhampered by any authority,[2] except, as we shall see, by that of the pope. In the words of Sir Maurice Powicke, the Charter "reveals a tendentious regard for conciliar government and for popular forms of justice".[3] It is therefore significant that in his bull of 24 August 1215[4] Innocent explicitly characterized the document "a loss of royal right" ("regalis juris dispendium") and a "disgrace to the English nation" ("Anglicanae gentis opprobrium"). The only way in which he could take action was in his function as pope, and not in that as a feudal lord.[5]

---

[1] II.i.13.

[2] Innocent's standpoint concerning the trial of a king by his barons was made perfectly clear on the occasion of John's condemnation in 1202. The Pope expressed his opposition in these words, according to Matthew Paris, *Chron. Majora*, vol. ii, p. 657: "Opponit dominus papa, quod barones Franciae non potuerunt judicare eum ad mortem, quia est rex inunctus, et ita sit superior: per barones tamquam per inferiores, non potuit ad mortem condemnari, quia major dignitas quodam modo absorbet minorem."

[3] F. M. Powicke, *Stephen Langton*, p. 123.

[4] Printed in Rymer's *Foedera*, tom. i, pp. 203-5, Bémont, *Chartes des libertés Anglaises*, pp. 41-44, and *Bullarium Romanum*, vol. iii, pp. 298-300.

[5] That the annulment was not based on feudal grounds, conclusively follows from the bull, surely the only document by which Innocent's action must be judged. For in the concluding words, summarising, so to speak, the whole issue (beginning with "unde compulsus est per vim. . . .") he did not assert himself as the feudal lord of John. That relationship was touched upon, it is true, but only in the *ex parte* statements of the bull, which recount the pleadings of John. It is

Two lines of approach suggested themselves to him. He could follow John's plea that the instrument was extorted (compulsion). Desirous as he was to render this noxious document harmless, the following question might have presented itself to him, Was there any canonical regulation which laid down in general terms that the pope *qua* pope could annul a compact of persons not primarily under his (temporal) jurisdiction, on the ground that the compact was the result of compulsion? Despite the apparent lack of any such general provisos, the ingenious mind of Innocent III could no doubt have found some way out of this difficulty,[1] but it is unlikely that his arguments would have carried real conviction.[2] Then, he could also argue that his authority as pope and the interests of the Church were violated by Magna Carta, but in this case he would have had to show how each particular chapter of the

---

also true that Innocent's bull *Mirari cogimur* (edited by Sir Maurice Powicke, *EHR*, vol. xliv (1929)) touched upon the feudal relationship (p. 91), but the concluding words ("unde insolentia. . . .") did not mention it. On the contrary, Innocent based his sentence of excommunication on the "periculum regni Angliae" and on the "subversia totius negotii crucifixi", but not on his being the feudal lord. In his letter to the barons (Rymer, p. 205, 25 August) Innocent said: "Utinam . . . attendissetis prudentius fidelitatis praestitae juramentum. .'. ." although this reference need not necessarily refer to the oath in Magna Carta. As G. B. Adams has shown, "Innocent III and the Great Charter" in *Magna Carta Commemoration Essays*, at pp. 31-32, 38-40, England was a "feudum censuale" and hence was held by a clearly definable money payment only. See also the report of Ptolomy of Lucca in his Annals, *Mon. Germ. Hist., Scriptores*, n.s., vol. viii, p. 100. Adams's conclusion has met with the approval of McIlwain, *Growth of Political Thought in the West*, pp. 231, 376, but with the disapproval of James Tait, *EHR.*, 1918, pp. 263-64, and Petit-Dutaillis, *Feudal Monarchy in England and France*, p. 338. Cf. also G. O. Sayles, *The Medieval Foundations of England*, pp. 395, 407, and Max Radin, "Myth of Magna Carta" in *Harvard Law Review*, vol. lx (1947), at p. 1080, note 90. It is noteworthy that Innocent did not repeat the words of John, namely, that the barons had acted "in praejudicium" of the papacy.

[1] It had been suggested that Innocent III might have attempted to take the line of the later *Decretales*, II.xvi (Ut lite pendente nihil innovetur). But it should be remembered that Innocent's own *Comp. III* did not contain this title and that the chapters I and II appeared only in the subsequent *Comp. II*. In any case, John's quarrel with his barons would not have been one amounting to a "lis" in the sense in which the term was used in *Comp. II* and in the *Gregoriana*.

[2] This jurisdiction must be clearly distinguished from the jurisdiction he would have exercised as a court of appeal, that is, as a judge in a disputed matter.

Charter constituted a violation.[1] This indeed was the way in which Alexander III proceeded when he condemned only *certain* articles of the constitutions of Clarendon. Here, according to the opinion of Alexander, papal authority and ecclesiastical interests were clearly violated, and therefore he was in a legitimate position to condemn individual chapters, and not the whole instrument. And Alexander could not have chosen any other way but that of individual condemnation, because they were not confirmed by a conventional oath: only an oral promise of observance was given. Exactly the same procedure of individual condemnation was followed by Gregory XI when he annulled the *Mirror of the Saxons*.[2] If there had been no oath in Magna Carta, Innocent would have had no choice but to select those noxious chapters which, in his opinion, constituted a violation of papal authority and of ecclesiastical interests. As matters were, the very last chapter of the Charter neatly contains the oath covering all foregoing provisions—and this gave Innocent precisely the basis upon which he could legitimately assert his papal jurisdiction. Had not Innocent himself declared that every oath must be presumed to have been taken without the authority of the pope, and that it was consequently left to the discretion of the pope to decide on the validity of an oath?[3] The oath of John was extorted, because taken under pressure. There was no need for Innocent to argue closely and in detail—hence, the diction of the bull appears at first so unsatisfactory;[4] it was sufficient for him that an oath was extorted, and this oath necessarily rendered the whole document null and void.

Once again, Innocent III was greatly helped by canonistic theory which he as a statesman merely applied to a concrete case. Alexander III appeared to have been far more cautious

---

[1] An exceedingly difficult task: how was he to prove that papal authority or ecclesiastical interests were adversely affected by the provisions governing forest jurisdiction, the appointments of bailiffs, sheriffs, etc., the establishment of a common wine measure, the purely technical stipulations concerning assizes and writs of *praecipe* and so forth? Of course, each of them could have been made an issue of morals and in this way papal jurisdiction could have been invoked "ratione peccati", but this would have been quite unconvincing.

[2] See *Bullarium Romanum*, vol. iv, p. 577, col. 2.

[3] See *supra*, p. 69.

[4] Cf. Adams, loc. cit., p. 26: "To determine the legal basis of the Pope's action, one turns first of all to the bull itself, but the answer which it gives is too indefinite to be satisfactory."

in matters relating to oaths, for he declared—II.xxiv.8—that even if an oath was extorted on the ground of fear, that oath should be kept, unless its observance was detrimental to the salvation of the soul.[1] But the contemporary of Huguccio, Bazianus, declared, as Gilbert reported in his gloss, that an extorted oath need not be kept at all.[2] Alexander's proviso that the salvation of the soul was to be the criterion for the observance of this kind of oath, was lost sight of,[3] and this view reflected the state of canonistic doctrine at the time of Innocent's annulment. Consequently, he did not make the observance of the Charter's provisions dependent on the endangering of the soul—a claim which even he might have had difficulties in raising. Another trace of canonistic thought can be discerned in this annulment. Tancred[4] maintained that the pope could, "ex justa causa", absolve anyone from the observance of stipulations, entered into on oath or grant a dispensation from keeping the oath, always provided that a just cause could be shown by the pope.[5] And surely Innocent, if challenged, would have been able to

[1] Alexander III in *Decretales*, II.xxiv.8:"Duximus tibi respondendum, quod non est tutum quemlibet contra juramentum suum venire, nisi tale sit, quod servatum vergat in interitum salutis aeternae." But it was precisely by a reference to this Alexandrian decretal that the *Quaestiones Londinenses* stated that even if an oath was extorted by violence it should be kept: "Ex juramento per violentiam extorto obligatur quis," BM Royal 9 E VII, fol. 193 verso.

[2] "Bazianus tamen dicebat, extortum juramentum non esse obligatorium, nec aliquem peccare, si veniat in contrarium," quoted after Schulte, "Die Compilationen Gilberts und Alanus" in *SB der kaiserl. Akad. d. Wiss.*, phil. hist. Cl., vol. lxv, p. 615.

[3] Later thirteenth-century doctrine, however, returned to the Alexandrian "interitus salutis aeternae", and it seems, to judge by the *glos. ord.* on II.xxiv.8 that an oath extorted by fear was obligatory, provided that it did not concern the salvation of the soul: "Communior est opinio et verior (scil. than the one of Bazianus) quod juramentum metu extortum est obligatorium, quia voluntarium, XV q. I merito, dummodo sit tale juramentum, quod sine interitu salutis aeternae servari potest, ut hic dicitur expresse." Fourteenth century theory, however, became much vaguer and focused the attention on "iniquitas". cf., for example, the gloss on *Sextus*, I.iv.I: "Juramentum non debet esse vinculum, iniquitatis, id est, non debet obligare aliquem ad observandam iniquitatem"; the gloss on *Clem.* V.v, reverted to the old doctrine: "Juramentum semper servandum est ex eo, quod sine periculo animae servari potest."

[4] In his gloss on II.xxiv.18—*Comp. III*, c. 4, eod. tit.

[5] "Tancredus dicit, quod ex justa causa potest quemlibet absolvere, XV q. VI auctoritatem, et dispensare potest in voto et illud commutare in aliud, quod magis sit Deo acceptum . . . et in juramento et ex eisdem causis potest dispensare," *glos. ord.*, II.xxiv.18.

declare as "just causes" the extortion of the promises, John's promise of a crusade, the diminution of royal rights and the disgrace to the English nation. The pope's authority therefore came into full play, because an oath was extorted, and an oath that concerned the observance of something that was, in the words of the bull, "vile and wicked".

CHAPTER IV

PAPAL PLENITUDE OF POWER: THE IDEA

THE papal claim to wield supreme and unchallengeable power in spiritual as well as in temporal matters demands the attention of the ecclesiastical and political historian. The contest between pope and emperor, though a constitutional quarrel between the two heads of medieval society, was the outcome of an ideological dispute. This dispute was possible, however, only in a medium that was imbued with the spirit of Christian cosmology.

The contest must be viewed against this background. For the struggle between pope and emperor could come to a head only when the former was able to put forward claims which made the emperor a mere tool in the hands of his antagonist. These claims, being based upon transcendental ideas, were, so to speak, removed from the sphere of sensual evidence and capable of expansion by means of logical speculation. In other words, the arguments on the papal side were weapons against which the imperial side had little to set. Pope and emperor fought with unequal weapons: the former could and did resort to transcendental arguments supported by the authority of the scriptures, whilst the latter, besides the Roman law, had only at his disposal an army which is, and always has been, unsuccessfully employed against the ideological fortifications of an adversary. A comparison of the times of the Ottos with those of, say, Alexander III or Innocent III, makes the fundamental difference of each respective position quite plain. The victory of the force of arms and the victory of the force of ideas faithfully reflects the respective victories of empire and papacy. The ascendancy of the papacy under the rulership of its powerful monarchs is directly attributable to the stimulating effects of the twelfth-century Renaissance. "That century's mighty stirring of the human spirit," to use one of Rashdall's happy phrases, was bound to show itself in the fructification of political thinking and to give men the assurance of the potency of the forces of ideas and the comparative impotency of the force of arms.

Without anticipating the detailed presentation of the papal and canonistic argument, we must here ask the pertinent question, Were their arguments based upon "the firm bedrock of belief" or were they an effluence of reason? The answer cannot be given by denying the one and affirming the other alternative. The explanation is that both arguments were employed, the scriptural as well as the philosophical. Naturally, as lawyers the canonists would not place exclusive reliance on the biblical material: they also resorted to some Aristotelian arguments, and in this combination lies not only the attractiveness of canonistic theory, but also its true value. The theologian, such as St. Bernard or Hugh of St. Victor, would naturally argue on the exclusive basis of scriptural and patristic literature—the canonist would take these into account also, but, at the same time, superimpose on them a legal-philosophical framework; whilst the political writer, such as Egidius Romanus or James of Viterbo, would consider these two bases as of secondary importance and emphasize the purely political argument. But in spite of the diversity in method and approach, the three have one feature in common, that is, the working on an *a priori* basis. The *petitio principii* is perhaps the most striking feature of all medieval scholarship, and is nowhere more glaringly marked than with the canonists in particular and the papalists in general. Very properly has Hegel declared that "the character of all philosophy in the Middle Ages was a thinking, an understanding, a philosophizing with a premise". Indeed, the a-hypothetical method of enquiry was hardly known to medieval people.

Papalist writers not only claimed a supremacy of the pope in spiritual matters—something that is outside the scope of this enquiry—but also and to an equal degree his supremacy in all temporal matters. In fact, the supremacy of the pope in spiritual matters was a point that aroused no more than a transitory interest amongst medieval writers: all the more interest was evoked by, and all the more energy was spent on, the proof that the pope was superior to the emperor in all temporal aspects of life. "Omnes subsunt ei jure divino"—everybody is subject to his jurisdiction—"parem non habet super terram"—nor has he any equal on earth. Both these statements, recurring over and over again in canonistic writings, have to be taken literally: the idea of hyperbole was foreign to the canonists. The pope is "rex omnium omnibus imperans". His laws demand obedience by everyone: they are not territorially restricted in their validity or applicability, as imperial laws are. The dominion of the pope extends over the whole world, irrespective of its religious beliefs—the power of the emperor, on the other hand, is co-extensive with, and restricted to, the Christian world.[1] The deposition of emperors and kings, the release of their subjects from the oath of fidelity, the taking away of empires and kingdoms, all these are merely expressions of the medieval conception of papal plenitude of power. Even in purely mundane matters everybody has the right of a direct appeal to the papal curia, thereby overriding the ordinary course of justice. There is an appeal from the emperor to the pope, but none whatever from the pope to the imperial court, for "the pope is not to be judged by anyone", and that holds good whether the cause be civil, criminal, spiritual or one concerning life and death of the accused.[2] In whatever rational and scholarly manner the civilians might have replied to this vast and all-embracing claim to papal jurisdiction, the canonists retorted by employing the ancient stratagem of branding their ideological contestants as sophisticated speculators.[3]

This papal power transcending everything on earth and responsible to nobody, was vested in a man not inappropriately styled "admirabilis". But the sensation of astonishment which medieval men might have experienced in looking through the catalogue of exclusive papal prerogatives, changed into one of awe when they came to realize that the pope was not a mere

---

[1] The territorial limitation of the emperor's power was deduced from civil law itself, see, for instance, Martinus de Fano, "Tractatus de brachio seu auxilio implorando per judicem ecclesiasticum" in *Tractatus*, tom. xi, pars 2, No. 20 fol. 417: "Ipse imperator asserit se tantum habere jurisdictionem et imperium, ubi Christiana fides tenetur, ut l. generaliter, C. De episc. et cler., ubi colligitur, quod Romanum imperium in tantum protenditur, in quantum Christianitas extenditur: facit l. cunctos populos, C. De summa trin." Reference is furthermore made to *Authenticum, collatio* I, tit. vi.

[2] As so often, Huguccio was a notable exception, see his *Summa*, on *Dist*. xcvi, c. 6, fol. 171 verso of LC 2: "A saecularibus judicibus non est appellandum ad papam." This statement was not repeated by any other canonist and must be considered unique. But see Richard de Lacy's views in App. H.

[3] See Antonius de Butrio, *Com.*, IV.xvii.13, fol. 54, No. 49: "Potest haberi recursus ad papam, quando est inter puros laicos etiam; et hoc est verum sive sit civilis, criminalis, sive sanguinis sive spiritualis. Quod facit contra legistas, qui . . . (sunt) sophistici."

vicar of Christ or of St. Peter, but a true vicar of God on earth. For it was he who "vices Dei gerit in terris", who was invested with God's powers on this earth.[1] Can we wonder, then, that resistance to the pope's commands was classified as resistance to God's commands and entailed the usual strictures, above all, the ever applicable punishment of excommunication? The statement of St. Paul that whoever resists the power, resists the ordinance of God (Rom. xiii.2) was interpreted, in the wake of St. Bernard's admonition to Conrad, in such a manner that it came to mean, whoever resisted the power of the pope, resisted God's ordinances.[2] In the conception of the canonists, the pope was truly God on earth.

We are impelled to ask ourselves, How was it possible to propound a view embracing projects of such dimensions, and how could its pursuit lead to a partial and temporary victory of the papacy over the empire? The answer to these questions must show that the imperial defenders were not in a position to marshal those forces which would have been necessary to dislodge the papal claims from their position. Military prowess can never be of any avail in a battle of this kind, and no one was better aware of this truism than the imperial contestants. One might perhaps attribute the victory of the papacy to the medieval inclination to mysticism and to the unquestioning acceptance of acknowledged authority. But this explanation would not lead us far, nor does it, in spite of its plausibility, carry much real conviction. For on the other hand, the emperor could still boast his real power manifested as it was in military strength, concrete alliances, real possessions and the authority of Roman law which made him not only a successor of the Roman emperors, but also the lord of the world, the "dominus mundi". It would indeed be idle to underestimate the actual and ideological forces working for the cause of the emperor. Moreover, the medieval inclination to mysticism appears a somewhat shallow assumption: the age was also characterized by a concreteness bordering on crudity. The resort to such general explanations, as medieval mysticism, medieval acceptance of

---

[1] Innocent III in *Decretales*, I.vii,3, and, following him, the common opinion, see, for example, Bonaguida de Aretio, "Tractatus de dispensationibus", in *Tractatus*, tom. xiv, fol. 173, No. 81.

[2] See also C. XI, q. iii, c. 97; Gregory VII, *Bullarium Romanum*, vol. ii, p. 79, and Alvarus Pelagius, *De Planctu Ecclesiae*, liber I, fol. 54.

authority, and the like, does not answer our initial question: Why was the authority of the emperor disregarded in favour of that of the pope? Or to put this question differently: What reasons can be adduced to show that the papal arguments made a greater appeal than those of the imperialists? This question throws us back upon the basic problem: Why was there such a claim for the superiority of the pope over the emperor? Why was this truly tremendous power claimed at all?

In the endeavour to find an answer to these fundamental questions we turn quite naturally to such solemn and well-considered pronouncements as the bulls, decrees, letters of the popes, and other papal documents. For the most part they are incorporated in one of the collections and thus made the law governing the Church. But the study of these pronouncements will not greatly enlighten us. In particular, we shall obtain a somewhat distorted picture, if we rely exclusively on the bulls, and so forth. Dealing as they usually do with some practical issue, they are too fact-tied and too concrete in their immediate application to provide a basis for the answering of our questions. The righteous indignation to which historians only a little while ago gave vent, is only too understandable: the reproach of popish machinations and interferences, the heartfelt suspicion of popedom's sinister designs, and many other reactions are so easily revived after studying this outward expression of the papacy's intention. The apparent motives of many of the papal bulls and decrees appear to be those of aggrandisement, lust for power, cupidity: fundamental explanations we will search for in vain in these pronouncements. And yet, no legislator lays himself so much open to the antagonist and critic as to say in his enactments what the reasons, what the true motives were that prompted him to issue a particular law. To lay bare these motives and reasons is the business of the legal philosopher and the political historian. Every legislator, whether ancient, medieval or modern, is caught in the network of the ideas within which he lives. Rulers are as much the "victims" of prevailing ideas as their humblest subjects. Everyone of their pronouncements exhibits the traits and sometimes betrays the origin of the conceptions which they have, often quite unconsciously, absorbed. However formal a pronouncement may be, it is merely a symptom of an underlying state of mind that is usually hidden from the consciousness of the author of the pronouncement.

The aim of all historical enquiry is explanation and the promotion of the understanding of those mental processes which appear in these fact-tied, concretely applicable expressions of papal power. It is true that a number of bulls, decrees, and so forth, are at first sight apt to arouse passionate fury and indignation at popish pretentiousness: they may indeed be adduced to demonstrate popedom as the mightiest disturber of the peace on earth. This, I repeat, is a natural and inevitable consequence of taking the bare word of a law, bull, and so on, at its face value.

Now, our enquiry can be materially helped by a consultation of the canonists. That is not to say that we shall find a cut and dried answer to our questions in their writings. That would indeed be a dangerous assumption. But we are on more familiar ground with them. As commentators and glossators and interpreters they were bound to go behind the letter of the papal decree and thus they had perforce to touch the main problem which confronts us, Why did not the popes content themselves with a merely spiritual supremacy? The canonistic writings explain the structure of the ideas from which sprang papal pronouncements. The canonists tried to explain papal laws, not so much by means of purely legal terms as by exposing the philosophical foundations upon which these decrees rested. An explanation of the law, they were convinced, is satisfactory only if its ideological framework is seen in its proper perspective. Nevertheless, we shall look in vain for a systematic theory in canonistic writings, especially in relation to a delicate problem such as the one we have thrown up. Our task is to view canonistic theory as an entity to extract the relevant ideas from the whole canonistic edifice. We have to reconstruct their ideas in such a manner as they would have done themselves, had they worked, not analytically, but systematically, in which case the answer to our questions would have been found at the very outset of their works. As it is, the answer must be gleaned from widely scattered contexts, and the reconstruction is therefore all the more difficult.

In these canonistic writings we shall plainly discover that the controversy Church versus State or papacy versus empire was considered as nothing else but as the political aspect of the ancient antagonism between mind and matter. "Just as the soul is superior to the body, in the same way the pope is superior to the emperor." This formula gives the answer in a nutshell,

"Sicut se habet corpus ad animam, ita imperator ad papam."[1] The canonistic writings furnish abundant evidence for their opinion that it is ideas which shape and govern the world, not material facts: these latter were considered as mere symptoms of underlying ideas. The typically dialectical twin concept of "anima—corpus" gives the clue to the understanding of at least a good deal of medieval political theory. The philosophical axiom was utilized for political purposes. The interpretation of medieval political theory, particularly in the papalist field, must necessarily begin at this point. The things pertaining to the mind and the things pertaining to matter, though complementary, were symbolized by the pope and the emperor. The canonists proclaimed the superiority of the mind, hence of the pope, and the inferiority of matter, that is to say, of the emperor. The inequality of mind and matter was faithfully reflected in the corresponding inequality of pope and emperor.

According to canonistic doctrine the term spiritual embraces everything that pertains to the soul: the antithesis is the corporeal. Although at first sight the spiritual power may be said to confine itself to purely spiritual, and the temporal to purely temporal things, the task of the secular ruler does not, however, exhaust itself in the purely mundane administration of his State. For, provided that the secular power fulfils its task properly, it must direct its attention to the spiritual well-being of its subjects, that is, to direct them "principally and eventually" into the paths of virtue. This function belongs, however, to the realm of the spiritual. Every secular power should see its main function in providing the conditions most conducive to happiness.

The decision to assign greater worth to the spiritual than

[1] To a certain extent foreshadowed in Anselm's *Collectio Canonum*, ed. F, Thaner, pp. 7, 15, 38 ff. Anselm's collection dates from about 1083, see P. Fournier, "Les collections canoniques romaines de l'epoche de Grégoire VII" in *Memoires de l'Académie des Inscriptions et Belles Lettres*, vol. xli (1918), p. 299, and A. Fliche, *La Réforme Grégorienne et la Réconquête Chrétienne*, p. 184.

In the wake of the canonists, St. Thomas Aquinas, *Summa Theologica*, II, ii, qu. 60, art. 6 (ad tertium) states: "Potestas saecularis subditur spirituali, sicut corpus animae, ut dicit Gregorius Nazianzenus, oratione 17, et ideo...." A check-up will not corroborate St. Thomas's reference. All St. Gregory said was "Quod enim corpori cibus est, hoc in animo est sermo," Migne, *Patr. Graeca*, vol. xxxv, oratio 17, col. 966. It would have been remarkable, had this statement been made as early as the fourth century.

to the temporal affords an instance in which the canonists were in complete agreement. They argued in the manner of a typical *petitio principii* that although both were ultimately derived from God (Rom. xiii.1), the spiritual could claim a worthier mode of divine descent than the temporal. The superiority of the spiritual was, secondly, deduced, from the consideration that it furnished a better and more appropriate equipment for attaining man's goal than its temporal counterpart. To all seeming, the strongest reason for the superiority of the spiritual appeared to lie in the difference of the aspects of man with which either power had to deal. It was man in his natural and corporeal state who was subjected to the temporal authority, whilst the object of spiritual power was man perfected by grace, that is to say, man who had become a member of Christ and a son of God. This difference in the conception of man, the one viewing him as a material and corporeal lump, the other as a dignified member of Christ's fold, illustrated the relative position of either power.

Nor were utilitarian reasons absent from the canonistic argumentation. For they argued that a further reason for the superiority of the spiritual might be deduced "ex utilitate", that is to say, the spiritual could achieve more than the temporal and had more ways of achieving its ends than the temporal. Consequently, the spiritual power ruled far more subjects than the temporal authority, for lay as well as clerical persons were under its jurisdiction: in fact, everybody who in any way— "qualitercumque"—belonged to the Church was under its jurisdiction.[1] Herein lies the reason, we may remark parenthetically, for the territorially unrestricted application of canon law, and for the territorially restricted application of civil law. Nor should the role which the spiritual played in its function as a "causa temporalis" be forgotten. According to the canonists, the temporal aim of life was a "natural felicitude", but this was ordained only as a step towards the attainment of the spiritual aim, which was a "supernatural beatitude". Therefore, the temporal existed for the sake of the spiritual—"ideo temporale est propter spirituale finaliter"—and was subordinated to the latter in its aim and function. The "anima" was made for the

[1] Reference was usually made to C. IX, q. iii, c. 17, but an unbiased interpretation of this passage of the year 498 would not confirm the correctness of the canonistic view.

sake of service to God, the "corpus" merely for the sake of the "anima". The aim of the temporal was considered as secondary as compared with the aim of the spiritual. The dignity of the soul of course far exceeded that of the corporeal adjunct.[1] Hence the often repeated declaration that the existence of the empire depended more on the prayers of the clerics and of the Church than on any military power the emperor might marshal.[2]

Relying upon these premisses it was indeed not difficult for the canonists to exalt the spiritual power embodied in the pope far above the power and dignity of his secular rival. Every human power, the argument ran, was imperfect and amorphous, unless perfected by the spiritual power. The practical demonstration of this perfection was the papal approbation, confirmation and consecration of the emperor's person. Consequently, all human power in the hands of infidels was shapeless and imperfect, since it was not moulded by the spiritual power. The significance of the controversial function of imperial coronation and so forth lies in the perfection of the temporal power by the spiritual authority. "Kings are anointed by the pontiffs, because it is through the spiritual power that what is called temporal is perfected and formed aright."[3] The temporal was merely the handmaid of the spiritual and functioned as its auxiliary. The inevitable conclusion to be drawn from such a presupposition was that the spiritual authority had complete and unrestricted power over the temporal. For, as Innocent III had declared, secular princes had been given earthly power alone, whilst ecclesiastical rulers had power in heaven as well.[4] The former were merely concerned with human bodies, the latter had human souls under their jurisdiction. Thus he exclaimed: "Unde quanto dignior est anima corpore, tanto dignius est sacerdotium quam sit regnum." And from whatever angle the position of the emperor *vis-à-vis* the pope was considered, it always turned out that the latter transcended his rival in dignity, although

[1] C. XII, q. i, c. 24, and the gloss of Bartholomaeus Brixiensis, ibid.

[2] Cf. the Archdeacon (Guido de Baysio) on *Dist.* i, c. 11, fol. 5, and C. XXIII, q. viii, pars 4 (Gratian).

[3] "A pontificibus reges unguntur, quia per spiritualem potestatem perficitur et formatur, quae temporalis dicitur."

[4] See Baluzius, *Epistolae Innocentii III*, tom. i, tit. 2, p. 548: "Principibus datur potestas in terris, sacerdotibus autem potestas tribuitur et(!) in coelis. Illis solummodo super corpora, istis super animas." (Migne, *Patr. Lat.*, vol. ccxvi, col. 1013.)

this conclusion might not have been indicated by mere outward appearances. Hence, the receiving of the tenth was "worthier" than the paying of it; but the receiving of benediction put the recipient on a lower level than the giver—and this was the relation of the anointed emperor to the anointing pope.[1]

The inferior position that was assigned to the temporal led the canonists to avow that every inferior virtue was necessarily contained in a superior. The same thought rendered in a more popular cloak said that whoever had the greater, had at the same time the smaller.[2] Therefore, the spiritual also embraced the temporal—the spiritual power thus stood above the temporal. The political aspect of this thought was: "Ecclesia continet imperium."[3] A further consequence of this scholastic standpoint was the superior manner in which the spiritual power dictated to the temporal: that is to say, by directing and ordering its policy, and not by taking on itself the execution of its own ordinances. Temporal power should be employed for the furtherance of spiritual ends. The temporal was to be the "instrument" of the spiritual. That the bodily substance was subject to the soul's guidance was also fully admitted by the gentile philosophers. It was pointed out that Christians in particular should take this idea to heart, since all their temporal actions should be undertaken with a view to the future, eternal life as the ultimate end of man's existence. The Christian's temporal life was to be orientated by the idea of a future, that is, spiritual life.[4] Therefore, the Church with this

---

[1] Innocent III, loc. cit.; "Dignior autem est, qui decimas recipit quam qui tribuit; et minor, qui benedicitur quam qui benedicit. Dignior est ungens quam unctus." (Migne, loc. cit., col 1012.)

[2] Or as the publicist Egidius Romanus had it: "Ipsa spiritualia trahunt ad se corporalia de facti natura," *De Ecclesiastica Potestate*, lib. iii, cap. 6.

[3] Or as the theologian, Magister Herueus (Hervé de Nédellec) expressed it: "Potestas papalis includit id, quod excedit omnem auctoritatem humanam," *De Potestate Papae*, contained in Durandus, *De Ecclesiastica Jurisdictione*. On Herueus see Bellarmin-Labbe, *Scriptores Ecclesiastici*, p. 471, and Raynaldus, *Ann. Eccl.*, ad annum 1323, 58-60. He was a staunch Thomist at a time when Thomism was still deemed a dangerous system of thought; he vigorously assailed Duns Scotus, see Maur Burbach, "Early Dominican and Franciscan Legislation concerning St. Thomas" in *Medieval Studies*, vol. iv (1942), pp. 138-58, at pp. 151, 153.

[4] See, for instance, Durandus, *De Jurisdictione Ecclesiastica*, (Troyes, 1516, no pagination), Qu. III: "Corpus ordinatur ad animam etiam secundum gentiles philosophos, et temporales ordinantur ad spiritualia." This tract is also contained

ultimate aim of man in mind, directed the policy of the secular State.[1]

The application of this idea led directly to the conception of the emperor as a mere instrument of the pope. In this theory of the structure of the spiritual—embracing as it did also the temporal—we find the explanation of why the Church refrained from exercising its right of dealing directly with purely temporal matters, and why it refused also to inflict punishment, especially the death penalty. It was agreed on all sides that the inferior character of the temporal necessarily branded the actions taken within its compass as inferior also. In other words, the administrative and executive actions of the secular

---

in Cardinal Petrus Bertrandi, "De Origine Jurisdictionum", printed in *Tractatus* tom. iii, fol. 29 verso—32 verso, at fol. 31. Petrus Bertrandi used this tract of Durandus in its totality when he spoke at the council of Vincennes in 1329, see his tract No. 13, fol. 31 in fine. On the question of the composition of this tract see also O. Martin *L'Assemblée de Vincennes* 1329 *et ses Consequences*, pp. 64-66, Baluzius, ed. Mollat, *Vitae Paparum*, vol. ii, pp. 284-85, and O. Martin, "Note sur le De Origine Jurisdictionum attribué à Pierre Bertrand" in *Mélanges Fitting*, vol. ii, pp. 104-19, cf. also J. Roy, "La conference de Vincennes et les conflicts de jurisdiction (1329-50)" in *Mélanges Léon Renier*, vol. i, p. 346. The proceedings of the council are reported also in Mansi, *Concilia*, tom. xxv, cols. 883-88 (the reference to Bertrandi on col. 884), and by Raynaldus, *Ann. Eccl.*, ad 1329, No. 75 ff. See further his "Liber contra Petrum de Cugneriis" in Goldast, *Monarchia*, tom. ii, pp. 1361 ff. (de Cugneriis was the royal advocate at the conference). On the life of this very eminent canonist see Schulte, *Quellen*, vol. ii, pp. 235 f. Durandus himself was a formidable opponent of St. Thomas Aquinas and of his theology: he himself was a professor of theology at Paris, and afterwards a "lector S. palatii" at the curia in Avignon, before he was made a Bishop of Meaux. As a Dominican professor of theology he openly attacked Thomas's theological opinions and thus greatly contributed to the embarrassment of the order. On this question see J. Koch, "Durandus de S. Porciano" in *Beiträge zur Geschichte der Philosophie des Mittelalters*, vol. xxvi (1926), pp. 1-436, at pp. 395 ff., A Hofmeister, *Papsttum und Kaisertum*, pp. 290, 294 and Burbach, art. cit., pp. 153-56, and also G. Walz, "Historia canonizationis S. Thomae de Aquino" in *Xenia Thomistica*, vol. iii (1925), p. 128, and F. Ehrle, "L'Agostinismo e l'Aristotelismo nella scolastica del secolo XIII" ibid., pp. 527 ff.

[1] See Durandus, op. cit., Qu. III: "Spiritualis jurisdictio ecclesiae se habeat ad jurisdictionem saecularem sicut ars, quae considerat finem se habet ad artem, quae considerat illud, quod ordinetur ad finem, puta militaris ad equestram et equestris ad rei publicae utilitatem. Constat autem, quod ars, quae considerat finem, *imperat* arti, quae considerat illud, quod est ad finem, sicut ars militaris, quae considerat victoriam, *imperat* equestri, et similiter est in aliis, ut dicitur Io ethicorum."

government were deemed of too mean a character to be dealt with by the spiritual power. Herein lay the real reason why the Church, following canonistic doctrine, desired to control the policy of the civil power, but refused itself to execute secular policy. Moreover, the execution of the death penalty—a rather delicate topic—was necessarily left to the civil power.[1] If a bishop should have criminal jurisdiction in a particular instance, he should delegate the matter to a secular court, so as to avoid passing the death sentence. This was the advice Johannes Teutonicus gave.[2] And before him, Tancred had stated in most general terms that the Church had committed to kings and emperors "executionem gladii quoad judicium sanguinis".[3] It would be too "indecent and unworthy of the spiritual power", to quote another writer literally,[4] "if it concerned itself with the vile works of government, since to the spiritual power belong the more dignified and more powerful works". A genuine contempt for the temporal power the activities of which the canonists considered too sordid for the spiritual power to contaminate itself with, is a feature which characterizes all the glosses, commentaries and tracts. In this context St. Bernard's rhetorical question was resorted to, Which power is the worthier and greater, the power to forgive sins or to divide estates?[5]

But precisely because the work of the temporal power was

[1] In this sense *Decretales*, III.1.5 and 9 may be interpreted, but see also *Sextus*, III.xxiv.3.

[2] Johannes Teutonicus, in his *Apparatus* on *Compilatio Quarta*, tit. Ne cleric., c. sententia (c. 2), fol. 223 of D 4.

[3] *Apparatus* of Tancred on *Comp. III*, De judiciis, c. Novit ille (c. 13), fol. 131 of D 4: "Verumtamen executionem gladii quoad judicium sanguinis imperatoribus et regibus etiam commisit ecclesia."

[4] Pelagius, loc. cit., fol. 55 verso. Durandus, op. cit., Qu. III, referred to Exod. xviii.22 when he said that it was not fitting for the ecclesiastical authority to deal with the minutest detail: "Habens potestatem et auctoritatem jurisdictionis non utitur ea in propria persona, nec decet quantum ad omnia, imo minora debent committi minoribus et mediocra mediocribus et majora supremis, sicut consultum fuit Moysi."

[5] "Quaenam tibi videtur major dignitas et potestas, dimittendi peccata an praedia dividendi?" *De Considerat. ad Eugenium Papam*, lib. I. Canonistic theory basing itself on *Decretales*, III.i.9 (Innocent III) claimed that ecclesiastical justices were not only forbidden to pronounce the death sentence, but also "dare consilium"; moreover, "nec interesse, nec dictare nec scribere sententiam". The necessary proceedings should be handed over to the laymen: "sed aliis debent vices suas committere," Bernardus Parmensis on *Decretales*, III.i.9, see also cap. 5. On this point see also Richard de Lacy in Appendix H.

considered so menial, it was nevertheless essential work which the canonists deemed indispensable—just as we deem certain lowly tasks so to-day. This consideration, incidentally, was a strong weapon in the hands of the majority of canonists in their fight against that extremist minority, who desired the abolition of all temporal power and the installation of officials directly responsible to the pope for each of their actions. The office of an emperor was believed necessary in order that this menial work should be performed. The contemptible nature of the temporal authority was furthermore deduced from the first epistle of St. Paul to the Romans (I Rom. vi.4) where the apostle is said to have written: "If you have judgments of things pertaining to this life, set them to judge who are least esteemed in the Church." Now those least esteemed—the Latin has in fact "contemptibiles"—were of course the laymen. The term "contemptibiles", after the fashion of Gratian, was invariably interpreted: "id est, laici."[1] It was therefore only logical that these repugnant duties should be executed by the "contemptibiles". Temporal affairs were unworthy of the pope's attention—this was the gist of St. Bernard's message to his protegé, and his argument was repeated over and over again. The advisability of permitting the temporal power to do what was useful for the spiritual power, emerged from the consideration that this arrangement freed the spiritual power from the tedious and burdensome tasks which could only impede its chief function. The temporal administration would be a serious brake on the liberty of the spiritual power, hampering perhaps its capability of swift action. On this point some canonists advised moderation. It was said that man was not like God who was not impeded by ruling inferiors in His government of superior beings. Man, however superior in his function, was in need of aid: the spiritual power was "insufficient", that is, inadequately equipped for the performance of the minutest temporal affairs. This aid could be exacted from a willing inferior, such as the temporal power. For, as Isidore put it, if the persuasive power of the priest proved insufficient to prompt man to do what he ought to do, then he must be made to do it by the force of power.[2] Hence, the institution of a civil power on

[1] See C. XI, q. i, c. 47.
[2] C. XXIII, q. v, c. 20: "Caeterum, intra ecclesiam potestates necessariae non essent, nisi ut, quod non praevalet sacerdos efficere per doctrinae sermonem, potestas hoc impleat per disciplinae terrorem."

earth was not only advisable, but also necessary, for the proper functioning of the spiritual power. "Non superfluit potestas principum temporalium in ecclesia."¹

The relation between the ecclesiastical and the civil power was believed to have a parallel in the relation between the idea and the fact. "Ideas govern the world's events" might have been an appropriate epitome of the canonistic outlook. They maintained that the spiritual ruled the corporeal—"in ordine rerum spiritualia regunt corporalia", or to use the semi-metaphysical language of the canonists: the celestial ruled the terrestrial—"coelestia regunt terrena". Experience proved, continued the canonists, that the inferior was always ruled by the superior, that is to say, the temporal must follow in the wake of the spiritual. The spirit had dominion over the human body, and therefore the spiritual power had dominion over the body politic. The typically medieval love of hierarchical classifications was demonstrated by the assertion that the cruder corporeal things were governed by the more subtle corporeal things, and the lower spiritual affairs by the higher.² And in the fashion of the contemporary realistic philosophy, the idea was pursued to its logical conclusion, viz. that every spirit was ruled by God: "Omnis spiritus regitur per Deum." Applied to the problem of pope and emperor this ideology admitted, of course, of one conclusion only: that the pope ruled the emperor. "Spiritualis potestas instituit et judicat temporalia."³ Even the heavens were invoked to justify the superiority of the pope in his function as the vicar of God. Just as the heavens contained all types of inferior matter, in the same way the pope presided over all types of terrestrial power, which of necessity was inferior to his. Some writers had the temerity to declare that the pope could say of himself: "All power is given unto me in heaven and on earth."⁴

But to make certain of their cause, the canonists also adduced

---

[1] Pelagius, fol. 56.
[2] "Et corporalia grossiora per subtiliora reguntur."
[3] Hostiensis, *Summa*, IV.xvii.13, and Panormitanus, *Com.*, II.i.13,, fol. 26 verso, No. 10.
[4] "Sicut enim coelum continet propter sui magnitudinem omnia haec inferiora, sic in potestate papali continetur omnis potestas sacerdotalis et regalis, coelestis et terrena, ut possit ipse dicere: data est mihi omnis postestas," Guilelmus de Amidanis, *Reprobatio Errorum*, p. 25 of Scholz, *Unbekannte kirchenpolit. Streitschriften*, vol. ii.

a pseudo-legal argument. They considered that whenever a principal object had been committed to somebody, each accessory appertaining to the principal, had been automatically committed as well. "Cui committitur principale, intelligitur committi et accessorium."[1] In the application of this tenet the principal matter was invariably represented by the spiritual, and the accessory by the temporal. Therefore, when Christ bestowed all spiritual power upon St. Peter and his successors, He necessarily handed over the temporal also as a mere accessory and the pope, if no more, was the vicar of Peter and of Christ. There is no need to labour this point or to dwell on its implications, far reaching as they were. It may suffice to mention the great importance which this pseudo-philosophical, pseudo-theological and speculative standpoint had in matters of jurisdiction concerning Church property. Accordingly, ecclesiastical jurisdiction of Church property was always based on the latter's "accidental" character. And, amongst other things, the conflict between Henry II and Becket concerned the disputed jurisdiction of the ecclesiastical court. Chapters one and nine of the constitutions of Clarendon put an end to the still only embryonic canonistic point of view, and they formed the beginning of a number of writs of prohibition, above all, the writ of prohibition "de advocatione" and "de laico feodo".[2]

The adventitious and accessory character of the temporal emerged also in the form of a means to an end. The spiritual power alone was invested with the knowledge of how to achieve the end for which all mankind was destined. This end was "the salvation and beatitude of the soul". Material goods, though given to us by God, were used either for good or for evil, that is, either for man's salvation or for his damnation. Now the canonists were convinced that the spiritual power alone knew best what use of temporal goods would lead to salvation, and what abuse to damnation. Injunctions and prohibitions regarding the use of material goods were therefore the business of the

---

[1] This rule was later laid down in Boniface's *Liber Sextus*, De regulis juris, regula. 43.

[2] See G. B. Flahiff, "The Writ of Prohibition to Court Christian in the Thirteenth Century" in *Medieval Studies*, vol. vi (1944), pp. 261-313, at pp. 274-75. "On the whole, the Church in England appears, in practice at least, to acquiesce in this view", p. 275.

spiritual power. For the Church had to teach the causes of sin to prevent misuse of material things.[1] And the conclusion was quickly reached that the temporal power must obey the spiritual power as regards the use of material goods. Their right use depended upon the ordinances issued by the spiritual authority. From here into the political arena was only a very small step.

It is certainly not difficult to see why the so-called instructional authority of the spiritual power was so easily extended to the purely political actions of the temporal power. The right use of material things was taught by the spiritual power: the latter was the rightful judge of everything temporal. This applied to an equal degree to the government itself. Princes, the argument of the canonists ran, easily deviated from the path which signified good government: they quickly became efficient tyrants. Nor had the canonists of the thirteenth and fourteenth centuries many difficulties in pointing to some concrete contemporary examples. Bad government, however, was not considered an exclusively political matter, but also a moral affair, for by choosing tyrannical modes of government princes made their subjects deviate from their rightful path. In fact, bad political government on the part of the princes entailed the loss of salvation on the part of their subjects. Whether the ruler be gentile, Jew or Christian—all succumbed to the temptation of ruling in a tyrannical way. And the reason lay, the canonists believed, in the possession of too great a power over their subjects. To wield immense regal power presupposed a corresponding degree of "virtue" in the person of the prince. The greater the power, the greater the "virtue" its holder should possess, and the right use of perfect power called for perfect virtuousness. "Perfecta autem virtus in paucis invenitur." This propensity to tyrannical government was rooted in the lust for power, the "vitium cupiditatis", which was the source of all evil.[2] It was in recognition of this fundamental defect that God refrained from setting up a king with unlimited power to rule the Jews. He gave them a judge and a governor, and it was

---

[1] Cf., e.g., Durandus, op. cit., Qu. III: "Cuius vel quorum est considerare de salute animae et de spiritualibus, sicut est praelatorum curam et regimen animarum habentium, ut sunt papa et alii episcopi et archiepiscopi, eorum est judicare de actionibus personalibus hominum, per quas possunt deviare a salute sua peccando contra quamcumque materiam. . . ."

[2] The canonists usually referred to I Tim. vi. 10, and *Dist.* xlvii, c. 7

only at a much later date that upon the petitions of an indignant people God granted the institution of a king (I Sam. viii.4, 19). The direction of the temporal power to ethically good governmental actions was consequently the business of the spiritual power. Their enthusiasm for the papal cause seems to have blinded the canonists, who obviously implied that the spiritual prince, the pope, was implicitly endowed with this virtue of good government and was himself in no need of guidance. Nay, we even find some canonists boldly asserting that the Holy See either received holy men or made men holy. Indeed, speculation was not conducive to an unbiased interpretation of contemporary events and personalities.

In consonance with the prevailing theory of punishment the canonists furthermore stated that fear of spiritual action would provide a salutary check upon the temporal government. Again, can we wonder that operating with such premisses as we have just briefly outlined, the canonists came to declare that, in the strict meaning of the term, there was no regal power before the advent of Christ, and that contemporary governments, like those of the Mohammedans and Arabs who refused to recognize the supremacy of the occupant of St. Peter's chair, could in no way be classed as lawful governments?

A further consequence of the canonistic ideas on the use of material goods was the theory concerning the rightful possession of these goods. Man, so they argued, could not possess anything justly, unless he submitted himself to the spiritual power.[1] In practice, then, this view eventually derived from St. Augustine's conception of justice, entailed the assertion that the jurisdiction of the spiritual power extended to purely temporal matters. This theory of possession was to lead directly to the idea of those canonists, such as Petrus Bertrandi who maintained that the pope was the rightful and lawful owner of the whole world.

The subservient position to which the imperial power was reduced by the canonists, was thus a necessary result of their attitude towards the spiritual and the temporal. Above all,

---

[1] Cf. the quite unambiguous statement of Guilelmus de Amidanis, loc. cit., p. 18 "Nullus juste et legitime possidet aliquid, nisi in possessione illius spirituali potestati se subdat." Cf. also Andreas de Perusio, *Contra Edictum Bavari:* "Cum saltem temporalia omnia principaliter ad summum pontificem, non ad aliquem saecularem principem debeant pertinere . . ." Scholz, op. cit., p. 72.

little imagination is needed to understand why the pope claimed the right to depose kings and emperors, whose governments if not in accordance with the policy that was to lead to the attainment of man's ultimate aim, were a liability to Christendom rather than an asset. Moreover, non-recognition of the temporal overlordship of the pope on the part of some secular princes was said to deprive them of any chance of salvation, since thereby they committed a mortal sin: this, it was pointed out, especially by Hostiensis, applied to the rulers of England, Spain and France.[1] Boniface's *Unam sanctam* formed the theory into a law.[2] Nor can any surprise be caused by the claim to the supreme jurisdiction "ratione peccati" over all men. Popes, canonists and other writers in the papal camp therefore conferred upon the pontiff the right to confiscate the property of notorious delinquents and disobedient sons of the Church—delinquency and disobedience being assessed by ecclesiastical criteria. Further rights bestowed were the right to expel anyone from a public post, the right to control executorship and inheritance, the right to incarcerate, to flog, to inflict servitude for life, or to condemn the unworthy to exile—all this and still more was contained in a properly conceived plenitude of power.[3]

That the popes were theoretically entitled to demand the support of the temporal arm for the furtherance of the Church's spiritual ends, also followed naturally from that fundamental position which we have tried to outline. Alvarus Pelagius was quite outspoken: "The Church can demand from the secular

[1] Hostiensis, *Summa*, I. vi. 34.
[2] See the Archdeacon's pupil, Egidius Spiritalis, *Libellus contra infideles* (Scholz, p. 109): "Numquid mortaliter peccent et sint in statu salutis rex Franciae, rex Angliae, rex Yspaniae, hanc subjectionem ecclesiae debitam etiam in temporalibus non recognoscentes, ut debent? Et certum videtur, quod mortaliter peccent et quod non sint in statu salutis, ut ex praemissis colligitur, et probatur per Unam Sanctam."
[3] "Quanta sit potestas ecclesiae etiam in mundanis, evidenter ostenditur et probatur. Potest enim exponere bona temporalia peccatorum notorie delinquentium et inobedientium, et ipsos peccatores inobedientes incligibles et intestabiles ac ad exercenda quaelibet publica officia inhabiles reddere, honore et successione privare, incarcerare, verberare, citra vindictam sanguinis carcerare sine periculo corporali, servitutem infligere, bona omnia confiscare...." ibid. A very similar point of view was expressed by Laurentius Hispanus in his gloss in *Comp. III*, tit. De haereticis, c. vergentis (c. 1), fol. 200 verso, s.v. "officia", and Tancred, ibid., s.v. "intestabilis".

power and its subjects any help, be it by arms or otherwise, for the furtherance of the ecclesiastical common weal."[1] And the help of the secular arm was generally demanded whenever the power of the ecclesiastical authority—the "potentia ecclesiae" —to enforce its sentences proved insufficient. This was particularly the case with so-called incorrigible offenders, viz. with heretics who were too hardened or numerous to be handled by the ecclesiastical court.[2] The constitutions of Pope Pius V were merely the logical conclusion of this doctrine. In them the pope commanded all secular rulers to obey the instructions of the cardinals commissioned with inquisitional proceedings.[3] Some extremists, such as Stephen de Tournay, considered that secular rulers were instituted only for the sake of suppressing heretics and schismatics.[4] Can we wonder that considering the contempt in which the function of temporal power was held, the exemption of the vast clerical army from the jurisdiction of the secular courts was an inevitable result of the canonists' views on the relation between "anima" and "corpus"?[5] The

[1] "Potest etiam ab ea (scil. temporali potestate) et ei subditis exigere auxilium et subventionem personarum et rerum pro communi utilitate ecclesiae," loc. cit. Reference was usually made to *Dist*. xcvii, c. 1, which only partially supports this important statement, and to C. XXIII, q. viii, c. 17, where St. Gregory explicitly spoke of armed support "pro utilitate reipublicae" only, and where he did not even mention the Church for which the armed support could be invoked. This letter was addressed to the "magister militum".

[2] See especially Martinus de Fano in his tract *De brachio seu auxilio implorando*, ed. cit., fol. 417, No. 2.

[3] These "Constitutiones" are printed in *Tractatus*, tom. xi, pars 2, fols. 207-208 verso.

[4] See *Summa Stephani Tornacensis*, on *Dist*. lxiii, p. 89 ed. cit.

[5] Nor could a cleric renounce the *privilegium fori* by a private compact, because the law giving a cleric this privilege belonged to the category of public law which could not be changed by private treaties. The *privilegium fori* was alleged to have been made in favour of the clerics at the expense of secular individuals. See Johannes Teutonicus in his gloss in *Comp. III*, tit. De foro compet., c. si dilig. (c. 4), fol. 132 of D 4, s.v. "pacto": "Nota, quod pacto privatorum non derogatur juri publico . . . ad hoc dico, quod si est tantum introductum in favorem aliquorum, bene potest quis renuntiare, sed si aliquod jus est introductum in favorem quorundam et in odium aliorum, illi non possunt renuntiare. Tale est hoc jus, de quo hic agitur, quod tam in favorem clericorum quam in odium laicorum statutum." Johannes also advanced another reason: by a private treaty the jurisdictional power of the bishop would be curtailed: "Item ex alia ratione non potest clericus consentire in aliquem judicem, quia ex hoc prejudicaretur suo episcopo." But a renunciation was possible by implication: "posset tamen dici, quod licet clericus per pactum non possit renuntiare suo foro,

cleric—anyone acquainted with medieval society knows the vagueness of the term—was a "res spiritualis", no matter how low his actual clerical standing might have been, and, accordingly, he was to be free from secular jurisdictional powers.¹ Incidentally, the designation of a cleric as a thing, though a spiritual one, allows us a useful insight into the mentality of medieval ecclesiastical legislators and writers.² In this context we may observe that the sagacious mind of Innocent IV, who was less inclined to philosophical speculation than his colleagues, asked the juristically pertinent question, Who actually exempted the clerics from secular jurisdiction? His answer was that God had exempted them. And the pope being the "vicarius Dei" was in a convenient position to express God's wish in the language of decrees and bulls, and nobody could object, Innocent

---

posset tamen tacite renuntiare foro respondendo coram judice laico". On the later doctrine see R. Génestal, *Le privilegium fori*, vol. ii, pp. 14 ff., and Professor C. R. Cheney, "The punishment of criminous clerks" in *EHR* 1936, pp. 215-36.

The compiler of the *Glossa Palatina* maintained that all those laws which exempted clerics from the jurisdiction of secular courts, were purely declarative in character: *Dist.* xcvi, c. si imperator, s.v. "discuti", fol. 37 of D 8: "Omnes constitutiones, quae emanaverunt, quod clerici non sunt judicandi, nisi ab episcopo, non sunt nisi juris declaratio."

It is interesting to compare with this last statement the history of clerical immunity, at least in the Saxon period and in the heart of the empire. Its basis then was royal favour. In order to furnish effective royal control, the Ottonians, above all Otto I, granted immunity to the churches and monasteries, and in this way they were "exempted" from the ordinary jurisdiction of the dukes and counts. On this aspect see the brilliant summary by Professor G. Barraclough, *The Origins of Modern Germany*, 2nd ed., pp. 34, 88. The exemption of the clerics and churches from all secular jurisdiction seemed to follow as a matter of course when the Gregorian reform movement spread and imperial power declined. See also Hinschius, *Kirchenrecht*, vol. v, pp. 409 f.

¹ So, for instance, Panormitanus, I. xxxiv.6, No. 4, fol. 111: "De jure divino papa et non imperator praeest spiritualibus, ex quo infertur, quod clerici sunt de jure divino exempti ab imperatore, cum sint res spirituales, eo enim ipso, quod quis ordinatur in clericum efficitur res sacra et transfertur in sortem domini. Et sic ipso facto eximitur a potestate imperatoris." This canonist complained of the vast number of clerics "to-day", individuals who had been ordained and promoted "indistincte"; therefore, the clerical status suffered in quality and prestige, whereas formerly it had been held "in maximo honore". Rufinus called the clerics "coelestes milites", *Summa*, on *Dist.* xxii, p. 41 ed. cit.

² Some writers referred to clerics in this way: "Imo clerici dicuntur esse de sorte domini et habere partem domini," Huguccio in his *Summa, Dist.* xxi, c. 1, s.v. "sorte", fol. 129 verso of P 72. Huguccio had of course in mind the wording of the Isidorian passage.

declared, to spiritual things belonging to the sole jurisdiction of the papal court.[1]

Although the work of the emperor was too sordid to be performed by the pope "regulariter et communiter", to the latter was conceded the right to interfere directly with *any* temporal affair in the same manner in which God Himself sometimes intervened in the governance of the temporal. We should also mention that the exemption of the clerics from military service was another logical sequel of the sordid character inherent in secular activities.[2] Another practical application of this canonistic tenet was the prohibition issued in the Fourth Lateran Council (1215) that no cleric might exercise any action that might be called surgical.[3] A little earlier Alexander III had forbidden monks to study medicine and the "vile" civil laws at a university.[4] We may however gather from the report of Alanus that this Alexandrian decretal was not too well received by the canonists, for they said[5] that it might very well be in the interests of the monastery, if the monks were allowed to attend lectures on civil law and medicine. These canonists interpreted the decretal in the following sense: if the monks went to the

---

[1] See Innocent IV, *Com.* I.xxxiii.2, fol. 156 verso, No. 1: "Sed quaeres, quis exemit clericos de jure imperatoris? ... Dicimus, quod exempti sunt a Deo ... cum clerici spirituales res sint, et ex toto corpus et animam dederunt in servitium et sortem Christi, per consequens papae in judicio et constitutionibus subsunt."

[2] The older doctrine was here, as in so many other respects, more cautious than that of the thirteenth century. If we take Rolandus (Alexander III) as a typical example of the older generation, it will appear that his refusal to allow clerics to bear arms was based on the sayings of the Fathers, especially those of St. Ambrose: "the arms of the bishop are his tears and prayers," *Summa Magistri Rolandi*, on C. XXIII, q. viii, p. 97, ed. cit. Philosophical speculations did not fall within the scope of this treatment: "Ex his praedictis auctoritatibus luce clarius constat, quod nulli clericorum licet vel per se vel per alium arma movere vel judicium sanguinis agitare."

[3] See *Decretales*, III.l.9: "Nec ullam chirurgiae artem subdiaconus, diaconus vel sacerdos exerceat, quae adjustionem vel incisionem inducit."

[4] ibid., cap. 3. This prohibition was later to be applied strictly, ibid., cap. 10 (Honorius III). Johannes Andreae in his gloss on *Sextus*, V.v.1, s.v. "expellant" therefore advised the professors of law or of physics to eject a nun who attended his lectures: "Sic doctor monacham audientem leges vel physicam de scholis suis expellere debet." The Honorian decree is glossed by Guilelmus Vasco: MS in Florence, Laurenziana, S. Croce, Plut. Vsin. 4, fly-leaf.

[5] Alanus was silent as to who they were, and to judge from the absence of any opinion of his own, it might have been he himself who held this opinion. There is no doubt that the gloss is Alan's, as the siglum is a clear "ala".

lectures with this intention, they would not violate the prohibition. "Hanc prohibitionem non intelligunt (scilicit quidam) in casu, ubi in tali intentione audire volunt."[1] This indeed was a most liberal interpretation which was nevertheless irreconcilable with the spirit and the letter of a rigid and narrow-minded law.[2]

The canonists' view on the structure of society faithfully mirrored the contrast between "anima" and "corpus". They applied this contrast to society and hence distinguished two separate bodies within the medieval commonwealth. The hierarchical order in society followed, the canonists believed, from the axiom that men were not equal: equality would militate against the natural order. "Intellige, ordo enim naturae est, quod non omnes sint equales."[3] The clerical order stood on a higher plane than its laical counterpart, as the Hungarian canonist, Damasus, succinctly stated: "Ordo clericorum dignior est coetu laicorum."[4] The universe could exist only under the presupposition of the inequality of men, that is, on the basis of a differential grading.[5] Accordingly, the two grades in society corresponded to two classes of citizens, each of which formed a distinct body of its own. "Within one and the same state," declared Stephen of Tournay, "and under the same king there are two bodies of citizens." "In eadem civitate sub eodem rege duo populi sunt."[6] These two bodies

---

[1] In the *Apparatus* of Tancred on *Comp. I*, tit. Ne cler., c. non magnopere (c. 2), s.v. "leges", fol. 38 verso of D 4. He introduced this passage: "Quidam tamen dicunt, quod pro necessitate ... monasterii liceat eis physicam et leges saeculares audire et hanc. ..." The preceding gloss came from the *Apparatus* of Richard de Lacy.

[2] On the political implications of the Honorian decree see now my paper in the *Juridical Review*, vol. lx, 1948, pp. 177 ff.

[3] Zenzelinus de Cassanis in his gloss on *Extravagantes Johannis*, Execrabilis, s.v. "qui mendicant". Curiously enough he corroborated this statement with a reference to the *Authenticum*, I.v.9.

[4] *Summa* of Damasus, MS. Vienna, National Bibliothek, 2080, fol. 103.

[5] *Id.*, ibid., "Nec universitas alia poterat ratione subsistere nisi ordo magnae differentiae eam servaret."

[6] Stephanus Tornacensis, *Summa*, p. 1, ed. cit., and Archdeacon, in his proemium to his *Apparatus* in the *Decretum*, fol. 1 verso, No. 2. Did Thomas Becket echo and adopt Stephen's words when he said: "Ecclesia Dei in duobus constat ordinibus, clero et populo"? (*Materials for the History of Archbishop Thomas Becket*, vol. v, p. 280.) Stephen wrote his *Summa* in the sixties of the century, according to Kuttner, *Repertorium*, p. 135, but before 1159, according to Schulte, p. xx of his edition.

were differently organized and presided over by different organs. They were the "ecclesia" and the "civitas". The clerical element and its laical counterpart led different kinds of life—"duae vitae, spiritualis et carnalis"[1]—the one regulated by the "jus divinum", the other by the "jus humanum". "Clerus" and "populus" were therefore two distinct bodies, each with a different calling ("diversa professio").[2] By their attempt to show also in the structure of society the contrast between "anima" and "corpus" and the inferiority of the latter to the former, the canonists overreached themselves: they cut the medieval body politic into two—admittedly unequal—sections that were clearly separated from each other, and hence had two kinds of jurisdictions and two laws. But all this remained pure theory: even within their own doctrinal edifice that view on medieval society was thrown overboard, for "ecclesia continet imperium", or negatively expressed: "Extra ecclesiam non est imperium."[3]

We may now proceed to an enumeration of some practical applications of the foregoing reflections. According to the canonists a direct jurisdiction of the ecclesiastical courts should take place in the following cases. These litigations were exempted from the jurisdiction of the ordinary civil court, although prima facie they would appear to be the latter's sole concern. In the first place came cases which were, as the technical term ran, "annexed" to, or connected with, a spiritual matter.[4] Moreover, not only jurisdiction, but also legislation

[1] The Archdeacon continued: "Et secundum duos populos duae vitae, secundum duas vitas duo principatus, et secundum duos principatus duplex jurisdictionis ordo procedit: civitas, ecclesia; civitatis rex, ecclesiae Christus; duo populi, duo ordines clericorum et laicorum; duae vitae, spiritualis et carnalis; duo principatus, sacerdotium et regnum; duplex jurisdictio, divinum jus et humanum."

[2] The Archdeacon in his *Com.* on the *Sextus*, V., Si sententia, fol. 130. Hostiensis, *Summa*, proemium, No. 13, constructed society on the pattern of Trinity and hence distinguished three bodies: the "genus laicorum", the "genus saecularium clericorum", and the "genus religiosorum clericorum".

[3] Johannes Teutonicus in his gloss on the cap. venerabilem, in *Comp. III*, s.v. "venerabilem", fol. 112 verso of D 4. The utilization of patristic literature for thirteenth-century political purposes emerges clearly in this particular instance. The canonists—all canonists following Johannes Teutonicus referred to this epitome—exchanged St. Augustine's "potestas" for "imperium". Augustine's "nulla potestas extra ecclesiam"—cited by Gratian in C. XXIV, q. i, post cap. 39—came to read: "Nullum imperium extra ecclesiam."

[4] Panormitanus, *Com.* on *Decretales*, II.ii.10, fol. 53, No. 8: "Potest enim ecclesia cognoscere de causa prophana, quando est connecta et conjuncta cum

was assigned to the ecclesiastical authorities, and legislation therefore embraced purely mundane and temporal matters in so far as they showed any connexion with the principal matter, that is, matrimony.[1] The outstanding examples were litigations (and legislation) about dowry,[2] an issue intimately connected with matrimony. The reason for the exclusive ecclesiastical jurisdiction in matrimonial litigations was the conception of matrimony as a "spirituale vinculum" rather than a "carnale vinculum". Dissolutions of marriages on the *dictum* of Christ that "What God hath joined together...." were therefore judicial acts which, precisely because of this command of Christ, could not come within the scope of a secular

---

causa spectante principaliter ad ecclesiam." The canonistic viewpoint was made law: *Decretales*, II.i.3, see text.

[1] See the gloss of the elder Bernardus Compostellanus, on tit. Qui filii sint legitimi, c. conquestus (in *Comp. I*, IV.xviii.1): "Sed quod ad dominum papam statuere de talibus, cum huiusmodi potius ad dominum imperatorem spectare videantur, ut dist. XCVI, cum ad verum? Respondeo, multum ad papam: cum ad eum de principali causa, scil. de matrimonio, statuere pertineat, non est mirum, si de eius sequela vel quasi accessorio statuat." This passage is transcribed by S. Kuttner, "Bernardus Compostellanus Antiquus" in *Traditio*, vol. i, p. 316. It is interesting to see that Azo, the great civilian teacher of Bernardus, could not resist the temptation of adding a curt "contra" to his pupil's gloss.

[2] See Bernardus Parmensis in his gloss in II.ii.10, Innocent IV and Hostiensis, ibid. But the gloss on *Decretales*, IV.xx.3, s.v. "accessorie" makes an important distinction. After first pronouncing the general principle that whoever decides the main issue (i.e. the principal matter), must also decide the "annexed issue" ("qui cognovit de principali, cognoscere debet de accessorio... et sic causa dotis ad judicem ecclesiasticum spectat"), the glossator continues to say that if dowry is the subject of litigation, whilst the validity of the marriage is not disputed, the secular tribunal is then conceded the right to decide this litigation; so, for instance, if the husband dissipates his wife's goods, or if he spends her dowry wastefully, or if he dies—in these and similar cases the decision is not to belong to the ecclesiastical judge. "Si vero constante matrimonio agat mulier de dote, quia forte maritus labitur facultatibus vel dissipat bona sua, vel quia mortuus est, tunc causa illa agi debet coram judice saeculari, quia modo causa dotis principalis est." Nevertheless, this competency of the secular tribunal is not one which he can claim as of right: the Church *delegates* the decision to the secular tribunal in such cases: "ecclesia enim favore dotis super ipsam causam delegat, quia reipublicae utile est mulieres dotes salvas habere propter quas (add: 'multis', LC 173, fol. 210 verso) nubere possint... papa simpliciter causam dotis committit secundum consuetudinem ecclesiae." The MS. LC 173 has this addition: "non de jure scripto", fol. 210 verso. In his *Com.* on this decretal Innocent IV in anticipation rejects the—rather conciliatory—opinion of the gloss: he claims that *in all cases* the decision belongs to the ecclesiastical judge: "Specialiter ad

judge. The pope, then, in dissolving marriages did not act as man—this was the ruling of Innocent III.¹

Other instances were the following. Gifts from secular princes or others of the faithful to a church or even to a mere cleric;² litigations concerning the tenth also fell within the compass of exclusive ecclesiastical jurisdiction³ as well as those about inheritance.⁴ Even if the principal question was temporal, the decision still rested with the ecclesiastical judge, if the domain of the spiritual was touched upon in even a side issue. "Et sic accessorium spirituale fortius est quam etiam temporale principale."⁵ Although this doctrine, too, was only embryonic in the twelfth century, Henry II fully grasped its far reaching implications and attempted to preserve his own jurisdictional domain.⁶ In fact and in theory, the idea that the *jus patronatus* was an annexe of a spiritual cause, and hence that litigations as to advowsons and presentations must be brought before the ecclesiastical court, was flatly rejected in England; in fact by Henry II in his Constitutions, and in theory by Bracton whom

---

ecclesiam pertinet cognoscere de dotibus, quia ad ecclesiam pertinet defensio dotium." But Innocent IV denies that litigations concerning inheritance should be brought before the ecclesiastical justices. Needless to say the civilians were highly perturbed by these claims of the canonists, see, for instance, Baldus, *Decretalium volumen commentaria*, fol. 155 of the edition, Venice, 1595, and Lucas de Penna, *Com*. c.XII.29.1 No. 5.

¹ *Decretales*, I.vii.2.

² The assize *Utrum* and subsequent English legislation tried to curtail ecclesiastical jurisdiction.

³ All these litigations were later expressly assigned to the ecclesiastical court for ecclesiastical jurisdiction by Clement V, see *Clem*. II.i.2. The ecclesiastical justices should also be approached, if by observing civil law sin would be committed, as, for example, in the case of so-called "natural obligations", see Panormitanus, *Com*. on *Decretales*, II.i.13, fol. 29 verso, additio quinta: "Concludo, quod ubi ex juris civilis observatione nutiretur peccatum, ut in obligatione naturali, quae oritur ex consensu, potest ad ecclesiam recurri." See also Bartolus, "Ad Reprimendum", who maintained a very similar point of view.

⁴ Ecclesiastical interference was claimed on the grounds of faith, see Alanus, in *Compilatio Prima*, tit. De judeis et sarac., c. judei (c. 5), fol. 51 of D 4, s.v. "haereditatis": "De haereditate se intromittit papa ratione fidei." On Innocent, see note 2, p. 99.

⁵ Hostiensis, *Summa*, IV.xvii, col. 1230, No. 9: "... trahit ad se principalem jurisdictionem temporalem, si id, quod de jurisdictione spirituali est, in ea incidat, et sic accessorium...."

⁶ See Constitutions of Clarendon, caps. 1 and 9.

we may well take as a classic witness.¹ This is not to say that the papacy, above all, the great canonist-pope, Alexander III, did not address decretals to Henry in which this exclusive jurisdictional right of the ecclesiastical court was laid down. Although the relevant decretal—II.i.3²—did not seem to have had all the desired effect in England, it nevertheless formed the basis of important canonistic doctrines. Huguccio seems to have been the first to develop the theory that the *jus patronatus* was an issue exclusively belonging to the jurisdiction of the ecclesiastical court. The *jus patronatus*, he said, was to be taken as a spiritual matter—"spirituale censetur propter connexitatem"—because things which adhered to religious matters, assumed a religious nature: "quia, quae religionis adhaerent, religiosa sunt: ex tali cohaerentia sumit suam naturam."³ But the English canonist Alanus, commenting a few years later than Huguccio on another Alexandrian decretal —III.xxxviii.21—designated the handling of the rights of patronage by his fellow-countrymen as "vulgare Anglicorum".⁴ As regards English conditions the testimonies of Alanus and Richardus were given full credence by contemporaries: "Quibus tamquam anglicis est credendum."⁵

[1] See P & M, vol. ii, pp. 136-38, Reuter, *Alexander III*, vol. iii, pp. 154 ff., K. Böhmer, "Das Eigenkirchentum in England" in *Texte und Forschungen zur englischen Kulturgeschichte* (Festgabe für Liebermann), p. 348 f. Cf. also Innocent III in *Decretales*, III.xxiv.7.

[2] Ulrich Stutz and Pietro Vaccari maintain that this Alexandrian decretal was designed "to integrate and modify civil law", see U. Stutz, "Papst Alexander III gegen die Freiung langobardischer Eigenkirchen" in *Abhandlungen d. preuss. Akad. d. Wiss.*, (phil. hist. Kl.), 1936, No. 6, pp. 10 ff., and P. Vaccari, "Nota sul diritto canonico nei suoi rapporti col diritto civile nei secoli XII-XIV" in *Zeitschrift, kanon. Abt.*, vol. xxvii (1938), pp. 348-63, at p. 352.

[3] See *glos. ord.*, *Decretales*, II.i.3, reporting the theory of Huguccio. The MS. of the gloss, LC 173, fol. 67 verso, has no reference to Huguccio. This decretal of Alexander III (in the first place addressed to Henry II) was embodied in the decrees of the Third Lateran Council and also in the *Compilatio Prima*, II.i.5. But, according to the compiler of the *Glossa Palatina*, Bernardus Compostellanus and Melendus held that the *jus patronatus* was a spiritual thing in itself: proemium ad C. I, q. i, fol. 39 of D 8.

[4] See Alanus in his gloss on *Comp. I*, III.xxxiii.27, and *glos. ord.* on the later III.xxxviii.21. In theory at least it was maintained that the right of patronage could not be sold, because it was a spiritual thing, see, for instance, Alexander III in *Decretales*, III.xxxviii.16, and Bernardus Parmensis, ibid. and on cap. 6, eod. tit.: "Res sacra non recipit aestimationem."

[5] Vincentius in his gloss on the decretal "which begins with the cheerful words"

Closely allied to the "ratio annexitatis" which, as we have seen, subordinated the temporal to the spiritual, was the claim to ecclesiastical arbitration and jurisdiction in cases of a breach of a peace treaty concluded between two secular rulers.[1] Peace, the argument ran, was a spiritual bond—a "spirituale vinculum" because an effect of charity[2]—and if, in addition, it was confirmed by an oath, its breach was a matter which could only be dealt with by an ecclesiastical tribunal. We may here recall the application of this idea by Innocent III to the dispute of John and Philip in 1204,[3] but we should also recall that in 1237 lay persons in London violently protested against this kind of claims to exclusive ecclesiastical jurisdiction. It was claimed that breach of faith, perjury, defamation, and the like, should not go before the ecclesiastical tribunal.[4] And the writ *Cir-*

(Maitland, *Roman Canon Law*, p. 126, where the greater part is translated) *Qua fronte*, tit. De Appellationibus, *Comp. I.*, fol. 22 of D 4. Alan and Richard, according to the report of Vincentius, maintained that the archbishop's proceedings were the "consuetudo anglicorum". In LC 163, however, Tancred signed this gloss, not Vincentius, fol. 31: "Hic do papa respondet secundum consuetudinem anglicorum, et hic notaverunt R. et ala., quibus tamquam anglicis est credendum." Incidentally, it is noteworthy that the reference to Thomas Becket was omitted in *Decretales*, II.xxviii.25; the reference is in the original compilation of Bernardus Papiensis, see also fol. 21 verso of D 4 (c. 41), and fol. 30 verso of the *Apparatus* of Richard, W 122 and also LC 163, fol. 31, and LC 29, fol. 20 verso. In W 122 there is also a copy of the famous lengthy "examination paper" (Maitland, op. cit., p. 124), which the Bishop of Ely asked Alexander III to write: fol. 91 recto—92 recto: this is also in LB 105, fol. 269-70 verso.

[1] See Laurentius in his gloss on tit. De judiciis, c. novit, s.v. "pacem" in *Comp. III*, fol. 131 verso of D 4: "Ad ecclesiam enim spectat servare pacem, et facere servari."

[2] Ephes. iv.3. Antonius de Butrio in his *Com*. on *Decretales*, I.xxx.7 fol. 18, No. 24: "Pax est vinculum charitatus. Charitas autum est dilectio Dei et proximi sui. Et cum charitas sit specialis virtus, qua salvamur, et fides, ideo circa pacem et juramentum specialius cognoscit ecclesia." In the same sense, Hostiensis, and Panormitanus, ibid., fol 26 verso, No. 8.

[3] *Decretales*, II.i.13. It is interesting to note that in his commentaries on this passage, Innocent IV (fol. 194, No. 7) deduced the right of papal jurisdiction from the mere declaration of John who maintained that the French king held the controversial province "in periculum suae animae, cum ad me pertineat". Upon this contention John asked for a papal pronouncement to compel Philip "ad poenitentiam". See also Johannes Andreae in his gloss on the *Sextus*, II.xiv.2.

[4] *Annales Monastici* (Burton), vol. i, p. 256. Flahiff, art. cit., p. 293, draws attention to the infectious example of Frederick II and the league under Pierre Mauclerc, which spread to England where the effort was renewed in 1247 to limit the ecclesiastical jurisdiction; cf. also Matthew Paris, *Chronica Majora*, vol. iv, p. 614.

cumspecte agatis of Edward I may therefore well be considered as a practical step towards a demarcation of the always fluid boundary between the spiritual and the temporal.[1]

The fundamental theory of the canonists furthermore entailed the conception that all crimes were purely spiritual issues and as such also fell within exclusively ecclesiastical jurisdiction. The contemporary identification of crime with sin made it still more easily for this claim to be put forward. For on the ground that every crime was sin, the canonists had little difficulty in demanding that "de peccato" the pope had the right to censure any Christian, of whatever standing. That this, in practice, entailed criminal jurisdiction over kings and emperors is not difficult to understand. This idea manifested itself fully in Innocent III's statement to which we have just referred. We cannot therefore be surprised, if the civilians made attempts to limit the jurisdictional powers of the Church to purely "ecclesiastical crimes". Petrus de Bellapertica, though himself bishop of Auxerre, but later a chancellor under Philip IV (1306), for instance, considered a competency of the clerical tribunal established if the crime concerned "the Catholic faith" in the strict meaning of the term: "Crimen ecclesiasticum sit tantum, quando tractetur de fide catholica." For, as his devoted pupil, Cynus, reasoned, if the Church were to exercise criminal jurisdiction wherever sin was involved, the whole structure of society would be upset. Rather angrily Cynus concluded that on this ground "the Church usurped all jurisdictional powers in criminal matters".[2]

But let us look a little deeper into the canonistic and papal claim that the pope should judge everyone on the ground of sin. What, we may ask ourselves, were the arguments which

---

[1] See especially Flahiff, art. cit., pp. 307-9, and B. Graves, "Circumspecte Agatis" in *EHR*, vol. xliii (1938), pp. 15-16. Appropriately enough, this writ is appended to the *gl. ord.* of Bernardus Parmensis in LC 173, fol. 303, in a late thirteenth-century hand.

[2] See Cynus, *Com. ad Codicem*, C. I.iii.33: "Petrus tenet, quod crimen ecclesiasticum sit tantum, quando tractetur de fide Catholica. Nam si ecclesia cognosceret ubicumque est peccatum, jam turbaretur rerum officia, quod esse non debet ... unde illud est crimen ecclesiasticum, quod immediate pertinet ad ecclesiam, ut crimen haeresis ... quod immediate respicit fidem ... ecclesia sibi usurpavit ratione peccati totam jurisdictionem." Bartolus, on the other hand, followed the canonistic lead, see, e.g., C. I.ii.7: when writing this commentary he might have been too near to Rome to express his real thoughts openly.

the canonists advanced to justify this vast, virtually unlimited jurisdiction "ratione peccati"? Durandus, the Frenchman, summed up the whole question neatly. The Church, he declared, had power to judge not only those actions which offended against "the articles of faith" and against the sacraments, but also those actions which constituted a mortal sin. Durandus was of course perfectly aware of the possibility of extending clerical jurisdiction to purely secular matters, but since, as we shall see, the present mortal life was considered to be merely the preparation for the future spiritual life, all actions within the former must be judged from the point of view of the final end. To quote Durandus literally: "We must judge those things, 'quae debent ordinari ad finem, quia ratio . . . sumitur ex fine'."[1] The means, then, by which the end was to be attained, should be viewed from that angle alone.

Moreover, as we have seen, even the gentile philosophers had declared that the body was to be orientated by the exigencies of the soul: "Corpus ordinatur ad animam". Therefore, "temporalia ordinantur ad spiritualia". From this followed, then, that all temporal actions of Christians should be directed by the requirements laid down for achieving eternal life: "Omnes actiones Christianorum debent ordinari ad consequendam vitam aeternam." And any temporal action might lend itself to a deviation from the path which assuredly led to eternal salvation. Hence, in the most general terms Durandus stated that the ecclesiastical authorities had power to judge all those actions "per quas possunt deviare a salute sua peccando circa quamcumque materiam sive contra articulos fidei et sacramenta sive contra bonos mores, peccando in seipsum vel in proximum, verbo vel facto seu quocumque alio modo." The practical, biblical example adduced was that of St. Paul who was said to have excommunicated notorious fornicators.[2] Properly speaking, Durandus concluded, the appropriate law court for any Christian was the ecclesiastical tribunal: "Omnes Christiani, inquantum sunt Christiani, pertinent ad forum ecclesiae." The jurisdictional powers of the civil law court were merely subsidiary.

In view of the ambitious character of this claim to jurisdiction "ratione peccati" no surprise will be caused when

[1] Durandus, *De Jurisdictione Ecclesiastica*, Qu. III.
[2] He referred to I Cor. v.II, etc.

Innocent III's somewhat modest statement "We do not intend to judge feudal affairs"[1] was improved upon by the canonists. They maintained that Innocent omitted to say "directe", that is, that he meant to say he would not judge feudal matters directly, because "indirectly" he should be considered to be the judge even of these purely temporal affairs. The Spaniard, Vincentius, therefore, in his gloss on those Innocentian words stated: "Directe, sed indirecte cognoscendo an peccet, et inducendo ad poenitantiam ... et ita per consequentiam feudum restituat."[2] This gloss was almost literally adopted by Bernardus Parmensis: "Tantum ratione peccati ... et sic per consequentiam cogit (scilicet papa) restituere feudum."

A concrete application of the pseudo-philosophic thesis that the spiritual also embraced the temporal lay in the rather practical—and highly controversial—matter of the legitimation of illegitimate children. Here the civilians[3] usually denied to a legitimation by the spiritual power any effects in the temporal sphere. They maintained that the pope was entitled to legitimate a child only in regard to the spiritualities. In order to acquire full civic status, the child was still in need of a legitimation by the temporal power. For the canonists there was no doubt that a legitimation effected by the spiritual authority automatically extended its benefits to the temporalities also: no further action was needed, in order to make the child a full member of civil society, once the spiritual power had bestowed upon it the advantages of a legitimation in the spiritual sphere. This standpoint followed quite logically from the idea that the inferior (temporal) was contained in the superior (spiritual) and was clearly expressed by Johannes Teutonicus in his gloss in the *Compilatio Tertia*—and Johannes was by no means a papal extremist. In his gloss he said: "Dic, quod dominus papa non habet potestatem legitimandi in temporalibus, sed *eo ipso* quod legitimatus est in spiritualibus intelligitur legitimatus in temporalibus, unde per quandam consequentiam."[4] But Laurentius

---

[1] *Decretales*, II.i.13: "Non intendimus judicare de feudo." This was said in the communication to the French prelates concerning the dispute between John and Philip.

[2] *Apparatus* of Tancred on *Comp. III*, De judiciis, c. novit ille, s.v. "judicare de feudo", fol. 131 of D 4.

[3] Cf. my *Medieval Idea of Law*, pp. 91 f.

[4] See the gloss of Johannes Teutonicus in *Comp. III*, tit. Qui filii sint legitimi, c. per venerabilem (c. 2), s.v. "potestatem", fol. 193 of D 4.

Hispanus added a curt "contra" to this statement of Johannes. Belonging as he did to the moderate section of the canonists, Laurentius declared that the pope's legitimation of a child could have effect in the secular sphere only, if the pope had been commissioned by the emperor: "Contra, quia non potest legitimare aliquem quoad forum saeculare, ut si habeat temporalem jurisdictionem, nisi princips hoc ei commisit."[1] Equally curt was the opposed verdict of the Englishman; Guido Brito asserted that if the pope could legitimate in regard to spiritualities, all the more could he do so in regard to the temporalities: "Papa potest legitimare quoad spiritualia, multo fortius in temporalibus."[2] And the Hungarian canonist, Paulus Hungarus, quite succinctly pointed to the underlying reason for all this. For the legitimation of a child as to the spiritualities necessarily included the temporalities, because the latter were inferior to the former. Thus the Hungarian stated: "Nota, quod in majori conceditur, licitum esse videtur etiam in minori."[3]

Lastly, according to the established doctrine of the canonists, the idea of justice as a spiritual concept necessitated the interference of the ecclesiastical power in purely mundane matters. This was asserted to be a real necessity not only in those cases in which a secular judge was merely alleged to have participated in a miscarriage of justice in a trial—anyone acquainted with legal proceedings will grasp the profound implication of this dogmatic view—or alleged to have maliciously acted to the detriment of one party, but, what is more significant, it also held good with regard to the unilateral declaration that the civil judge had failed to do what he ought to have done in compliance with the ordinances of the ecclesiastical power and with the exigencies of the common good.[4] Precisely because of their general nature these claims not only provided ample material

---

[1] Laurentius, ibid., following the gloss of Vincentius who also adhered to Johannes, fol. 193 verso.

[2] Guido Brito in his *Casus*, on cap. Venerabilem, fol. 39 of W 159.

[3] Paulus Hungarus in his *Notabilia ad Compilationem Tertiam*, on c. Per veneravilem, fol. 24 of W 159. He continued: "Si quis est legitimatus ad spiritualia, etiam ad temporalia, sed non convertitur."

[4] C. XV, q. i, c. 3. Laurentius in his gloss on tit. De foro compet., c. licet (c. 1) in *Comp. III*, fol. 131 verso of D 4, enumerates nine specific cases in which the ecclesiastical court is to interfere; some more cases were added by Johannes Teutonicus, ibid., cap. ex tenore (c. 2), fol. 132.

PAPAL PLENITUDE OF POWER: THE IDEA

for friction between the theoretical jurists and the practical lawyers, but they also penetrated deeply into the sphere of practical politics and political theory.[1] For it was on the basis of these studiedly vague and flexible demands that emperors and kings were deposed and excommunicated and others put into their places. The reigns of thirteenth-century popes were eloquent testimonies of the concrete realization of this canonistic demand. That the pope was entitled to take over the government of the secular power in the case of a vacancy, again follows conclusively from these vast claims, especially from the one based upon the idea that the spiritual as the higher notion embraced the temporal as the lower. In short, the supreme pontiff was to possess complete and exclusive jurisdiction over spiritual and temporal affairs of the whole world. Papal plenitude of power embraced every conceivable aspect of human life.[2] In other words, the pope was the vicar of God on earth: "Summus pontifex Dei locum tenet in terris." Consequently, whenever a king felt himself aggrieved by the action of another king, or an emperor by that of another emperor, the aggrieved party could take his complaint to the pope for arbitration. This was clearly set forth by the Hungarian canonist, Paulus.[3] His Italian contemporary, Benencasa, would not fall behind him when exclaiming: "Ad ipsam (scilicet Romanam ecclesiam) de omni parte mundi appelletur."[4]

In the light of these fundamental considerations the overexploited Donation of Constantine appears in a somewhat new light. It is not here proposed to deal with its contents, but only with its position in the general pattern of canonistic doctrine. The canonists were not content tediously to repeat the so-called facts of the Donation, but attempted to interpret it on the basis of their fundamental conceptions of the spiritual and the tem-

---

[1] See *infra*, chapter VI, at pp. 182 f, 188, 193, 194, where some passages are transcribed.

[2] The Archdeacon's pupil, Egidius Spiritalis, in his *Libellus contra infideles* (Scholz, op. cit., vol. ii, p. 106) said: "Summus pontifex in toto orbe terrarum non solum in spiritualibus, sed etiam in temporalibus obtinet jurisdictionem plenariam."

[3] See Paulus Hungarus, in his *Notabilia*, tit. De judiciis, c. tria, fol. 20 verso of W 159: "Nota, quod si rex a rege vel princeps a principe injuste offendatur, potest offensus conqueri domino papae et denuntiare ecclesiae."

[4] Benencasa in his *Casus ad Decretum*, ad C. IX, q. iii, c. 17, fol. 128 of W 159.

poral. And the Donation was found to have been a miraculous confirmation and proof of the correctness of their views. Through its unquestioned historical veracity the Donation formed the link between their abstract philosophic reasoning and the realities of life. Here the canonists found the much wanted connexion between human and divine law. All their foregoing reflections found welcome confirmation in the allegedly stark and naked historical facts.

That the superiority of the spiritual, that is, of the ecclesiastical, was based on divine law, was a point that was in no need of further elaboration by the canonists. Their philosophic speculations on the nature of the spiritual and the temporal had, they were convinced, the sanction of the divine law. In fact, it was on the ground of these speculations that the superiority of the ecclesiastical power was asserted. No lesser authority than Innocent III had declared in one of his letters that priesthood was instituted by divine ordination: priesthood itself was an efflorescence of the divine law. On the other hand, the secular power could claim no divine descendancy, but was instituted by human force.[1] Once again, the contrast between the celestial and the terrestrial clearly emerged, and herewith also the contrast in the respective degrees of dignity. Sacerdotal power was thus made an issue of divine law.

But there was a human confirmation of all this. For the pope was able to declare, the canonists argued, that his power rested not only upon divine, but also upon human law. Through the Donation of Constantine the pope's superiority was also grounded in human law. It is this interpretation of the Donation which makes it appear somewhat novel and attractive. The canonists explained the Donation as the human manifestation of the divine law, and, so it appeared to them, as an imperial anticipation and confirmation of the curial point of view. As a legal act the Donation indisputably belonged to the sphere of human law. Now this human law, whereby Constantine handed over to Pope Sylvester the terrestrial empire and imperial insignia, signified a confirmation, an imitation and veneration of the divine law. By this act Constantine desired to show his

---

[1] See Baluzius, *Epistolae Innocentii III*, tom. i, tit. 2, p. 548 (ed., Paris, 1682): "Sacerdotium institutum fuit per ordinationem divinam; regnum fuit exortum at petititionem humanam." A few lines down he said that "regnum (constitutum fuit) per extorsionem humanam."

veneration for, reverence and submission to, the ecclesiastical power. For the canonists there could be no possible doubt that the transaction was performed by divine providence: for "the king's heart is in the hands of the Lord" (Prov. xxi.1). The emperor did not confer any authority upon the pope, since this was always possessed by the latter, but merely confessed to his own inferiority openly and publicly. The temporal admitted its inferiority to the spiritual—the emperor to the pope. Some canonists argued that the Donation might also be interpreted as the translation of the desire of the emperor that the pope might more effectively exercise the powers which, according to divine law, he already possessed. During the persecution by Constantine's predecessors the full exercise of papal power had been impossible, they argued further, and therefore Emperor Constantine merely translated into practice what had always been the pope's right. Having in this way based papal power upon human law also, the canonists conceived that hence was constituted a still stronger papal right of direct interference in temporal matters; in particular the vacancy of the imperial throne made the pope the true temporal ruler. We will return to this point later, but we may point out here that the passage in canon law—II.ii.10—which purported to be the chief legal source of the papal right in the case of an imperial vacancy, did not mention the Donation at all. Innocent III was too cautious and shrewd to base his claim upon this slender foundation. But the canonists and all writers in the papal camp were unanimous in agreeing that Innocent III could not have claimed this right without the Donation of Constantine.

Let me conclude with one or two observations. In the first place this question is certainly uppermost in our minds, What exactly was the basis of the canonistic views on "anima" and "corpus"? or to put it differently, How was it possible that the theory of the relative worth of mind and matter gained such almost universal acceptance, not only in medieval, but also in modern times?[1] In an attempt to furnish an answer we must

[1] It may not be out of place to give a short extract from an important statement of modern ecclesiastics on the points which we have touched in this chapter. The extract is taken from "The Prayer of several archbishops and bishops of Gallia, Germania, Austria, Italia, Anglia, Hibernia and America" from 10 April 1870, on the occasion of the Vatican Council which provoked the debate on papal infallibility. (Quoted from Schulte, *The Power of the Popes*.)

("The medieval popes) exercised a power derived from the public rights of

necessarily resort to the source of all medieval wisdom and the corner-stone of every kind of medieval reasoning—the philosopher. Whether the writers were papalists or imperialists, legists or canonists, they were all under the spell of the Stagirite's short treatise *De Anima*.[1] Because the immense influence of Aristotle's tract is commonly underestimated, the explanation and interpretation of medieval political thought tends to be somewhat superficial and unsatisfactory. But we need not blame our contemporaries for failing to point to this source of information, since only a handful of medieval writers explicitly referred to the tract, and strangely enough, these writers were almost all in the anti-papalist camp and quoted the *De Anima* to beat their antagonists, so to speak, by their own weapons. The close

---

the orient and from that great benefits accrued to the Christian nations. But as those popes, even the most learned of them, judged of past events according to the standard of their times and were often led astray by false accounts of popes of former centuries who had dethroned emperors, they firmly believed as they enunciated in their decrees and rescriptions that God had delegated to them the right to give commands and judgments from the standpoint of sin in all temporal transactions." After a reference to *Unam sanctam* the statement continues: "The popes had down to the seventeenth century publicly taught that power in temporal affairs had been given to them by God and had condemned the reverse opinion."

"We teach: certainly, the dignity of the two powers is unequal, for, as the heavens overhang the earth in the same way the eternal gifts which man gains by the spiritual power are higher than those gained by the temporal, upon whose maintenance and augmentation the principal aim of civil authority is centred, but each of the two powers, however, is, in the peculiar demands made upon it, the highest of its kind under God, and is not subjected to the other in its functions."

After thus propounding the former heretical dualistic standpoint the clerics go on to say that there is no divine right for popes "to dethrone kings or to sever the allegiance of their subjects from them. The power of the popes of the middle ages had been vested in them by the peculiar formation of the public rights of their times, whereas, on account of the changed circumstances, both private and public, such rights had, with the basis upon which they rested, passed away."

"It would be impossible to reform civil society in conformity with the rules laid down in Unam Sanctam."

This "Prayer" is signed, amongst others, by Cardinal Rauscher of Vienna; Cardinal Schwarzenberg, archbishop of Prague; Bishop Hefele, the eminent Church historian; the Archbishops of Agram, Olmütz, Munich, Bamberg; the Bishops of Augsburg, Trier, Breslau, Rottenburg, Mainz, Osnabrück, etc.

[1] It should be borne in mind that this tract was amongst the first of Aristotle's work to become known: it was current before 1210, see Professor M. D. Knowles, "Some recent advance in the history of medieval thought" in *Cambridge Historical Journal*, vol. ix (1947), pp. 33-34.

relationship between the "anima" and the divine was a chief tenet in this treatise. The spiritual, according to Aristotle, was something divine (Θεῖον).¹ The spiritual was the most valuable and the most distinctive of man's attributes.² Chiefly in this Aristotelian tract, but also in the Nichomachean Ethics and other of his writings known in the Middle Ages, we find the ideological roots of the canonistic theory of mind and matter, of the spiritual and the corporeal, of the "anima" and "corpus"; above all, the inferiority of matter was one of the main axioms of Aristotle's *Metaphysics*.³ But this link with ancient Greek philosophy would not alone have accounted for the wide acceptance of the theory. We must, secondly, take into account the unquestioned authority of Holy Writ. In fact, it seems that Aristotle and Holy Writ taken together formed the speculative basis of the canonistic theory. Hellenistic thought and Christian cosmology⁴ combined, lead without difficulty to the theory of the superiority of mind over matter, of the spiritual over the temporal. Holy Writ was considered Truth. The character of this premiss as the embodiment of truth precluded questions such as, Is this or that idea reconcilable with the reality of life? However anti-papalist a particular imperialist might have been, the Old and New Testaments were to him no less than to his political adversary perfect truth. Herein we may find the second important reason for the ascendancy of canonistic theory.

This observation gives us an opportunity of sketching the

¹ *De Anima*, i.4; ii.2.
² ibid., iii.3. *Politics*, i.5; vii.1, etc.
³ In his profound investigation, "Studien über den Einfluss der aristotelischen Philosophie auf die mittelalterlichen Theorien über das Verhältnis von Staat und Kirche", in *SB d. Bayr. Akad. d. Wiss.*, 1934, Mgr. M. Grabmann shows the influence, especially of Aristotle's Metaphysics, Nichomachean Ethics and Politics, on the formation of political theories, but it seems that he somehow underestimated the influence of the *De Anima*, see p. 25. Here as in all modern writings the canonistic literature is completely left out of account, apart from a casual mentioning of Johannes Monachus, p. 99, Zarabella, p. 138, and Petrus de Ancharano, ibid. None of the great canonists of the thirteenth century, nor those representative of the following century, are taken into consideration. That they leaned heavily on Aristotle's ideas of the aim of the State, of virtue, of subordination etc., as set forth in the *Politics*, appears too obvious to call for any comment.
⁴ Particularly as presented in St. Augustine's ideology, so, for instance, in his *De Anima et eius origine*, or in his letters, cf. epistola CLXVI. In these works we find the relationship between *anima* and *corpus* depicted against a purely metaphysical background.

chief difference between papalist theory as it was developed after the acceptance of Alanus's teachings, and the anti-papalist doctrines. We must not, however, leave out of account the anti-papalist share of responsibility for this ascendancy of canonistic doctrines. Indeed, we must bear in mind that the anti-papalist would not and could not dispense with scripture as a basis of reasoning which he too considered to be beyond the pale of human criticism. Although, in other respects, the anti-papalist was diametrically opposed to the papalist, scripture was to him also an indispensable basis for argumentation. It is an interesting phenomenon in the history of thought that both canonist and imperialist employed one and the same premiss. That this was at all possible, might be attributed to the many apparently contradictory passages easily to be found in the scriptures, above all, in the gospels themselves. In the opinion of the subtle scholastic thinker of the Middle Ages there were as many passages which supported the canonistic point of view, as there were others flatly contradicting it. Now, this difficulty was solved by the ingenious and sharp-edged instrument of dialectics, which enabled both the papalist and anti-papalist to point to the divinely inspired source of wisdom as an irreproachable basis of his particular theory.

Hence, in the choice of this basis alone we can detect no fundamental divergence between the ideological camps. Indeed, considered only from this aspect, their essential divergence was but faintly marked. It is only when we look a little deeper into the structural framework of the two schools that we can perceive the deep gulf that separates them. The cleavage between the two was constituted not by difference of interpretation of the common basis, but by difference in approach. This was the principal feature which distinguished the two opposing schools. Juxtaposed to the biblical and metaphysical line of approach, the only one acceptable to the papalist, the anti-papalist chose also the positive non-transcendental method of enquiry focusing his attention on the reality and actuality of political life—in this latter sphere leaving all speculation out of account. The canonistic approach was monistic, the imperialistic was dualistic. The papalist travelled in a one-way street and maintained a hierachical subordination of the temporal, the emperor, to the spiritual, the pope. The anti-papalist travelled in a dual-carriage way and insisted on the equality of the temporal with the spiritual. The monism of the canonists and the dualism of the imperialists followed naturally from their difference in approach. Perhaps nothing reflected that difference of outlook better than the metaphorical relationship between Church and State accorded by the imperialist and canonist: to the canonist the Church was the mother of the empire, to the imperialist the Church was the sister of the empire. The canonists adhered to the conception of a political government of the world based upon one principle—the spiritual alone—whilst the imperialists rested their political structure on two principles—the spiritual as well as the temporal. Can we be surprised, then, when we find the imperialist somewhat lightly charged with heresy? He was liable to incur this charge because he relied upon two principles instead of the orthodox and traditional one. "Duo principia ponere haereticum est."[1]

[1] *Decretales*, I.i.1 and 2, and C. XXIV, q. iii, c. 39. In some very isolated cases we find anti-papalists who also adhered to a monism which was, however, the very opposite of the one propounded by the canonists. The spiritual principle of the papalists was supplanted by the temporal one: "anima" and "corpus" and hence pope and emperor changed places in their relative positions; the former was hierarchically subordinated to the latter, in temporal as well as in spiritual matters. Perhaps the earliest exposition of this monistic principle as conceived by the anti-papalists, we find in the anonymous *Tractatus Eboracenses*. Its author denied that the ecclesiastical authority should rule the souls only, and the secular prince the bodies: the two could not be separated in practice, *Mon. Germ. Hist. (Libelli de Lite)*, tom. iii, p. 663. Christ, the author maintained, combined the regal and sacerdotal functions, but the former weighed heavier than the latter. He also considered that the keys of the heavenly kingdom "magis ad regiam potestatem pertinent quam ad sacerdotalem", p. 672. Sacerdotal power was instituted, not by God, but by royal authority and was subject to the latter, p. 667. The King alone was the "vicarius Dei". In the *York Tractates* we find the execution of the monistic principle which subjugated the Church to the State. The role which the papalists assigned to the Church, was here taken up by the State. Even the argument of the greater dignity reappeared here in an inverted sense: "Major et sanctior videtur unctio et sanctificatio et potestas regis quam sacerdotis," p. 670. The State guided the Church. For an account of these very interesting tracts, see H. Böhmer, *Kirche und Staate in England und in der Normandie im xi, und xii. Jahrhundert*, pp. 177-216, F. Kern, *Gottesgnadentum und Widerstandsrecht*, pp. 299-304, Carlyle, *History of Political Theory in the West*, vol. iv, pp. 273-82, and Z. N. Brooke, *The English Church and the Papacy* pp. 157-60. It is well known that Marsiglio used Aristotelian principles to prove the subordination of the Church to the State. On the importance of Aristotelianism for medieval political theory see de Lagarde, *La Naissance de l'esprit laique*, 2nd ed., 1948, pp. 166 ff.

CHAPTER V

WORLD MONARCHY

A VERY cursory glance at present-day international relations necessarily leads to the idea of a sovereignty which every state guards as one of its most vital and basic rights. The idealists in our midst are undaunted by the apparent stubbornness with which States and statesmen cling to the conception of the sovereignty of the political entities; the idealists put forward a remedy that must command our respect: the establishment of a world government in the shape of an international organization in which the constituent members have voluntarily and virtually abandoned their sovereign status. For the idealists, a race as persuasive in theory as elusive in practice, hold that the conflicts and disputes between States could speedily be brought to an end, if individual States were servants of a world community rather than complete masters within their own frontiers. To realize this end the States should abandon their exclusive right to determine the fate of their own citizens and should defer to the commands of a central world government. Perhaps the most significant criterion of the already over-developed idea of sovereignty is of a negative kind, the conception, namely, of non-interference in national matters. The old Romanistic principle "What pleases the prince, has the force of law" has developed into the modern principle "What pleases the State, has the force of law". Within its own national frontiers the State can do as it pleases, and no outside political entity is allowed to raise a perhaps very justifiable protest against some internal legislation. The history of the last decades provides convincing examples of where the logical pursuance of this principle is bound to lead. The touchiness and suspicion with which certain contemporary States meet the faintest hint of interference with their own national affairs is indeed a most remarkable feature of twentieth-century political and international relations. But this demand for non-interference is also strongly reflected in the degree of suspicion accorded to representatives of parties and ideologies which somehow deviate from the accepted or imposed national ways of thinking. The charge that this or that political or religious ideology has its headquarters outside the national frontiers is perhaps the strongest weapon in the hands of its antagonists. The free and unchecked movement of the representatives of ideologies not friendly or favourably to the established pattern of society or to the accepted philosophy of life, is frowned upon by the die-hard protagonists of sovereignty. Hence, the idea of sovereignty is not merely a political concept in the strict meaning of the term, but it also contains strong emotional elements which to disregard would be foolhardy. The idea "national sovereignty" appears to be the most fundamental and vital concept in present-day relations between what are euphemistically called independent political entities.

Although to some extent foreshadowed in the later Middle Ages, this concept is of comparatively recent date. And the general picture of the political structure in the Middle Ages exhibits definite tendencies towards the establishment of a world government. Nevertheless, in considering this trend we must be on our guard not to look upon the thirteenth century with the idealistic eyes of the twentieth. We must furthermore keep in mind that the medieval conception of a world government was identical with that of an absolute world monarchy, the only form of government that appealed to, and was favoured by, the medieval mind. Moreover, this world monarch was a truly theocratic institution and its protagonists abhorred the idea of a limited monarch and shuddered at the mere thought of his responsibility to anybody. A democratic composition of the central government was not even discussed, although in other fields of the political debate the democratic derivation of the prince's powers was very much in the foreground. The medieval world monarchy, to use a strong, though appropriate word, arrogated to itself the powers to command and issue binding decrees to all nations. And since it was the pope who was to play the role of a world monarch, his dominion was not therefore restricted to the confines of Christendom, but extended to all members of all nations, wherever they might be found and whatever creed they might embrace. This is the gist of the canonistic doctrines relating to a world ruler, doctrines which had been fully developed half a century before the publicists took the field. Hence by unjustifiably disregarding the canonistic groundwork, the modern reconstruction of medieval political thought takes as its point of departure the age which marked the end of the creative period of the canonists and the beginning of the period in which their ideological successors, the publicists, came to the fore.

Yet, we are faced with the question that also considerably engaged the attention of the thirteenth-century canonists, the question, namely, Why was the pope to be the world's monarch? Did not the Roman laws say as explicitly and plainly as possible that the emperor was the "dominus mundi"? The idea of a double headship was incompatible with the tenet invented for quite a different purpose, the tenet that it was heresy to have two principles: "Duo principia ponere, haereticum est." There was room for one monarch only, one who alone was empowered to command and direct everybody in the world. The insistence on the monistic principle is certainly apt to arouse our criticism, but for medieval minds the principle of unity was an overriding requirement. Just as within the empire the medieval canonists were unable to conceive Church and State as two co-ordinated entities, in the same way in the wider international sphere they were unable to brook a plural headship. Unity, not multiformity, was the watchword in medieval canonistic and in pro-papalist civilian doctrine. The division of governmental functions, the division of responsibility and of offices, were ideas quite alien to the political conception of the Middle Ages. One ruler on earth, just as one ruler in heaven—this was the political aim and concept. There is one God, one faith, one baptism—"unus Deus, una fides, unum baptisma".[1] The heavenly government constituted the ideal of the medieval political thinker. In his opinion the terrestrial should simply be a copy of the celestial government. There was one celestial ruler and, consequently, there ought to be one terrestrial ruler.

The groundwork and thought pattern was once again Aristotelian. Some of the profound and precise thinkers amongst the papalists openly referred to the philosopher's *Metaphysics* and *Politics*[2] and declared that in a state of nature the lower creatures were ruled by higher, and all of them by one: this idea of an hierarchical government of the universe, so ancient and yet so medieval, was borrowed from the principle of sub-

---

[1] Ephes. iv.5. C. VII, q. i, c. 6.
[2] Books xii and i respectively.

ordination in an organized army: here too it was the one supreme leader who directed the movements of his subordinates. All plurality of leaders and rulers was thought of as objectionable and, for reasons of expediency, everyone should be subjected to the rulership of one. And this one was conceived of metaphysically as God, the supreme ruler.[1] But, apart from this theistic concept, one more argument in support of the monarchical principle was advanced: every wise king would strive to avoid the division of his kingdom and strive for unity. "Every kingdom divided against itself is brought to desolation."[2] Why should not this principle be applied to the government of the whole world, questioned the papalists in their alluring manner. On the contrary, one world ruler would be a guarantee of peace and prosperity. They supported their argument by referring to the human body which possesses only one head. It would be monstrous to conceive of an entity with two heads.[3]

But this denial of a dual headship still fails to answer the fundamental question, Why was this one ruler to be the pope? In their treatment of this topic of political theory we may see clearly why the canonists, despite the comparative youth of their science, were in a stronger position than their civilian colleagues. Parenthetically we may here observe that the civilians never seriously approached the conception of a world government, at least in the comparatively developed sense in which the canonists conceived it. For the latter were able to refer to the law to no lesser a degree than to theological and transcendental considerations. Therein lay their strength—and weakness. For it was admitted on all sides that there was one God only, one heavenly ruler who shaped the destinies of mankind. Could any secular ruler claim to be God's vicar on earth? God existed for Christians, Gentiles, Jews and Mohammedans alike—all their lives were in His hands. The pope alone of all living creatures was in a position to say of himself that he held

---

[1] Cf. Durandus, *De Origine Jurisdictionum*, Qu. I: "In naturalibus inferiora reguntur per superiora et multitudo per unum; denique totum universum ad modum exercitus ordinatur sub uno principe, qui est Deus, ut dicitur XII metaphysicae ... pluralitas principantium non est bona." The term "principans" was used a considerable time before Marsiglio, in whose *Defensor Pacis* this idea gained particular significance.

[2] Matt. xii.25; Luke xi.17. C. XXV, q. ii, c. 4.

[3] Cf., for example, Hostiensis, *Summa*, IV.xvii, Rubrica, col. 1231.

the vicariate of God. Whatever the position of the emperor might be—whether a delegate of the people or a divine instrument—and whatever basis any other rulers might claim for their government—whether acquired by force, usurpation, treaty or marriage—none could demand that respect which that transcendental speculation bestowed upon the pope. He was, the canonists and the popes themselves avowed, the "vicarius Dei", an office which no other mortal, however presumptuous, could reasonably claim, let alone hold. In unmistakable language, Innocent III had affirmed that he was not the vicar of man, but the vicar of God on earth.[1] And before him Clement III had postulated that "all earthly princes" must be subject to the ecclesiastical jurisdiction.[2] Moreover, the psalmist had sung that "the earth is the Lord's, and the fulness thereof, the world and they that dwell therein".[3] And this the papalists quickly applied to the pope arguing that *"therefore the earth is the pope's and the fulness thereof and the world"*—"ergo et papae est terra et plenitudo eius".[4] God had created everything and ruled everything and, consequently, the divine government lay in the hands of His vicar.[5] Some of the more extreme amongst the canonists even went so far as to declare that the pope was not only God's vicar on earth, but also His successor.[6] Indeed, the Roman law served as a welcome prototype from which the canonists openly borrowed the typically imperialist notion of the emperor as the "dominus mundi" and fitted this notion into their own framework. Thus, the pope became a "coelestis imperator" who was endowed with the "coeleste arbitrium".[7] The emperor was left far behind, as his supreme rulership was confined to the boundaries of Christendom. According to the canonistic interpretation, the emperor himself had by his own legislation restricted his dominion to

---

[1] "Romanus pontifex non puri hominis, sed veri Dei vicem gerit in terris": *Decretales*, I.vii.3.

[2] *Decretales*, I.xxxiv.4.

[3] Ps. xxiv.1.

[4] Cf., e.g., Alvarus Pelagius, *De Planctu Ecclesiae*, lib. i, cap. 13, fol. 3 verso.

[5] See, for example, Zabarella, *Com.* on *Decretales*, III.xxxiv.8, fol. 201 No. 8.

[6] Cf. the gloss on *Decretales*, I.vii.2, s.v. "vicarium".

[7] See the gloss of Bernardus Parmensis on *Decretales*, I.vii.3.

the Christian lands.¹ The pope was to be not only, through the Donation of Constantine, "vere et proprie monarcha occidentis", but also, as we shall presently see, an oriental monarch.

Some more specific reasons were brought forward by the canonists to show that the pope alone was the world's rightful master. It was undeniable, they maintained, that the common father of all mankind was Adam who was created by God alone. The making of Eve from the body of Adam signified the creation of the Church by God, for Christ was nothing but the successor of Adam—the "secundus Adam"—and it was since Christ that the visible Church originated. Adam's relation to Eve was like that of Christ to His Church. Now the pope was also Christ's vicar, and therefore in a sense Adam's successor as the father of mankind. Thus the papalists had little difficulty in making the pope the master of the world, whether Christian or otherwise.

> Credimus, quod papa, qui est Christi vicarius, potestatem habet non tantum super Christianos, sed etiam super omnes infideles, cum enim Christus habuerit super omnes potestatem.²

Moreover, Christ had said to St. Peter "Whatsoever thou will bind...." with which commission the pope was given authority over everybody, not only over Christians. For a proper interpretation of Christ's *dictum* "Feed my sheep"— "pasce oves meos"³—shows, as the gloss had already indicated, that Christ wished to say "Feed the sheep, as if they were mine"—"pasce oves ut meos".⁴ From this premiss the conclusion was swiftly reached that Christ had bestowed upon the pope power over the faithful as well as over infidels. "All men," said Pope Innocent IV from whom the main ideas of papal world government were derived, "faithful and infidel alike are

---

[1] See, for instance, Martinus de Fano, "Tractatus de brachio seu auxilio implorando" in *Tractatus*, tom. xi, pars 2, No. 20, fol. 417 verso: "Ipse imperator asserit se tantum habere jurisdictionem et imperium, ubi Christiana fides tenetur ut lex generaliter, C. De episc. et clericus, ubi colligitur, quod Romanum imperium in tantum protenditur, in quantum Christianitas extenditur." The passage referred to is *Cod. Just.* I.iii.
[2] Innocent IV in his *Com.* on *Decretales*, III.xxxiv.8, No. 3, fol. 429 verso.
[3] John, xxi.16.
[4] Innocent III, *Decretales*, I.xxxiii.6, and *glos. ord.* in the same words.

through their creation the sheep of Christ."[1] The correctness of this view the canonists thought could be proved by Christ's declaration, namely, "And other sheep *I* have which are not of this fold".[2] The overlordship of the pope was one *de jure*, although in some cases it could not be exercised *de facto*. "Nobody can claim to be outside the fold of the Church and therefore everybody is subjected to the jurisdictional powers of the Church" was one more saying of the canonists.[3] Nor did the papalists, again following the lead of the great canonist-pope, Innocent IV, omit to refer to the familiar passage in Jeremiah where God has said: "I have set thee over the nations and over the kingdoms."[4] For a canonist of the thirteenth century no doubt could possibly exist that these words were literally applicable to the pope. With some extreme canonists we even find a tendency to assert a chronological precedence of the Church and its ruler over any earthly kingdom, thereby basing the pope's superiority not only upon theoretical and legal considerations, but also upon those of time.[5]

Our investigation into the theory of papal world government has so far left out of account the actual political events against which we have to set these purely theoretical speculations of the curialists. For every political doctrine is prompted by actual circumstances or at least stimulated by the not too remote possibility of creating those circumstances which are favourable to the execution of the plan appearing under the cloak of an abstract theory. The papalist claim to world monarchy was the direct result of the stimulus afforded by the crusades. They had shown to the alert and sensitive canonistic mind the immense possibilities that existed for the expansion of papal power. It is true that the crusades were primarily heralded as campaigns to take possession of land that was of greatest emotional importance to Western Christianity; this made of course the strongest appeal to the people at large. But the crusades had only wetted the appetite of the curialist political thinkers and of the papacy

[1] Innocent IV, on III.xxxiv.8, fol. 429 verso, No. 4.
[2] John, x.16.
[3] See Panormitanus, *Com.* on *Decretales*, I.vi.34, fol. 111, No. 6: "Nemo potest dicere se alienum ab ovili ecclesiae, omnis ergo creatura subjecta est ecclesiae."
[4] Jer., i.10.
[5] Cf. Alvarus Pelagius, lib. i, cap. 36, fol. 8: "Ex his manifeste apparet, prius fuisse ecclesiam quam aliquod justum vel injustum imperium temporale."

itself. It was soon discovered that by a logical elaboration of the ideas which first prompted the enterprise of the crusades papal powers and supremacy could be extended so that it might, at least in theory, embrace the whole of what was known as the universe. In other words, the crusades were considered only a stepping stone in the direction of the eventual establishment of a fully fledged world government. But we should not for a moment assume that the crusades served as a model for the setting up of a papal world monarchy: the employment of brute force was a feature that did not gain much favour with the canonists. They preferred subtler methods, some of which would nowadays be termed the method of infiltration. That is not to say that the canonists did not justify the crusades *ex post*, but that they at least never propagated the employment of force as the ordinary and regular method for the extension of papal power. Only in the very last resort, that is to say, when all the means of so-called "peaceful penetration" had been exhausted, did they advise calling upon the secular arm to carry out what their own efforts had vainly tried to achieve.

This policy of infiltration, sometimes appearing under the guise of protecting individuals subject to curial jurisdiction, sometimes showing itself as open interference, and not infrequently carried out by the activity of emissaries, was, as far as we can see, first conceived by Pope Innocent IV. We may now turn to these practical aspects of papal world dominion. According to Innocent IV, the general maxim for the jurisdiction of the pope over non-Christians should be that whenever and wherever God had reason to inflict punishment or to deal in any way with mortals, the pope as God's vicar had the same right and power. All power, Innocent declared in this context, "est apud Deum et sic apud ipsum eius vicarium". Hence, whenever a gentile, wherever he might live, defied the natural law, he could legitimately be tried and punished by the pope. To avoid any confusion we should bear in mind that natural law was that set of rules which was contained in the Old and New Testaments. This right of the pope to punish such offences by non-Christians was, in the theory of Innocent IV, copied from the manner in which the Lord had dealt with Sodom.[1] For since God's judgments should be examples to man—"judicia Dei nobis examplaria"—no reason could be adduced

---
[1] Gen. xix.4 ff., Innocent IV, loc. cit.

to show why the pope could not and should not do likewise: "Non apparet, quare papa hoc non possit et etiam debet." The punishment of idolatry committed by infidels, was also the concern of the pope. This, too, was conceived as an offence against the natural law, because it is natural to worship one God only rather than the images of imaginary deities.[1] The punishment of Jews provided another example of the power of the pope over non-Christians. Whenever Jews committed an offence "contra legem" that is, against the New Testament, especially when they defied the Christian moral code, they were legitimately subject to the pope's jurisdiction. The chief offence was the medieval crime of heresy—and this, Innocent IV said, was committed by the authors of a number of Jewish writings. Therefore some popes have rightly ordered the burning of these books, such as the Talmud, and commanded the punishment of those who wrote them or spread their doctrines.[2]

In this context mention should also be made of the decree of Clement V (1311) in which he prohibited the holding of Mohammedan services in countries inhabited by Moslems, but ruled by Christian princes. Clement ordered these rulers to issue laws whereby the public invocation of Mohammed and the annual pilgrimages to his shrine were to be forbidden. Mohammed's name was to be obliterated in those countries, and those Moslems defying these laws should be punished in such a way that their punishment would be an appropriate deterrent for future offenders.[3] This Clementine decree was in fact merely a specific application of the decree passed in the Fourth Lateran Council (1215) in which decree the secular princes were called upon to direct Jews and Saracens to wear distinctive badges in public.[4] Bernardus Parmensis correctly observed that the temporal authority was thereby made responsible for carrying out an order which concerned a purely spiritual affair.[5]

---

[1] "Papa potest punire infideles, si colant idola. Naturale enim est, unum Deum solum creatorum colere, et non creaturas," loc. cit.

[2] See, for example, Zabarella, loc. cit., No. 15.

[3] *Clem*. V.ii, cap. un.

[4] Cap. 68, and *Decretales*, V.vi.15; cf. also Alexander III's decree, ibid.: cap. 4.

[5] Bernardus on V.vi.15, s.v. "animadversionis", and cap. 5, s.v. "excommunicationis".

Into this category of papal jurisdiction also fell the condemnation of the famous *Mirror of the Saxons* (*Speculum Saxonum, Sachsenspiegel*) by Gregory XI in 1374. It is interesting to see that before passing this sentence, Gregory XI consulted the doctores juris utriusque. This legal work marked a turning point in the history of medieval Germanic law; it was declared null and void and its use by the ecclesiastical tribunals and by secular justices was prohibited. Anyone using it was to be excommunicated. The main reason for the annulment was the alleged denial of papal power. The *Mirror* denied the pope or anybody else the power to excommunicate a validly elected and crowned emperor, although the *Mirror* itself left this papal right untouched in three cases: the right of excommunication was not denied, if the emperor's faith appeared dubious; if he cast his wife away; or if he destroyed churches.[1] Obviously the *Mirror* tried to restrict papal censures to purely spiritual matters and to exclude excommunication from the field of politics.

In the case of excommunicates who scorned the ecclesiastical sentence of excommunication or who persistently failed to recant, the ecclesiastical authority—usually the pope himself—was given the right to issue binding instructions to the secular prince that he should compel the recalcitrant excommunicate to ask for re-admission into the fold from which he had been excluded. The goods of the excommunicate were to be confiscated and he himself arrested, if he continued to disobey the papal command. If the prince himself failed to obey, he also was faced with excommunication and expropriation.[2] Reference was made to St. Louis who had laid down that if an excommunicate had failed to recant within the period of one year, he

---

[1] *Bullarium Romanum*, vol. iv, pp. 573-76. Although Gregory XI recognized that these laws had been observed for a long time, he condemned them (they were "detestable", p. 574, col. 2), because by observing them God would be offended, justice would be miscarried, canon and civil(!) laws disregarded "enormiter", natural law perverted, "and, what is still worse, the apostolic power denied".

[2] Durandus, op. cit., Qu. III: "Ad secundam rationem": "Aliquis laicus juste excommunicatus per ecclesiam contemnit excommunicationem longo tempore nec vult redire ad gremium ecclesiae; certe ecclesia potest praecipere domino temporali, sub cuius dominio excommunicatus manet, quod compellat eum per captionem bonorum et etiam personae, si nota sit, ut satisfaciat et reddat ad obedientiam ecclesiae; et si dominus temporalis recusat hoc facere, potest et debet excommunicari." Obviously this was an extension of the rule laid down in *Decretales*, V.vii.13 (cap. 3 of the Fourth Lateran Council).

should be compelled to do so by the secular authority.[1] In the Fourth Lateran Council it was laid down[2] that if the prince would not purge his country from heresy, the pope should be informed of this; he would then proceed to release the subjects from their oath of allegiance and would, furthermore, throw the country open to occupation by Catholics. The shrewd political mind of Innocent IV clearly saw that in a great number of cases popes did not exercise their jurisdictional powers, although the "potestas faciendi est apud eum", but this inactivity was justified either by physical impossibility or by the possibility of giving scandal or by the disproportionate nature of the risk involved.[3]

We have so far confined ourselves to the exercise of jurisdictional powers over individuals some of whom were not or were no longer considered to be Christians. Let us now see how the political power of the pope might affect collective groups, the Mohammedan nations, for instance. Firstly, mention must be made of the claim to unmolested activity on the part of papal emissaries. According to the established canonistic teachings, missionaries and other papal representatives must be allowed free entry into non-Christian countries and must be able to enjoy unrestricted movement in them. The canonists clearly acknowledged that these non-Christian countries were political entities which were territorially under the jurisdictional power of some other potentate. This recognition follows from the way in which the question was usually put: "I ask, whether the pope can issue the order to infidels to admit the 'praedicatores evangelii' into their countries?"[4] The question was invariably answered in the affirmative. Innocent IV—and with him all the canonists—even went so far as to declare that if these non-Christian countries refused permission for the emissaries to enter, they could be compelled to do so. The reason for this view, Innocent IV stated, was that

---

[1] Durandus, op. cit.

[2] Cap. 3: "... ut ex tunc ipse (scil. papa) vasallos ab eius fidelitate denunciet absolutos et terram exponat catholicis occupandam." On the interpretation of this decree see Maitland, *Roman Canon Law*, p. 162.

[3] "Vel propter pericula vel scandala, quae inde obveniunt vel evenire timerentur, potestas tamen faciendi est apud eum," No. 5.

[4] Zabarella, *Com.* on *Decretales*, III.xxxiv.8, No. 19, fol. 201 verso: "Quaero, an potest mandare infidelibus, quod admittant praedicatores evangelii in terris suis?"

"every rational creature is made to praise God".[1] Consequently, their refusal constituted a punishable act.[2] But if the pope were not in a position to inflict punishment on these infidels, the help of the secular arm should be invoked and war declared upon them, the declaration of war being the exclusive prerogative of the pope. This held good whenever a lawful command of the pope to non-Christians was disobeyed.[3] A right to compel the non-Christians to embrace the Christian faith, was denied by Innocent and the canonists, since in these matters they were to be left to their own free choice.[4]

The emphatic claim to unfettered missionary activities was paralleled by the likewise emphatic denial of the right of entry into Christian territories of non-Christian emissaries, especially Mohammedans. "Pro constanti tenemus," declared Innocent IV, that they were to be strictly refused the possibility of entry. One might ask, he said, why could they not claim admittance in the same way—"eodom modo"—as the Christian emissaries? "We must not" said Innocent answering his own question, "put ourselves on the same level as those people, because they are in error, and we walk in the path of truth."[5]

A corollary of this effluence of papal power was the thesis of the right of direct interference with the internal legislation of non-Christian countries. The pope, in short, assumed the role of a protector of all Christians wherever they might be found. He was to exercise his authority "sine limitatione loci et personarum"; this held good in whatever country and under whatever ruler Christians might live: they owed direct obedience to the pope alone: "ideo omnes Christiani, ubicumque sint, debent ei obedire."[6] Perhaps we should add that the criterion of papal interference left out of account the not unimportant

[1] "Omnis cretura rationabilis facta est ad Deum laudandum." He referred to Peter Lombard's *Sententiae*, lib. ii, dist. 1.

[2] "Si ergo prohibeant praedicatores, peccant et ideo puniendi sunt."

[3] Loc. cit., No. 9: "Si papa non potest de facto eos punire? In omnibus praedictis casibus et in aliis, ubi licet papae eis aliquid mandare, si non obediant, compellendi sunt brachio saeculari et indicendum est bellum contra eos per papam, et non per alios."

[4] Loc. cit., No. 8, fol. 430 verso.

[5] "Sed dices, numquid et eodem modo debet papa admittere illos, qui vellent praedicare legem Mahommedi? Respondeo, non enim ad paria debemus nobiscum judicare, cum ipsi sint in errore, et nos in via veritatis, et hoc pro constanti tenemus."

[6] Durandus, op. cit., Qu. III.

question of whether there was a conflict of loyalty in the particular case.[1] Whilst Innocent IV confined the papal right of interference to those countries which had at any time been ruled by Christian princes, but had been wrested from them and placed therefore under a non-Christian government, later canonists, such as Cardinal Zabarella, asserted this right of the pope unconditionally—"in aliquo casu",[2] regardless of whether or not the country was ever in Christian hands. According to the established teaching of the canonists the pope was entitled to issue orders and decrees to these non-Christian countries to the effect that the Christians under their jurisdiction should not be unjustly molested in their activities—though the canonists wisely and diplomatically refrained from a definition of the nature of these activities. Were they merely religious, or did they also extend into the political arena? In the latter case, was the issue of a divided loyalty given due appreciation? Here the canonists were silent and simply said:

> Papa potest facere praeceptum et constitutionem, quod non molestant Christianos injuste, qui subsunt eorum jurisdictioni.[3]

Moreover, the pope was given the right to exempt the Christians from the non-Christian jurisdiction of their rulers.[4]

Now, it is interesting to see that the legal basis for this certainly far-reaching theory were passages which expressly

---

[1] There is, however, an interesting case of divided loyalty in the *Glossa Palatina*. The gloss on C. XV, q. vi, c. 4, says that if the soldiers of an excommunicate king refused to obey his call, even if the enemy had invaded the country, they would not incur infamy according to the "jus poli", although they would do so according to the law of the land. "Dicit (scilicet Bernardus Compostellanus antiquus), quod si non juravent excommunicatum talem, si inimici intrarent terram eius, incurrerent infamiam secundum leges suas, licet non debeant jure poli; non tamen veniat ille ad exercitium, vel si venerint, recedant," fol. 91 verso of D 8. That the siglum "b" stands for Bernardus Compostellanus antiquus in this compilation, was conclusively proved by Professor Kuttner who discovered this *Apparatus*, although at first ascribing it to Johannes Teutonicus, see "Eine Dekretsumme Johannes Teutonicus" in *Zeitschrift, kanon. Abt.*, vol. xxi, pp. 141 ff., *id Repertorium*, pp. 82-91, and above all his article in *Traditio*, vol. i, pp. 277-340.

[2] Zabarella, on III.xxxiv.8, No. 18, fol. 201 verso.

[3] See, for example, Innocent IV, loc. cit., No. 7.

[4] Innocent continued: "Imo, quod plus est, potest eos eximere a jurisdictione eorum et dominio in totum."

dealt only with the position of Jews and pagans either as domestic masters or as public officials. Generally speaking, these regulations aimed at restraining Jews from gaining power over Christians, but only within the *Respublica Christiana*, an understandable point of view. There is nothing in these passages originally passed by the Fourth Lateran Council[1] to suggest that they were meant to be applied to whole communities. In other words, these rules concerned individual cases within the Christian commonwealth, in which the exercise of papal legislation could not be disputed. What the canonists did was to apply these regulations to whole countries, and to all non-Christians wherever they lived.[2] If, therefore, the non-Christian princes treated their subjects badly, the pope was entitled to deprive these rulers of their jurisdictional powers and of their title to rule altogether.[3] It was, however, usually agreed that only in extreme cases should this right of direct interference be exercised, as, for instance, in the case of a danger to the Christians and of the creation of grave scandal.[4] Both these criteria were of course flexible.

Whilst regulations obviously designed for use within the medieval commonwealth furnished the legal basis of this claim of interference, the political support for this theory was found in the conception of the pope as an emperor. We have said that Innocent IV restricted the papal right of interference to those countries which were once under Christian domination. He assigned to the pope the role of a quasi-imperator who by reason of his overlordship could claim jurisdictional powers over all Christian princes, hence also over those countries which were at one time under the rule of a Christian prince. But as there was now no possibility of the emperor's exercising the right of interference, this right now devolved upon the pope. "Unde licitum est papae ratione imperii Romani" to interfere, said Innocent IV, but "si non potest facere *tamquam imperator*", he could do so "ex aliis praedictis causis", that is to say, on the grounds of the pope's overlordship of the world. It is plain

---

[1] Cap. 69 of the Fourth Lateran Council.
[2] The passages were: *Decretales*, V.vi.2, 16, 18, 19.
[3] "Imo si male tractarent Christianos, posset eos privare per sententiam jurisdictione et dominio", Innocent IV, fol. 430.
[4] "Tamen magna causa debet esse, quod ad hoc veniat, debet enim papa eos quantum potest, sustinere, dummodo periculum non sit Christianis, nec grave scandalum generatur," fol. 430, No. 7.

that this loophole left open by Innocent IV, did not escape the attention of later canonists who conveniently lost sight of the supposed function of the pope as a "quasi-imperator".

These considerations lead us straight on to the political explanation of the crusades. The strong emotional appeal which the crusades made to the people did not unduly stir the hearts of the more rationally and politically inclined canonists. The consideration that the Saracens held the Holy Land in *illicit* possession, furnished the juristic thesis for the campaigns. That country was consecrated by the birth, suffering and death of Christ, where now, however, not Christ, but Mohammed was worshipped. It provided the pope with a just motive for attempting to regain the Holy Land. The political thesis was that the country was wrested from the hands of the Roman emperors after the death of Christ, and therefore "by reason of the Roman empire" it was legitimate for the pope to regain a jurisdiction which the emperor once possessed, but which he himself was unable to recover. The pope in his role as a quasi-imperator, had the right to re-conquer those territories. In conclusion Innocent IV advanced the general theory that whenever and wherever Roman emperors—not necessarily Christian Roman emperors—had once exercised their power, it was the exclusive prerogative of the pope to reclaim those countries as belonging to him.[1] The very plausible objection that Constantine had handed over to the pope the occident only, and not the orient, was brushed aside by the scholastic distinction between "proprietas" and "tuitio": the Donation of Constantine had bestowed upon the pope the "proprietas" of all occidental countries, but had left the papal "tuitio" of oriental lands untouched.

But could not the reverse also be maintained, that is to say, that infidels were entitled to regain those countries and territories which they had once ruled, but which were now in Christian hands, in particular Southern Europe? Every medieval canonist put this question, and every one of them gave the same negative reply: there was to be no reciprocity,[2] because

[1] "Haec ratio (scil. imperii Romani) sufficit in omnibus aliis terris, in quibus imperatores Romani jurisdictionem habuerunt," loc. cit., No. 7.

[2] Cf. Innocent IV who again was the first to consider the possibility of reciprocity: "Sed dicas, quare non eodem modo licet eis repetere terram istam, scil. Italiam vel alias, ubi dominati fuerunt infideles?" No. 10, fol. 430 verso.

the peoples themselves who inhabited these countries had been converted to Christianity. And in any case, the supreme consideration was that the cause of religion was the highest and loftiest reason for any human action. "Summa est ratio, quae pro religione facit."[1] Now it is certainly not without interest to point out that for this significant statement only one passage was cited and that was from Roman law, but this passage dealt with a subject quite irrelevant to the present topic. The juristic aid for the papalist theory had to come from Roman law.

This brings us to the question of the legitimacy of conquering non-Christian countries which at no time were under a Christian rule. Here we meet with two schools of thought, the one moderate and led by Innocent IV, and the other rather extreme and initiated by Hostiensis. The difference between these two schools was not so great as it might appear, for they both had a number of premisses and basic reasons in common, and it was only in their final conclusions that they differed. The moderate party maintained that Christians had no right to conquer non-Christian countries, the extreme section affirmed that this right existed. "Is it permissible," the canonists asked, "to invade territory (other than the Holy Land) that is possessed by infidels?"[2] "In veritate," the answer was given, "in truth, the earth is the Lord's and the fulness thereof: the world and they that dwell therein."[3] For the Lord was the creator of all and everything, and He Himself had subjected the whole universe to the control of the rational creature.[4] From the beginning this world was "the common property" of all its inhabitants, and it was not until after the introduction by primaeval men of certain customs that different peoples appropriated different parts of the world. In this slowly emerging acquisition of private property no evil tendency was envisaged. On the contrary, this urge for appropriation was all to the good, since it was only natural that common property was neglected by everyone and that it was also a source of discontent,[5] for it is said, "every place whereon the soles of your

[1] Zabarella, loc. cit., No. 21.
[2] Innocent IV, No. 1: "Sed numquid est licitum invadere terram, quam infideles possident vel quae est sua?"
[3] Ps. xxiv.
[4] "Ipse enim est creator omnium, idem etiam ipse Deus haec universa subjecit dominio rationalis creaturae, propter quam haec omnia fecerat."
[5] Innocent, loc. cit.

feet shall tread shall be yours".[1] But no right of occupation was conceded, if there was previous possession of land by some other individual or group of individuals, because this would violate the legal and ethical maxim, that one should not do to one's neighbour what one would not wish to be done to oneself.[2] The Old Testament also proved, it was furthermore argued, that nations could have their own chosen leaders, as in the case of Saul and many others. Hence Innocent IV recognized realistically enough that nothing obnoxious could be seen in the mere fact of infidels possessing and ruling countries, unless of course certain actions on the part of their governments made the further possession sinful. For property and rulership were given to every rational creature, Innocent was convinced, and Christ Himself said: "The Father maketh his sun to rise on the evil and on the good, and sendeth rain on the just and on the unjust."[3] It was for these reasons that Innocent IV and his school of thought denied to the pope any right of conquering non-Christian countries.[4] It seems, however, that Innocent only grudgingly refused to give his sanction for a conquest of a non-Christian country, for immediately afterwards he continued literally: "But we believe nevertheless that the pope who is the vicar of Christ, has power not only over Christians, but also over all infidels, since Christ Himself had power over everybody."[5] Here Innocent left his argument and enumerated those specific cases in which the pope could interfere "ex potestate" with the internal legislation of non-Christian countries.

It was at this point that Hostiensis continued Innocent's argument. While adopting the canonist-pope's basic tenets, he took up the argument where his forerunner had left off. Through the advent of Christ, according to Hostiensis, every human being, every dominion, principality and jurisdictional power had been taken away from the infidels and had been handed to

---

[1] Deut. xi.24.   [2] Matt. vii.12.

[3] Matt. v.45. This realistic view is in pleasant contrast to that expressed by Hostiensis and especially by the publicist Egidius Romanus, *De Ecclesiastica Potestate*, lib. ii, c. 1, p. 96 of the edition of Scholz.

[4] "Propter hoc dicimus, quod non licet infidelibus auferre dominia sua vel jurisdictiones infidelibus, quia sine peccato ea possident."

[5] "Sed bene tantum credimus, quod papa, qui est vicarius Christi, potestatem habet, non tantum super Christianos, sed etiam super omnes infideles, cum enim Christus habuerit super omnes potestatem."

the faithful, and all this "de jure et ex justa causa".[1] This translation of power was first made to the person of Christ Who combined the functions of priesthood and kingship,[2] and this sacerdotal and kingly power was then transferred to the popes. On the strength of this premiss Hostiensis saw no difficulty in asserting that all infidels should be subjected to the faithful: "Infideles debent subjeci fidelibus." But he took realities into account and made a certain degree of concession. If, he said, the rulers of infidels' countries "recognize the principality of the Church"—"si dominium ecclesiae recognoscunt"—the pope should leave them alone. By virtue of this recognition or, in other words, on sufferance of the Church, the infidel countries should be allowed to have property and jurisdictional power. If they were content with this position and did not abuse this privilege given to them by the Church, they could be left in peace.[3] But if infidel countries did not recognize the Church's dominion, overlordship and power, and did not obey its commands, they must be considered unworthy of their possessions and sovereign rights, and they should give up these rights which they only acquired by occupation and force.[4] It is worth while pointing out that the existence of this theory substantially detracts from the supposed originality of Egidius Colonna's system, for the views of this publicist were almost verbally anticipated by this canonist.[5] One of the staunchest adherents of Hostiensis was the glossator of the *Extravagantes* of John XXII, Zenzelinus de Cassanis, who asked whether Christ's commission to St. Peter included supreme powers over infidels and non-Catholics as well. His answer was a strong affirmative.

Something in the way of a compromise between these two theories was achieved by later canonists. It was agreed that force should not be employed to subjugate these pagan countries to Christian rule, but that they should be won over by the effects of missionary activity, that is, by peaceful penetration. Only

---

[1] Hostiensis, loc. cit.; this point of view was also adopted by Zenzelinus de Cassanis in his gloss on *Extravagantes*, V, cap. un., s.v. "commisit".

[2] "Et fuit facta translatio in personam Christi filii, Dei vivi, qui non solum sacerdos fuit, sed etiam rex."

[3] "Et si his contenti non sunt vel abutuntur, sibi imputent, quia privilegium merentur amittere."

[2] Hostiensis, loc. cit.

[5] Cf. Hostiensis, loc. cit., and Egidius Romanus, op. cit., lib. ii, cap. 11, p. 98 ed. cit.

when the right of entry was refused to the emissaries, should force be used.[1] Canonistic thought in the fourteenth century also somewhat receded from the Innocentian and biblical reasons for the legitimacy of infidel possessions and governments. A more juristic justification was put forward, which provides a pleasant contrast to the extravagant views of the publicists, such as Egidius Colonna, who stated that infidels had no legitimate title to these possessions, because they did not pay tributes to the Church.[2] According to the canonists, however, the infidels were thought of as being capable of acquiring property and rulership by means of prescription. It was quite true, the argument ran, that the countries came into possession of the infidels by means of fire and sword—"ferro ac vi"—but this had taken place such a long time before that one was justified in legally condoning that acquisition through "diuturna praescriptio". Moreover, it was increasingly recognized that some of these infidel countries had never accepted the truths of the Old and New Testaments and that it was therefore incorrect to apply to them the thesis of Hostiensis that through the advent of Christ all power had been transferred to Christians. The idea of using force found no adherents in the papalist camp, and even Hostiensis himself seems to have been somewhat doubtful on the wisdom of its use, as so many princes, he declared, snatched from one another their legitimate possession, and despite the palpable injustice of such conduct they were absolved by their confessors who thereby only countenanced such conduct.[3]

This idea of an immemorial prescription was not evolved without some ulterior motive. A deeper insight into canonistic political thought shows us that this tolerant attitude towards pagan countries had some very definite motives. As we shall see in the next chapter, the political thinkers of the curialists maintained the superiority of the pope over the emperor, and this very largely by virtue of the Donation. The papalist thesis

---

[1] Zabarella, loc. cit., No. 24, fol. 201 verso: "Alios autem infideles in pace degentes, etiam illos, quos servos tenemus, non per bellum vel violentiam aliquam, sed per praedicationem debemus convertere, et si praedicatores non admittunt, debeant compesci."

[2] See *De Ecclesiastica Potestate*, p. 97 ed cit.: "Nisi tributum solvat, injuste possidet, quicquid habet."

[3] "Christiani principes inter se bella movent et violenter occupat unus id, quod alius juste tenebat, et absolvuntur tales a confessoribus, qui palpant crimina."

asserted that Constantine had handed over the rulership of the West to the pope: he was alleged to be the master of those territories which a legitimate Roman ruler used to hold. It was this point which the anti-papalists made the target of a well-planned attack. For they declared that the Roman empire was founded by force and that therefore the pope received the government of an illicitly acquired territory. That was certainly a frontal attack. The blow had to be parried. Hence, in their defence the canonists declared that immemorial possession of territories by pagan countries conferred the title of legitimacy upon their governments. And in any case, the canonists asked, was one certain that the Roman territories were acquired by force? Surely some of them were licitly acquired as gifts or in other ways, and, to quote one canonist literally: "When we are in doubt we presume that the Romans acquired their empire justly."[1] Some papalists tried to ward off the attack by boldly asserting that the Roman empire rose through the political wisdom and ability of its rulers.[2]

The argumentation of Hostiensis proved extraordinarily fruitful. His manner of reasoning and of showing the power of the pope on the basis of some selected and skilfully interpreted passages of the New Testament exercised a stimulating influence on contemporary canonistic thought. It may be that the fertility of the germ which he had sown in his theory, was not recognized by its author, but the canonists treading in the footsteps of the great master, fully appreciated the extreme richness of his thoughts. For the ideas of Hostiensis led directly the conception of dominion, as it was systematically developed by Cardinal Petrus Bertrandi. His theory may well take its place besides the much-praised works of Egidius Colonna, Fitzralph, the archbishop of Armagh, and Wyclif, who also made the concept of dominion the focal point of their political tracts. In his treatise, *De Origine Jurisdictionum*,[3] which is as

---

[1] See Antonius de Butrio, *Com.* on *Decretales*, III.xxxiv.8, fol. 151, No. 8: "Nec obstat, si dicatur, quod ecclesia teneat possessiones et terras in occidente vel alibi, quae per violentiam fuerunt occupatae, et sic illicite per imperatores Romanos . . . ideo praesumere debemus in dubio, quod juste quaesiverunt."

[2] Cf. Durandus, op. cit., Qu. I, in fine: "De imperio autem Romano clare patet ex cronicis et diversis historiis, quod insurrexit per potentiam et saecularem prudentiam."

[3] Bertrandi's tract, although printed in *Tractatus*, tom. iii, fol. 29 verso—32, under the title of *De Origine Jurisdictionum*, represented an almost literal

comprehensive as it is little known, he devoted the fourth and last chapter to the apparently innocent question, of whether the spiritual power should *dominate* the temporal power. This chapter was added by Chappuis as an appendix to the gloss of Johannes Monachus on Boniface's *Unam sanctam*. The cardinal's theory, in contrast to that of Egidius,[1] was juristically formulated and clothed in more sharply definable terms.

Bertrandi's arguments set forth to prove the secular inferiority were all of the old, well known pattern, and in this part of the chapter no original contribution to political thought can be found. It was only when he came to examine the statement that every human creature was subject to the pope that his system showed ideas which were politically and juristically original. The presupposition for the understanding of universal subjection to the pope's jurisdiction was that there were two kinds of *dominium*, the one a dominion according to divine law, the other a dominion according to human law. The former was a "dominium divinum", the latter a "dominium legale" or "humanum". The divine dominion was of course that which God had over every human creature,[2] for He was the creator of all mankind and of the universe itself.[3] At this point Petrus Bertrandi took up the idea of Hostiensis that through the advent of Christ all power had been transferred to Christ's successors and consequently to the popes. "Properly speaking," said the

---

adoption of Durandus's tract *De Jurisdictione Ecclesiastica;* the fourth and last chapter of Bertrandi's tract was his own. See also *supra.* p. 85 n. 4.

The MS. in Edinburgh University Library, Db V 12 (fifteenth-century hand, probably French) to which no reference seems to have been made by modern authorities, also presents the whole tract as Bertrandi's own creation and even uses Durandus's title. Incipit, fol. 1: "Libellus petri bertrandi de jurisdictione ecclesiastica penitentiali quam spirituali ... iste liber est compositus et translatus de ytalico in latinum...." Explicit, fol. 46: "qui (dem?) libellus de jurisdictione ecclesiastica per petrum bertrandum in concilio conveniantibus praelatorum franciae regni eiusdem verbo tenet(?) per ipsum deputatum ex parte ipsorum recitat, etc." For a description, see also Borland, No. 143. The MS. is very badly stained through damp.

[1] See, for instance, *De Eccl. Potestate*, p. 98 ed. cit. (Sacramental theory.)

[2] "Dominium divinum est illud, quod est apud Deum super omnem creaturam."

[3] "Ipse autem Deus est creator omnium universorum." Egidius Romanus also referred to the Psalmist, who might be quoted as evidence *against* the universal dominion of the Church, see lib. ii, cap. 11, p. 99 ed. cit.

cardinal, "all creatures whether human or otherwise or whether Christians or pagans, were in the possession of Christ." Therefore all the divine dominion was in the hands of the pope. This kind of dominion was, according to this canonist, "verum dominium".

The other kind of dominion was the human or, as the "legistae" preferred to call it, the legal dominion which was not dominion in the strict sense of the term, although it was loosely styled dominion. Even before the "jus gentium" there was a dominion, as the civil lawyers themselves were bound to admit. And this dominion which was in existence before the "jus gentium" was the true dominion. The "jus gentium" merely fixed the limitations, separations and divisions of property, which were first introduced by primaeval men. Before this time everything was common property. It was merely by virtue of a divine concession that God permitted the use of those separated and divided dominions. They were conferred upon human creatures by God: "Dominium humanum fuit a Deo collatum humanae creaturae." In other words, God whilst still in the last resort reserving to Himself in His hands the true dominion, that is, supreme power of disposing of property, bestowed the temporary use of this dominion upon men.[1] The last decision in respect of the true dominion thus rested with God and, consequently, with His vicar on earth. But, and this argument of the canonist was significant, the human dominion considered by itself, without regard to its origin, was a dominion and although the pope as God's vicar had the "potestas", i.e. the power over all dominion, he must not disturb man in the peaceful use of his human dominion. From the supra-human point of view the pope was the sole owner of the world, but he could not, without just cause, encroach upon the divinely conceded use of the world's goods.

Now it is not difficult to see that, firstly, the pope by reason of his divine ownership of the universe, stood above every earthly ruler, Christian and non-Christian, and it is significant that the cardinal unhesitatingly applied his political system to the whole cosmos. And secondly, the theory of papal encroachment upon the human dominion, juristically more valuable and politically more potent than Egidius's theory, fitted

[1] "Et sic reservato sibi universali et vero dominio omnium creaturarum huius dominii utilitatem concessit ab initio humanae creaturae quoad usum."

smoothly into the general pattern of medieval canonistic thought. In it the system of Hostiensis and also of Innocent IV found a welcome juristic addition. The canonists were henceforth provided with a politically as well as a juristically formulated weapon. When, therefore, the Roman law styled the emperor the "dominus mundi", the term was to be understood in the sense of a human master of the world: his power was necessarily subjected to the general directions of him who held the divine dominion of the world. But this was not only true as regards the Christian emperor, but also in respect of any ruler on earth who enjoyed the benefits of the divine dominion. Cardinal Petrus Bertrandi had at long last furnished the long awaited theoretical justification for the practice that had grown up in connexion with the expropriation of goods held by heretics. It is of course true that in a number of his letters St. Augustine had urged that those who had withdrawn from the Church should no longer be entitled to hold property.[1] The older doctrine relied mainly on the Augustinian *dicta*, but failed to show a juristically tenable justification for the expropriation. And when Magister Rolandus (Alexander III) insisted on the judicial sentence as an indispensable requirement for expropriation, he cannot be said to have thereby advanced the theory of expropriation.[2] In the writings of the thirteenth-century canonists we find the standing phrase, "Have Catholics proper authority to deprive heretics of their dominion?"[3] The reply was strongly in the affirmative, because, to quote literally, "the Church had given general authority to Catholics to exterminate the heretics".[4] But apart from this so-called "general authority" given by the Church, we do not find a justification for this deprivation of property. Through the theory of dominion it was possible to stigmatize heresy as a "just cause" for the

---

[1] See C. XXIII, q. vii, c. 1-4. The actual economic conditions of the age of course contributed very largely to the creation of this point of view. On contemporary economic conditions see H. Pirenne, *Economic and Social History of Medieval Europe*, (ed. 1947), p. 13.

[2] See *Summa Magistri Rolandi*, on C. XXIII, q. vii, p. 96 of the edition F. Thaner.

[3] See, for example, Goffredus de Trano, *Summa*, De haereticis, fol. 200, No. 4: "Numquid catholici possunt haereticos propria auctoritate spoliare?"

[4] "Videtur, quod sic, ecclesia enim generalem auctoritatem eis praestitit, ut

papal withdrawal of the divine concession from heretics. The thirteenth and fourteenth centuries were truly in need of a theoretical justification for the confiscation of heretical property.

---

eos exterminent." See also *Summa Stephani Tornacensis*, on *Dist.* lxiii, p. 89 (ed. Schulte): "Propter haereticos et scismaticos, qui catholicam impediant electionem principes interesse jussi sunt, ut quod gladius spiritualis non poterat, carnalis reprimeret."

CHAPTER VI

POPE AND EMPEROR

THE highly organized state of modern civilization is characterized by the ever growing and ever expanding powers which the State exercises over the individual. It is the individual personality that claims, on the one hand, protection of its interests and, on the other hand, a latitude in his own actions *vis-à-vis* the organized community of which he forms an integral part. The reconciliation of these two inherently conflicting claims constitutes what is known as the problem of freedom. The conflict is one between an organized entity, the State, and an unorganized body of citizens. The former—rightly or wrongly—claims something approaching omnipotence in its actions, and it is this claim to omnipotence that is disputed either in its entirety or in its extent, by the individual. "He" tries to ward off anything he may call an infringement on his freedom by "them". Whether sailing under the flag of collectivism and individualism, or under that of totalitarianism and democracy, socialism and capitalism—the name does not matter—the problem still remains the same: the individual against the group.

This is an interesting development in the history of political and perhaps also in that of social thought. For the place which is now taken by the individual, was in medieval days occupied by the Church. Then it was not State versus the individual, but State versus the Church, emperor versus pope. In our own days the Church has receded into the background as a political factor, but the other institution, the State, has survived and prospered. In medieval days, however, the two combatants were nearly equally matched. In their lectures, public disputations, commentaries, tracts and glosses—whether originating in the minds of civilians or of canonists—the somewhat idealistic point of view was maintained, namely, that the *sacerdotium* and *regnum* were the two pillars of the medieval society that constituted the *Respublica Christiana*. The one should assist the other in the execution of its functions.¹ These two institutions were both said to be divinely ordained and should be vigilant not to overstep the frontiers set by a divine ordinance, which met with an all too vague interpretation. Perhaps no other passage in the huge body of medieval law was so much quoted, so hackneyed, so over-interpreted as the *Novella* of Justinian in which he stated with deliberation that the supreme mercy of God had bestowed upon mankind the two greatest gifts, that is, the *sacerdotium* and the *imperium*, the one ministering to the divine, the other presiding over, and caring for, the human. Justinian's final declaration that both proceeded from one and the same principle proved of crucial importance. A very similar idea was expressed in the old canon law,² and the famous passage of Pope Gelasius³ may be taken in this sense.⁴

Both the imperialist and the curialist accepted Justinian's passage and the canonical ordinances, and both interpreted them differently. In particular, the passage of Justinian provided the main common denominator of papalist and anti-papalist doctrine—otherwise they had little in common. The imperialist, it is true, conferred a plenitude of power upon the emperor, but however extreme he might have been, he never wished to arrogate any powers to the emperor in the spiritual sphere in which sole supremacy was conceded to the pope. The weak point of this political system, as one can readily see, lay in the difficulty of drawing the line of demarcation: where did the temporal end, and where did the spiritual begin? The civilians as well as the earlier generation of canonists took the Justinianean passage to heart and were earnestly bent on realizing the strict

---

[1] *Authenticum, collatio* I, tit. vi, praefatio.

[2] *Decretum Gratiani*, C. XXIII, q. iv, c. 45, and Gratian himself in his *dictum post cap.* 41, C. II, q. vii; "Notandum est, quod duae sunt personae, quibus mundus iste regitur, regalis videlicet et sacredotalis. Sicut reges praesunt in causis saeculi, ita sacerdotes in causis Dei. Regum est corporalem irrogare poenam, sacerdotum spiritualem inferre vindictam."

[3] *Dist.* xcvi, c. 10. For the historical importance of this theory see J. Haller, *Das Papsttum, Idee und Wirklichkeit*, vol. i, p. 213, and L. Knabe, *Die gelasianische Zweigewalten-Theorie bis zum Ende des Investiturstreites*, 1936, *passim*, and Ulrich Gmelin, "Auctoritas, Römischer Princeps and päpstlicher Primat" in *Geistige Grundlagen Römischer Kirchenpolitik*, 1937, p. 143, note 207 and 147.

[4] "Duo sunt, quibuis principaliter hic mundus regitur, auctoritas sancta pontificum, et regalis potestas." But Gelasius here clearly maintained the greater dignity of the pontifical power.

separation of *sacerdotium* and *imperium*, of State and Church. where were to be two heads at the helm of the Christian commonwealth, each supreme in his own sphere. The civilians and early canonists attempted the execution of the dualistic principle.[1] Not so the thirteenth and fourteenth-century canonists. To them, as we have already had an opportunity of pointing out, the dualistic principle was anathema: "Duo principia ponere haereticum est," became the watchword in canonistic doctrine. Translated into the jargon of political language the watchword became: "It is heresy to postulate two co-vicars on earth."[2]

The papalists proclaimed for the pope a plenitude of power which, unlike the emperor's, comprised both spheres, the temporal as well as the spiritual. Papal plenitude of power *ex se* was considered to include the temporal as well. To quote one canonist who was especially extreme in his papalist views: "Just as the soul dominates the body, in the same way the pope dominates the emperor."[3] When we keep in mind the role which canonistic doctrine assigned to the temporal in the general pattern of their conceptional framework, we shall not find the inclusion of the temporal in the papal plenitude of power anymore startling than the idea of plenitude of power itself. According to the political design of the canonists, the emperor's powers—we are not entitled to speak of an imperial plenitude of power when considering canonistic conceptions—ranged as far as the pope wished them to go: the extent of the authority of the emperor depended on the extent to which the pope conceded to the emperor the exercise of those powers which he as pope was not desirous personally to exercise. In other words, the emperor's function was that of an "advocatus", "the most inferior servant of pope and Church", "ultimus servus papae et ecclesiae". The emperor was alleged to exercise his power at the bidding of the master as a mere subordinate official of the pope and the Church. From the standpoint of the monistic principle the superiority of the pope over the emperor was inevitable. Perhaps the difference between the civilian and canon-

---

[1] See, for example, Cynus, *Com.* on *Cod. Just.* I.i.1: "Temporaliter sub imperio omnes populi omnesque reges sunt, sicut sunt sub papa spiritualiter."

[2] See, for instance, Panormitanus, *Com.* on *Decretales*, II.i.13, fol. 26 verso, No. 12: "Sic et ponere duos vicarios equales in terris est haereticum."

[3] Panormitanus, loc. cit.: "Sicut ergo anima dominatur corpori, ita papa imperatori."

istic political systems emerged most clearly in the metaphor to which we have referred before: the civilian termed the Church the empire's sister—"soror imperii"—the canonist styled the Church the empire's mother—"mater imperii".[1]

The arguments in favour of the papal monarchy were applied with particular zeal to the relations of Church and State, and Aristotle's thesis on the character of the "optimus principatus" (in the second book of his *Politics*) was a highly favoured source of reference. And when driven into a corner and challenged by a reference to the explicit declarations in Roman law that the emperor was the "dominus mundi", the papalist had a ready answer: these laws, he declared, which impugned the papal plenitude of power, were ill conceived and wrongly issued. "Jura sunt male posita." Two could not have the undivided dominion of one and the same thing.[2]

For the civilian as well as for the canonist the theistic idea was fundamental. No power could claim respect or authority if it could not prove divine origin, however remote. Basing their claims on the previously mentioned passage of Justinian both the imperialist and the papalist could assert the divine origin of their respective idols, the emperor and the pope. But whilst the imperialist and early canonist stated that the pope and emperor alike had a directly divine origin,[3] the papalist of the mid-thirteenth century postulated an exclusively divine origin for the pope alone. The emperor was thought to receive his powers from God, indirectly, through the medium of the pope. This, in short, was the interpretation which that well worn *Novella* of Justinian received at the hands of canonists who were thoroughgoing papalists.

When we speak of the canonists in this context we must keep

---

[1] Cf. Accursius, *glos. ord.* on *Authenticum*, col. I, tit. vi, praef.

[2] Cf. Petrus de Ancharano, *Com.* on *Decretales*, II.ii.10, fol. 46, No. 10: "Duo enim non possunt habere eiusdem rei dominium in solidum nec in possessionem ... si ergo omnis potestas in coelo et in terra data est papae, multa jura, quas dicunt esse contrarium, sunt male posita. Dicit enim lex, quod imperator dominus mundi est...." Quite in the fashion of the day (1937) Ulrich Gmelin, loc. cit., pp. 2, 150, maintained that the claim to papal supremacy was the result of a natural development of Roman-indogerman principles culminating in the leadership idea: the leader drew his powers "from the blood of Nordic descent".

[3] See, for instance, *Cynus, Com.* on *Dig. Vet.* I.iv, 3, No. 1: "Imperium est a Deo ... et ab ipso Deo immediate processit, unde inter imperatorem et Deum non est ponere medium."

in mind that the name of Alanus, the great (and forgotten) English canonist, marked a turning point in the development of canonistic political thought. Before his time the view of Huguccio, the teacher of Innocent III, prevailed, and this view did not materially differ from the civilian standpoint. Huguccio taught that pope and emperor had likewise received the authority to rule mankind directly from God. Strangely enough, he did not rely on Justinian's *Novella* (although his conclusion was indistinguishable from it), but on the statement of Gratian, namely, that "the human race is ruled by natural law and customs",[1] and on the Gelasian principle as incorporated in canon law.[2] Combining these two tenets Huguccio maintained that pope and emperor were simply God's "instruments" and "artificers" ("opifices"): they were but "rectores et ministri", the one of the human, the other of the divine, law. Theoretically, then, Huguccio was logical in juxtaposing Gratian and Gelasius. He applied Gratian's "natural law and customs" to the Gelasian pope and emperor. Through his identification of natural with divine law, and of customs with human law, Huguccio had no logical difficulty in referring to both pope and emperor as "rectores et ministri", the former of the divine (natural), the latter of the human law. Within this conception God became the prime agent of the government of the world—the "actor", as Huguccio put it. In order to make his theory accessible to the less philosophically inclined of his students, Huguccio compared God with a hatchet that splits a piece of wood into two: the two pieces of wood symbolized divine and human laws.[3]

[1] Gratian ante cap. 1, *dist*. i.
[2] *Dist*., xcvi, c. 10.
[3] Huguccio on "humanum genus", fol. 116 of P 72: "xcvii duo. Ibi enim dicitur, quod mundus regitur pontificali auctoritate et regali potestate . . . (mundus) regitur tamquam per instrumenta; per illa regitur tamquam per rectores et ministros divini et humani juris; per dominum regitur tamquam per actorem . . . ab illis duobus et opificibus. Sic ergo mundus regitur ab illis duobus his duobus, id est, illi duo regunt mundum per haec duo (scil. jura), pontificalis auctoritas per jus divinum, regalis potestas per humanum, sicut lignum dolatur ascia, id est, per asciam, scil. instrumentum." Huguccio was quite consistent when, in a different context he declared, that as regards the "spiritualia" the emperor was under the jurisdiction of the pope, just as any bishop or archbishop: and this spiritual bond was established by the "juramentum fidelitatis": "Omnes enim episcopi et archiespiscopi et imperator jurant fidelitatem papae," *Summa, Dist*. xxiii, c. 6, fol. 133 verso of p. P 72. He corroborated this

A natural corollary of Huguccio's premiss was his refusal to attribute any constitutive effects to the emperor's coronation by the pope. According to him, the confirmation, consecration and coronation were formalities which merely changed the title. We may remark in parenthesis that if Cynus had not been obsessed by an inveterate hatred of the canonists, he would have noted that this canonist (and some others to be mentioned presently) had propounded "anti-papalist" views well over a hundred years before his and Jacobus de Arena's time.[1] "It seems," said Huguccio, "that the emperor is not emperor before he receives his crown from the pope." He contradicted this opinion, however, and continued: "But I say that he is not called emperor before he is crowned, for he is emperor not as regards the coronation and confirmation, but as regards his jurisdictional powers and the fulfilment of his duties."[2] Huguccio's basic tenet was the strict separation of Church and State, for Christ Himself had clearly distinguished between

---

statement by a reference to a bull of Celestine II of 29 December 1143 addressed to Petrus de Hongro, in which this pope only very casually mentioned the oath of fealty, see Theiner, *Codex Diplomaticus*, tom. i, p. 13. The tracing of this bull is difficult, as the scribe, instead of writing "Ego Coelestinus" wrote e°petr, in other words he substituted the third word for the second. This communication was not incorporated in any of the collections, and Huguccio's reference to it proves his outstanding knowledge of papal decrees. The same mistake was made by the scribe of the *Glossa Palatina*, on *Dist.* lxiii, Ego Ludovicus, fol. 26, of D 8, s.v. "tibi".

[1] See Cynus, *Com. in Codicem*, VII.xxvii.3. Cf. also Baldus in his *Consilia*, cons. 326, pars i, No. 1: "Corona nihil addit imperatori nisi coruscationem." Nevertheless, formalism in the medieval period seems to have been very marked. Before the receiving of the "biretta" no licence to teach was considered to have been given. Jacobus Butrigarius held this view and said "quod scholaris ante receptum birettum non potest actus magistrales exercere." Baldus witnessed one case in which a certain Johannes de Parigua refused to submit to the ceremony, "et ideo actus magistrales exercere non voluit et sic nec magistrare scolares", Baldus, on *Cod. Just.* VII.xxxvii.3, No. 6.

[2] Huguccio, *Summa*, *Dist.* xxiii, c. 1, s.v. "sicut jam": "Nota, quod non dicitur imperator, antequam accipiatur coronam a papa, sed dico, quod non ante dicitur imperator; est enim ante imperator, non quoad unctionem vel confirmationem, sed quoad impletionem et jurisdictionem." He corroborated this view by referring to ecclesiastical elections which gave the bishop-elect "ante confirmationem jus disponendi et administrandi res ecclesiasticas", ibid., s.v. "facultates", fol. 132 of P 72. Alanus, from his point of view (see text), denied that the bishop-elect had any administrative powers before coronation, see Alanus in the gloss in *Compilatio Secunda*, De electionibus, c. transmissam, s.v. "de talibus", fol. 63 verso of D 4.

secular and sacerdotal actions: according to Christ, temporal and spiritual functions were to be separated, "in order to promote humility and to prevent pride", for if either pope or emperor should be supreme in both spheres, he might easily become intoxicated with his own power. "Si enim imperator vel pontifex omnia haberet officia, de facili superbiret."[1] Huguccio then gave his own opinion. He rejected the doctrine that the emperor received his powers from the pope and declared that he received them from the princes who had elected him. The empire preceded the papacy in time.

> Ego autem dico, quod imperator potestatem gladii et dignitatem imperialem habet non ab apostolico, sed a principibus, et papa per electionem ... ante enim fuit imperator quam papa, ante imperium quam papatus.[2]

This view of Huguccio did not gain much favour with the later generations of canonists, although his idea was wholeheartedly approved at the time by an Englishman and a Spaniard and appeared also in the *Summa Cantabrigiensis*. Whilst the two former expressly referred to Huguccio, the latter did not mention him by name.

In his *Apparatus* on the *Compilatio Prima* the Englishman, Richard de Lacy (Richardus Anglicus) put forward a thesis which later became one of the most cherished arguments in the anti-papal camp, the thesis namely, that the powers of pope and emperor were derived from God directly. Huguccio's argu-

---

[1] The whole passage runs: "A Christo distincta sunt jura et officia imperatoris et pontificis, et alia sunt attributa imperatori, scil. temporalia, et alia, scil. spiritualia concessa sunt pontifici. Et haec facta sunt causa humilitatis, servandae et superbiae vitanda. Si enim imperator. . . ." *Dist.* xcvi, c. 6, fol. 171 of LC 2.

[2] ibid., fol. 171 verso. In view of this political point of view of Huguccio one might be inclined to see only a moderate influence of the teacher on the pupil Innocent III. But apart from his political theory Huguccio was a thorough-going and rather extreme curialist who provided Innocent III with the juristic equipment which was so skilfully handled by his disciple. It is in furnishing the thought pattern, and not in the actual political arguments and in his own interpretations that Huguccio's influence on Innocent III lies. It was not so much the contents of Huguccio's work as his method which influenced Innocent. Cf. also Schulte, *Quellen*, vol. i, p. 169: "In Huguccio hat die Methode, nach rein juristischer Casuistik Alles, auch die Moral, zu konstruieren, ohne jede Rücksicht auf die Religion, ihren Höhepunkt erreicht: die Kurie bedurfte fortan der Staatsgesetze nicht mehr."

ment that the empire was, in time, anterior to the papacy, and that the coronation merely involved a change of title, was dutifully quoted. Let us quote Richard's passage.[1]

> Solutio: Magister Huguccio dicit, et bene, quod a solo Deo habet potestatem in temporalibus, et papa in spiritualibus et sic divisa est jurisdictio. Prius enim imperator quam coronam accipiat a papa vel gladium ab altari, ut XCIII legimus; nam ante fuit imperium quam apostolatus.[2]

The Spaniard, Laurentius, expressed his approval in very similar terms and said:[3]

> Magister Huguccio dicit, et bene, quod a solo Deo habet potestatem in temporalibus, quamvis coronam accipiat a papa et gladium ab altari, ut XCIII legimus, nam ante fuit imperium quam apostolatus et ante imperator quam apostolicus. lau.

---

[1] Richard's *Apparatus* on *Comp. I.*, Qui filii sint legit., c. causam quae, fol. 64 verso of W 122. Richard very pertinently asked in this context what was the position of the kings in this scheme, since there were only two swords, the one belonging to the pope, the other to the emperor: "Sed, quid ad regem, cum tantum duo gladii ... ?" He answered that the kings received their power from the emperor to whom they were subjected in his temporal jurisdiction, just as they were under the pope in spiritual matters; in order to corroborate this statement, Richard referred to Luke ii.1: "exivit edictum a caesare". "Sicut spirituali gladio omnes sunt subditi papae, ita in saeculari omnes imperatori, ut VII, q. I, in apibus." A thoughtless scribe changed the evangelist's name into "Lucanus".

[2] The gloss on the same passage in the *Apparatus* on *Comp. I* in LB 105, fol. 196 is in literal agreement with the one quoted in the text (W 122), except that the scribe wrote here: "magister hugo." But in LB 105 the problem connected with territorial kings precedes this passage. (And significantly the author of this gloss in LB 105 reaches a conclusion contrary to that of Richard in W 122: "Sed contra patet." Above all, the empire was founded by force, and emperors have therefore no legitimate title to a universal empire. The "universitas civitatis" was in a far better position to confer royal powers than a universal emperor: "Nam universitas civitatis multo magis regiam jurisdictionem et imperium conferre potest." Lastly, there was no difference between royal and imperial power. because "rex eadem auctoritate, eadem consecratione et eodem crismate inungitur, non ergo potestatis diversitas". The conclusion this glossator reached was: "Animadversionem plenam habent reges." This is certainly an early expression of the later "Rex-Imperator" idea. On Richard see also Appendix H.

[3] Laurentius Hispanus in *Comp. I.*, Qui fil. s. leg., c. causam quae (c. 7), fol. 47 of D 4. The siglum of the gloss is: "lau."

To these writers must be added[1] the French inspired *Summa Cantabrigiensis*. Its author declared that the pope did not confer any powers upon the emperor, for it was from the army that the latter received his imperial powers. The author also rejected what was later the papalist doctrine, and said:[2] "Ergo una potestas non pendet ex altera, et ita est argumentum, quod imperator non habet jus gladii a papa, immo ab exercitu, qui fecit imperatorem ... alii dicunt, quod a papa habet jus gladii ... primam opinionem didicimus."[3] Johannes Teutonicus, though somewhat vacillating in his opinions, also maintained the emperor's independence of the pope. The emperor himself, Johannes declared, was instituted by divine authority.[4]

The vigorous pontificate of Innocent III exercised a decisive influence on the shaping of curialist theory. Huguccio and his English and Spanish followers were to sink into oblivion. The

---

[1] Rather inconsistently (see *infra* p. 195 n.3) the *Glossa Palatina* also maintained a point of view which would a few years later have ranked as an anti-papal thesis. For it said that the emperor received his powers immediately after his election, although he had not the title of an emperor: "Ex sola enim electione principum dico eum verum imperatorem, antequam papa confirmatur, arg. hic, licet non ita appelletur," on *Dist*. xciii, c. 24, fol. 35 of D 8, s.v "imperatorem". This gloss is not signed, although a later gloss in the same chapter bears the siglum "fa" (Johannes Faventinus?) The anonymous *Notabilia* in the Worcester Codex F 159 also state: "Nota a solo Deo et non a papa imperatorem postestatem gladii accepisse," fol. 157 verso, on *Dist*. xcvi, c. 11.

[2] See fol. 32 of T 0.5.17 (Kuttner's *Ecce vicit leo, Repert*., p. 59), on *Dist*. xcvi, c. 6; this point of view is repeated in *Dist*. xcvi, c. 10, fol. 32 verso: "Ergo neuter istarum potestatum pendet ex altera."

[3] Although in another place the author of the *Summa Cantabrigiensis* appears to hold the opposite point of view, it is nevertheless safe to assume that the standpoint as given in the text was his real opinion, for he referred to his gloss on *Dist*. xcvi, c. 6. In the gloss on *Dist*. xxii, c. 1 he said: "Ergo dominus papa habet potestatem super clericos et laicos, et ita est argumentum, quod imperator accipit materialem gladium a domino papa, de hoc diceretur diffusius XCVI cum ad verum," s.v. "terreni", fol. 12 verso of LC 137.

[4] See the gloss of Johannes Teutonicus on *Dist*. xcvi, c. 10, s.v. "auctoritas": "Neuter pendet ex reliquo, et ita est argumentum pro imperatore, quia divinutus consecutus est imperium." See also his glosses on *Dist*. x, c. 8: "Respondeo, quod utraque potestas ab eo processit, non quod una persona illa duo officia execeret vel gerere debeat; haec enim duo dona, imperium et sacerdotium, ab eodem principio sunt," with a special reference to the *Authenticum, coll*. I, tit. vi, praef. See furthermore his glosses on *Dist*. lxxxix, c. 7, and C. IX, q. iii, c. 16, as well as on the decretal "venerabilem" in *Comp. III*, fol. 112 verso of D 4: "Nam et habent (scil. teutonici) regimen romanae ecclesiae." In the gloss on tit. De judiciis, c. novit ille. *Comp. III*, fol. 131, s.v. "ex homine" he said: "Imperium a solo Deo est."

lead in canonistic political thought was henceforth to be taken by an Englishman who may well be considered the scientific framer of the extreme papalist point of view, which precisely a century later found such pronounced expression in Boniface's *Unam sanctam*. The theory of Alanus constituted the turning-point in the history of canonistic doctrine relating to Church and State. It is interesting to observe that the decretal which Alanus glossed and in which he set forth his views, did not at all lend itself to the exposition of political ideas, for that decretal of Alexander III dealt with a different point which had arisen in the matter of appeals.[1] But it would be wrong to suggest that Alanus created his theory *ex nihilo*, since some of his predecessors, notably Rufinus,[2] had put forward arguments and views which were not dissimilar to those of the Englishman, who himself might have drawn on some of the *dicta* of his compatriot Thomas Becket[3] and on those of the most accomplished gentleman of the day, John of Salisbury. But canonistic political doctrine hardly ever referred to any of them, in fact, I have not come across one reference to Rufinus or Thomas or John, and the "new" theory was commonly associated with the name of Alanus. This Alexandrian decretal was embodied in one of the pre-Gregorian collections, the *Compilatio Prima*. Apart from his own compilation of decretals, Alanus's chief fame rested on his having composed the *Apparatus* on this compilation; he wrote this work between 1201 and 1210.[4]

[1] *Comp. I*, De Appellationibus, c. si duobus (c. 7), which is in the *Gregoriana* II.xxviii.7. The contention of Kuttner, *Repertorium*, pp. 326, 337, that the MS. Bibl. Nat. Lat. 3932, contains the *Apparatus* of Alanus cannot be confirmed. The glosses do not bear the usual siglum of Alanus, nor does this *Apparatus* contain the important gloss on the chapter si duobus, see fol. 21 verso. That Alanus did in fact write the passage on this chapter is borne out by Tancred who expressly referred to it, see *infra* p. 150 n.6. Alanus is here quoted from MS Cod. Aug. XL, fol. 13 verso, Badische Landes Bibliothek, Karlsruhe; the passage is also transcribed by Schulte in *SB d. kais. Akad. d. Wiss.*, vol. lxvi, pp. 89-90.

[2] See *Summa Rufini*, on *Dist.* xxii, c. 1, p. 41 ed. cit.

[3] See Thomas's axiomatic expressions in *Materials for the History of Archbishop Thomas Becket*, vol. v, pp. 518-19: "Sciat ... et intelligat ... dominus meus, quia qui dominatur in regno hominum, sed et angelorum, duas sub se potestates ordinavit, principes et sacerdotes; unam terrenam, alteram spiritualem; unam ministrantem, alteram praeminentem; unam, cui potentiam concessit, alteram, cui reverentiam exhiberi voluit; qui vero his vel illis de suo jure subtrahit, Dei ordinationem resistit ... terrenis enim potestatibus non sunt commissae claves regni coelorum, sed sacerdotis." Cf. also ibid., pp. 356, 357, 358.

[4] For the date of its composition, see Kuttner, *Repertorium*, p. 325, note 1.

And just as this undeservedly neglected canonist anticipated by a century the ideas of *Unam sanctam*, in the same way the traditional canonistic theory of the superiority of the pope over the emperor can be traced to this English canonist rather than to Hostiensis or Innocent IV. These very eminent canonists elaborated and fortified the Englishman's doctrine by strengthening its foundations, but they did not themselves create the idea.

After marshalling all those arguments and passages from which the independence of imperial power could be deduced, Alanus continued the exposition of his theory by referring to those scholars who declared that the emperor received his powers from the princes who had elected him. Obviously, Alanus had Huguccio in mind. "Dicunt quidam, quod potestatem et gladium habet a principibus, quorum est imperatorem eligere ex jure consuetudinario." Alanus would have none of this. There were not to be two heads, the one in the spiritual, the other in the temporal field. He flatly rejected the dualistic principle. Neither in the spiritual nor in the temporal sphere was the pope subject to the emperor: "Verum tamen papa imperatori non subest quoad spiritualia nec quoad temporalia." For the Church and everything belonging to it were exempted from the jurisdictional powers of the secular authority. "Ecclesia enim et omnes res eius a laica potestate sunt exemptae." It was truer to say, Alanus argued, that the emperor obtained his sword from the pope. "Verius est, quod gladium habeat a papa," for there was only one body of Christians, and therefore that body should have one head only: "ergo unum solum caput habere debet."

This one head of the medieval commonwealth could be none other but the pope, for Christ Himself wielded spiritual and temporal power. He possessed both swords.[1] St. Peter, too, as

[1] Alanus referred to *Dist*. xcvi, c. 6, and C. I, q. iii, c. 9: the former passage contains nothing to corroborate Alanus's statement, but the latter does, although in a somewhat different sense. Alexander II here reproached the bishop and the people of Lucca for their venality in ecclesiastical appointments; in the words of the pope, they gave the ecclesiastical benefice to him "qui profano pecuniae munere illud emere studuisset". Alexander II stigmatized this procedure as "detestabile" and drew the bishop's attention to the example of Christ who had thrown the money lenders out of the temple (that is, the "sancta ecclesia"), an incident which the bishop should take to heart. This somewhat slender basis, upon which Alanus's theory rested, was to prove quite fertile in the hands of his adherents, see text.

the vicar of Christ, was in the possession of both of them.¹
Moreover, Moses also wielded both swords, and the pope was
merely the successor of Moses: "Item Moyses utrumque
gladium habuit, cuius sucessor est papa in novo testamento."
Our expectation that this statement would not go unchallenged
is confirmed by the Hungarian canonist, Paulus Hungarus, who
himself referred to the legists as denying the priesthood of
Moses.² The Spaniard, Vincentius, also reminded his readers
that a civilian gloss "quae in multis libris habetur" had denied
the priesthood of Moses—and of David.³

Begging the question in the typically medieval manner,
Alanus asked how Pope Zacharias could depose King Childeric
(A.D. 751), if the king had not been under the *temporal* jurisdiction of the pope,⁴ and our canonist quickly reached the conclusion that the king derived his power from the pope: "Propter
hoc dicatur, quod gladium temporalem habet a papa." Without
the pope there could be no legitimate imperial authority. The
pope, if he wished, could use both swords: "Utroque gladio uti
potest."

The foundation stone for the ensuing canonistic political
edifice was thereby laid. What was needed was the usual
biblical and historical basis for this view and the elimination
and explanation of those references which might endanger the
structure of this edifice. The suggestive character of Alanus's

---

This reference to the "temporal" activity of Christ was not a novel idea of
Alanus, since Huguccio, and others, had referred to it before him: but they
failed to draw any conclusions from it. Christ Himself, said Huguccio, had
distinguished between the two jurisdictions: "Quaedam fecit ut rex ... vendentes
et ementes de templo ejecit, quaedam fecit ut sacerdos, cum corpus suum in
coena consecravit et discipulis dedit ... in cruce oravit, quae omnia officia sunt
sacerdotis," on *Dist.* xcvi, c. 6, fol. 171 of LC 2.

¹ "Sed Petrum vicarium suum in terris in solidum constituit, ergo utrumque
gladium ei reliquit," Luke xxii. 38, see Tancred in his *Apparatus* on *Comp. III*,
De judiciis, c. novit, in the long marginal gloss, fol. 131 of D 4.

² Paulus in his *Notabilia* on *Comp. III*, De Majoritate, c. solitae, fol. 20 verso
of W 159.

³ Vincentius on *Comp. III*, ibid., s.v. "sacerdote", fol. 126 verso of D 4:
"Hinc collige quandam magnam glossam messe falcam quae in multis libris
habetur, C. De sum. trin., juris claras, quae negat Moyses et David sacerdotes
fuisse." The passage referred to is *Cod. Just.*, I.i.8.

⁴ Si quoad temporalia imperator sub papa non fuisset, ergo de eis sub papa
respondere non teneretur, at invenitur princeps a papa depositus ut XV q. VI
alius." This is wrongly transcribed by Schulte.

pregnant theory can easily be seen, if we look at an *Apparatus* which was composed (between 1210 and 1215) very shortly after Alanus had written his own. The hitherto undetected author or authors of this *Apparatus*[1] which was almost certainly a creation of the Bolognese school,[2] argued quite in the manner of Alanus, that by instituting St. Peter as His vicar, Christ had automatically instituted all the successors of St. Peter. "Therefore," the *Apparatus* continued, "Innocent to-day possesses also the temporal sword."[3] And Tancred, the faithful follower of Alanus, argued, in a typical *petitio principii* that, because the pope had plenitude of power, he was therefore God's vicegerent on earth. "Item in hoc gerit vicem Dei, quia plenitudinem potestatis habet."[4]

In fact, Tancred, the Bolognese archdeacon, was the first to refer to the English canonist explicitly. He approved Alanus's theory warmly in the gloss on the same decretal in which the Spaniard, Laurentius, had so warmly supported the political scheme of Huguccio.[5] Tancred added virtually nothing to the point of view of Alanus, except perhaps that the pope was the judge of the emperor and that he confirmed or rejected the result of an imperial election. The misgivings which Tancred might have felt about Justinian's *Novella* were set at rest by his declaration that a canon had greater weight than an imperial law. "Sed canon praejudicat legi."[6]

---

[1] S. Kuttner, *Repertorium*, pp. 67-75 who discovered this *Apparatus* "*Jus Naturale*". But now in *Traditio*, vol. i, p. 289 (and note 52) Kuttner maintains that this work was written by Alanus himself, but the proof that he adduces for this statement is somewhat tenuous. There does not seem to be sufficient reason to contradict his earlier statement in op. cit., p. 67, that this *Apparatus* "stammt aus der Bologneser Schule des beginnenden 13. Jahrhunderts, genauer aus den Jahren zwischen dem Erscheinen der Compilationes III, II und dem IV. Laterankonzil, also 1210-1215." In art. cit. he says: Alanus "must have composed it somewhat before 1210 and revised it shortly after that date": the mere fact that some of the newly referred to MSS. do not all (e.g. the Vatican and Klosterneuburg MSS.) cite the *Comp. III* (1210) can surely not be accepted as proof that Alanus himself "must have composed" the *Apparatus*.

[2] See preceding note.

[3] *Apparatus* "*Jus Naturale*" on *Dist.* xcvi, c. 6: ". . . si Petrum in terris vicarium constituit, ergo et omnes Petri successores. Ergo et hodie Innocentius habet de jure gladium materiale," quoted by Kuttner, op. cit., p. 68.

[4] Tancred in his *Apparatus* on *Comp. III*, de translat. episc., c. quanto personae, (c. 3), fol. 103 verso of D 4.

[5] See *supra* p. 145.

[6] *Apparatus* of Tancred on *Comp. I*, tit. Qui fil. sint legit., c. causam quae

The evidence necessary to strengthen the view of Alanus was amply supplied, and it is in this connexion that the *glossa ordinaria*, and the writings of Innocent IV, Hostiensis and Goffredus de Trano and the bulk of the eminent canonists, assume their true importance. The reference of Alanus to Christ's possession of both swords was bound to prove fruitful, for here was the biblical foundation for the idea that the pope was at once temporal and spiritual overlord. Most of the canonistic political theory was henceforth focused on the proof of a full papal plenitude of power. Biblical events and historical facts were invoked, interpreted and handed down to make the papalist structure immune from any anti-papalist attack. The strongest weapon in the hands of the anti-papalist forces was of course the attractive and historically plausible contention—set forth, as we have seen, also by the followers of Huguccio—that there was a temporal power long before there was any thought of a spiritual, let alone of a Christian power. Emperors, the argument ran, had existed long before the birth of Christ. How, then, could a pope or a canonist say with any shade of historical justification that the pope possessed plenitude of power in the temporal field? This argument, so formidable in its power to sway the waverers in the political camp, had to be countermanded. The views of the earlier canonists lent additional force to this anti-papalist tenet. But the reference of Alanus to Christ and Moses opened up the investigation into the Bible, and the canonists were not slow to discover that, according to their interpretation, the Old Testament especially contained the *desiderata*. The canonistic argument to prove the biblical basis of the pope's plenitude of power proceeded on the following lines.

God as the creator of the universe personally ruled heaven

(c. 7), fol. 47 of D 4: "Ego dico cum alano, sicut ipse notavit supra de app., si duob., quod imperator habet gladium a papa ... et solum petrum vicarium suum in terra constituit, ergo utrumque gladium relinquit. Item Moyses utrumque gladium habuit, cuius successor est apostolicus; praeterea judex eius est dominus papa, quia electionem confirmat et cassat, ut textus III de elect., per venerab., et etiam confirmatum deponit, ut XVI q. VI alius, et hoc totum invenitur expresse in quadam extravaganti Inno. III in genesi; est argumentum contra in authentica quomodo oporteat episcopos, sed canon paejudicat legi."

The decretal of Innocent III referred to by Tancred is contained in the *Registrum de Negotio Romani Imperii*, cap. xviii, in Migne, *Patr. lat.*, vol. ccxvi, colls. 1012-13.

and earth, the spiritual and the temporal, down to the time of Noah. Noah was the first man instituted as a "rector populi" who had rule over the temporalities, and he was also a priest. Although it was not explicitly stated that he was actually a priest, he nevertheless performed the functions of priesthood. He was the first who combined priesthood and kingship in one person. This state of affairs, according to the reading of the canonists, was continued under the patriarchs, the judges and kings, and lasted until the time of Christ. Christ was "the natural master and our king". That He also wielded temporal power could be conclusively gathered from the scene in which the money lenders in the temple were thrown out. This, the canonists maintained, was surely an action that belonged to the temporal sphere.[1] Because, as the glossator of the Constitutions of the First Council of Lyons, the younger Bernardus Compostellanus, argued, Christ had used both swords, the Church too was in a position to wield both of them: "Videtur, quod ecclesia utroque gladio uti possit, nam dominus utroque gladio usus est."[2] St. Peter, too, was said to have possessed the temporal sword, for we read in St. John's gospel that St. Peter cut off the ear of Malchus, again undoubtedly an action falling into the temporal domain. Moreover, the Acts reported that St. Peter condemned Ananias and his wife, Sapphira, on the charge of theft.[3] Now if St. Peter had this power over temporalities,[4] why should the pope not have it? There was no doubt for the canonists that the pope's powers rested upon those conferred to St. Peter by Christ Himself. The vicariate of the pope necessarily included all those powers which Christ had bestowed on St. Peter in the famous words, "Thou art Peter and upon this rock I will build my church,"[5] and "I will give

---

[1] Bartholomaeus Brixiensis in his gloss on *Dist.* x, c. 8.

[2] Gloss on the decree "Dilecto filio" (the later *Sextus*, V.xi.6), s.v. "vi", fol. 287 of the Lincoln Codex 173. For this *Apparatus* on the Constitutions of the First Council of Lyons (1245) and for the one of the Second Council of Lyons (1274) see Appendix.

[3] Durandus, *De Jurisdictione Ecclesiastica*, Qu. III.

[4] Cf. the Archdeacon on *Dist.* x, c. 8, No. 4, fol. 12 verso: "Uterque gladius Petro erat concessus;" also Durandus, op. cit., "Potestas data Petro et ecclesiae extendebat se ad delicta civilia et ad poenas civiles, et non solum ad spiritualia."

[5] Matt. xvi.18. Cf. in this context Gregory VII's second sentence of excommunication against Henry IV, see E. N. Henderson, *Select Documents of the Middle Ages*, p. 391.

POPE AND EMPEROR

unto thee the keys of the kingdom of heaven, and whatever thou shalt bind on earth, shall be bound in heaven; and whatever thou shalt loose on earth, shall be loosed in heaven."[1] Lastly, Christ's expression after His resurrection "All power is given unto me in heaven and in earth" was one more proof for the canonists of the temporal plenitude of power asserted by Christ Himself.[2] These biblical passages, then, were the very basis of the canonistic doctrine relating to papal plenitude of power in the spiritual as well as in the temporal sphere.[3] The pope, we must remember in this context, was not considered a vicar of St. Peter who was only a vicar himself, and there was no such a thing as a vicariate of a vicariate; but the pope was a true vice-gerent of God on earth. The appellation of the pope as the vicar of St. Peter was, as Johannes Andreae termed it, an "impropria locutio".[4] He was the vicar of Him to whom belongs "the world and they that dwell therein".[5] Many a canonist referred to the pope as "admirabilis" and, as they liked to quote contemporary English poetry, styled him "stupor mundi" after the English poet. Although no explicit reference was made to Geoffrey de Vinsauf, it is fairly certain that the canonists had in mind his lengthy laudatory poem addressed to Innocent III. The poem begins with the words: "Papa est stupor mundi."[6]

---

[1] Matt. ibid., 19: this was embodied in the *Decretum*, C. XXIV, q. i, c. 6, and served as a basis for the statement that the pope was the vicar of God, see Tancred, *supra*, ch. III, pp. 50-51. The reference to Matt. xviii.17, was not frequently made, see, for instance, Durandus, *De Jurisdictione Eccl.*, Qu. II.

[2] Matt. xviii.18.

[3] On all this see Innocent IV in his *Com.* on II.ii.10, fol. 197 verso, Nos. 3-4.

[4] Gloss on *Clem.* II.vii, cap. un.: "Si alicubi invenitur, quod est Petri vicarius, illa est impropria locutio." It should be borne in mind that a papal legate, too, was invested with the plenitude of power. Obviously referring to the appointment of Hubert Walter as the papal legate in England, the author of the *Quaestiones Londinenses* stated: "Cancellarius legatus a domino papa per totam Angliam constitutus ... habebat plenitudinem potestatis et illius (scil. papae) auctoritate fungit," BM Royal 9 E VII, fol. 197 verso.

[5] See the gloss of Johannes Andreae on *Clem.* Proemium, s.v. "papa", and on *Clem.* I.ix.1 and II.i.1: "Papa est admirabilis quia vices Dei gerit in terris: est enim papa vicarus illius, cuius est terra et plenitudo orbis terrarum."

[6] The poem has 36 folio columns, MS. York Minster, xvi.Q.14. Inc.: fol. 106: "Incipit liber magistri Gaufridi anglici de artificio loquendo, scriptus ad papam Innocentium tertium". The "ap" of "papa" in the first line is erased. The poem ends fol. 111 verso where one line says: "Nec deus es nec homo, quasi neuter es inter utrumque"; another line: "... pater ergo vicarie Christi me totum committo tibi". This poem is followed fol. 112 by a tract of Gaufridus Arthurus.

The vicariate of the pope was based, as we have seen, on the so-called commission of Christ to St. Peter. Being the successor of St. Peter and the vicar of Christ, the pope became the vicegerent of God on earth. His powers contained in the vicariate were not those of man only.[1] The pope ruled and reigned as he pleased: "Unde omnia regit et disponit et judicat, prout sibi placet." He was truly the "vicarius Dei". Whoever could claim papal authority for his actions, could claim divine sanction.[2] The juristic construction chosen for this vicariate was that of Pope Nicholas II,[3] namely, that Christ had entrusted to St. Peter, the bearer of the keys, the laws of the earthly and celestial kingdom. "Terreni et coelestis imperii jura commisit." In this commission of Christ to St. Peter lay the papal plenitude of power. By virtue of this commission the pope was said to possess both swords "ex commissione Dei".[4] With the wording of the Roman law in mind the canonists termed the pope a "celestial emperor", and they advanced him to the unsurpassable height of an individual who has "all the laws within his bosom"—"omnia jura in suo pectore sunt".[5]

The thesis that the pope was a celestial emperor, was not of course a mere hyperbole on the part of the canonists. The emperor as depicted by Roman law was not bound by the law:

On Geoffrey himself see A. Gröber, *Grundriss der romanischen Philologie*, vol ii, p 389, and *Cambridge History of English Literature*, vol. i. p. 193. Geoffrey was also quoted by fourteenth century chroniclers, so, for example, by the Swiss chronicler, Johann von Winterthur, see *Mon. Germ. Hist., Scriptores*, n.s. vol. iii, "Die Chronik des Johann von Winterthur", ed. F. Baethgen, p. 157.

[1] See *Spec.*, lib. I, part i, De Legato, § nunc, No. 51: "Ipse est sucessor Petri et vicarius Jesu Christi vicem non puri hominis, sed veri Dei gerens in terris." Cf. also Tancred in *Comp. I*, De translat. episc., c. quantopere, fol. 103 verso s.v. "vicem": "Gerit vicem Dei, qui sedet in loco Jhesu Christi, qui est verus Deus et verus homo, ut instituit Innocentius III 'firmiter credimus'."

[2] See the passage transcribed *supra* ch. III, pp. 50-51.

[3] *Dist.* xxii, c. 1.

[4] "Ipse habet utrumque gladium, scil. temporalem et spiritualem, ex commissione Dei," *Spec.*, loc. cit., Nos. 50 and 52.

[5] See, e.g. Goffredus de Trano, *Summa*, De Rescriptis, No. 38, fol. 5, verso and the gloss of Johannes Andreae on *Sextus*, I.vii.1. Dealing with the question of why the pope's decrees were binding upon all, Huguccio said that in deciding a case and in laying down generally applicable rules not only knowledge was necessary, but also the power to carry out effective action: "Nam in definiendo et decidendo causas non solum scientia, sed etiam potestas est necessaria," *Summa* on *Dist.* xx, ante cap. 1, s.v. "exequantur", fol. 129 of P 72. Hence, councils, as such, which lacked the power, could not issue binding decrees.

he stood above it and was responsible to nobody—"legibus solutus est". If this applied to a mere emperor, how much more was it applicable to his celestial colleague. He too must be free from the vexatious observance of the law. There were to be no restrictions on the scope or contents of his actions. And yet, there was a number of prohibitive enactments especially addressed to the popes themselves, of which a good example was the canonical prohibition on selling ecclesiastical goods.[1] Was there not a contradiction? What sense, one might ask, was to be attributed to an enactment specifically restricting the pope's sphere of action, if, on the other hand, the pope was declared to be free from observing the law?[2] The canonists somehow perceived this incongruity, but the explanation they offered was anything but convincing. Huguccio, who seems to have been the first to deal with this thorny problem at great length and whose conclusion gained wide, if not universal acceptance, said that the passage referred to "appears to impose a law on the pope and therefore it seems that the pope can be judged for its violation".[3] But this, according to Huguccio, was not the correct interpretation. "I say," he continued, "that the pope does not impose a law on another pope, but on others," for "par enim parem ligare non potest".[4] Moreover, the prohibition on selling goods was not a genuine prohibition, because that enactment merely spoke of a "non licere", and

[1] C. XII, q. ii, c. 20.
[2] "Prima sedes a nemine judicatur." The formulation of this sentence, quoted over and over again, must be traced to a forger, see E. Caspar, *Geschichte des Papsttums*, vol. ii, pp. 107 ff. It may be that the idea itself was derived from Matt. xix. 28 although some writers deduced it from I Cor. ii.15; so, for example, Guido Vernanus in his commentary on *Unam sanctam*, transcribed by Mgr. Grabmann as an appendix to his "Studien über den Einfluss der aristotelischen Philosophie" in *SB d. bayr. Akad. d. Wiss.*, phil. hist. Abt. 1934, p. 155. Cf. also Alexander III's reply in *Liber Pontificalis*, ed. Duchèsne, vol. ii p. 401: "Ipsa (ecclesia) vero nullius judicio subjaceret", and W. Holtzmann, "Zur Geschichte Friedrich Barbarossas" in *Neues Archiv*, vol. xlviii (1930), pp. 384-413, at pp. 391-92.
[3] Huguccio in his *Summa*, *Dist*. xl, c. 6, s.v. "vapulaturus", fol. 147 verso of P 72: "Ibi enim videtur papa imponere legem papae in alienationem rerum ecclesiasticarum, et sic videtur papa posse judicari ab alio."
[4] "Sed dico, quod ibi papa non imponit legem papae, sed aliis, par enim parem ligare non potest." Fourteenth-century doctrine maintained that the pope could "indicate" the policy to his successors. See, for instance, Johannes Andreae in his gloss on *Sextus*, I.iii.15, s.v. "indicamus": "Indicare potuit, sed non legem imponere, quia par in parem non habet imperium." This "par-in-parem" was usually deduced from *Decretales*, I.vi.20.

hence breaking this law was not a crime, but only sin. "Tamen sit peccatum."

Similar problems confronted the canonists in other spheres of papal legislation. Canon law explicitly defined heresy as the only crime with which a pope could be charged.[1] Now the question was, whether the pope could simply issue a decree in which he annulled that passage, so that even the possibility of this charge was eliminated. "De facto," Huguccio said, the pope could do so, but not "de jure". The juristic explanation which Huguccio offered, was scarcely satisfactory: the pope was not entitled by law to promulgate a decree of this kind, "because he would thereby teach heresy"—"quia sic doceret haeresim". Moreover, if the pope practised heresy publicly and could not be brought to book for his heresy, "tota periclitetur ecclesia et confunderetur generalis status ecclesiae".[2] No doubt great canonist as he was, Huguccio felt uneasy when writing down this passage, for all he could say in conclusion was "I do not believe that a pope would act to the detriment of the Church," a statement that must have violated his juristic conscience. But here again, the same problem as before arose, that is, how could a pope bind his successors, for by making popes answerable for heresy, the law itself curtailed the field of papal activity? The explanation given is perhaps still less convincing than the previous one. This law (*Dist.* xl, c. 6) was in the nature of a privilege, Huguccio said, and contained no general provision for charging a pope with heresy. Generally speaking, the pope was not responsible for any crime committed, but if he were charged with heresy, he could renounce this privilege and voluntarily submit to the judgment of lesser mortals. Hence, according to canonistic doctrine,[3] that law was not a law in the ordinary sense, but one that merely expressed the

---

[1] *Dist.* xl, c. 6.

[2] "Item quaero, an papa possit istum casum excludere, ut nec in haeresi vel notorio crimine possit accusari? Respondeo, de facto sic, sed non de jure, quia sic doceret haeresim. Praeterea, si papa esset haereticus publicus, tota...."

[3] The explanation of the *Glossa Palatina* in *Dist.* xl, c. 6, was apparently rejected by the canonists: "Quaero, quomodo potuit hanc legem condere papa successoribus, ut accusaretur de haeresi: sed non constituit, immo declaravit," fol. 15 of D 8. This gloss may be from the pen of Bernardus Compostellanus. We may observe here that the opinion of the *Glossa Palatina* that the heretical pope should be tried by one of the cardinals, also remained an isolated statement. "Credo papam judicem habere certum cardinalem." A deposition of the pope by

privileged position of the pope in unmistakable terms. This interpretation by Huguccio certainly did credit to his juristic acumen, however little it might tally with the actual words of the passage which runs: the pope "a nemine est judicandus, nisi deprehendatur a fide devius".[1]

In close connexion with the conception of the pope's celestial emperorship stood the question of his power to declare any law, civil and canon, null and void. The more moderate section owned that the pope could not exercise his powers in declaring a civil law null and void; he could do this only with regard to canon law. The extreme party, however, claimed this right. Johannes Andreae proposed a compromise solution. He conceded to the pope the right of legislative interference with purely secular laws, if their observance would amount to an endangering of the soul; in default of this criterion no such right was to be given to the pope. In fact, this theory of Johannes Andreae was but an application of the principle that the pope had jurisdictional powers "ratione peccati".[2] Hence,

---

the college of cardinals was clearly stated by Huguccio, *Summa*, on *Dist*. lxiii c. 22, fol. 121 verso of LC 2: "Nam et cardinales possunt deponere papam pro haeresi, non tamen ipsi sunt majores quam papa."

[1] Naturally, the civilians had to deal with an identical problem. Although all of them declared the emperor to be above the law, they nevertheless attempted to prescribe some obedience on the part of the emperor to the law: "de necessitate" he was free, but "de honestate" he should observe his own laws, see *The Medieval Idea of Law*, pp. 93-94, Cynus, *Com. ad Codicem*, I.xiv,4, No. 2, Bartolus, ibid. No. 1: "Ipse enim submittit se legibus de voluntate, non de necessitate." Baldus, ibid., No. 1: Observance of the law by the emperor was a "debitum honestatis"; Salicetus, ibid., No. 1: the emperor's observance of the law "dignitatem suam non minuit, sed perpetuat et auget."

Since, according to legistic theory, a treaty made by the emperor with another state was a law, the question arose as to whether he himself and his successors were bound by this treaty. The question was answered in the affirmative and, if we can rely on Cynus's report, loc. cit., No. 7, the first to that reply was Guido de Suzaria. It is true, the legists pointed out—like the canonists—that "par in parem imperium non habet", but they declared that the emperor's successors should observe a treaty or a law of this kind, because, firstly, a treaty implied faithfulness on both sides, secondly, natural law enjoined observance of pacts and keeping faith even with enemies, and thirdly, "honesty" bound the prince to keep his own laws. See Cynus, No. 7, and Bartolus, No. 5, Baldus, No. 8. The civilians, despite their very noticeable tendency to exalt the emperor's position, nevertheless gently attempted to subject him to laws and treaties entered into by his predecessors.

[2] See the gloss of Johannes Andreae on *Sextus*, V De regulis juris, reg. 2, s.v.

judgment as to whether a particular civil law would lead to an endangering of the soul was again left to the pope, and in a somewhat circuitous way the pope was made the undisputed master of purely mundane legislative acts. After all, as Innocent IV had declared, the pope was the "judex ordinarius" of all and everyone.[1] He could be appealed to without taking the somewhat troublesome and laborious course of obtaining judgment from an inferior court of appeal.[2] Even so, the previously mentioned condemnation of the *Mirror of the Saxons* did not adduce a "ratio peccati" as a reason for the pope's interference.

Another sequel of the pope's celestial emperorship was the thesis that treaties concluded between secular rulers were as much subjected to the pope's authority as a mere law was which was promulgated by one of them. Following canonistic doctrine, Urban VI annulled all treaties concluded between Wenzel and Charles IV on the one hand, and the "schismatics" on the other hand. To quote the pope's words, "all confederations, alliances, leagues, and conventions" with whomsoever in the schismatic camp they had been made, were "ipso jure" null and void, even if the parties had taken an oath to observe the treaties. Moreover, the Urbanists, that is to say, those who held to the Roman pope and opposed his Avignonese rival, Clement VII, were forbidden to observe any treaty entered into between them and a secular prince who adhered to Clement's conception of the papacy.[3] This decree of Urban VI was merely a specific application of the principle so clearly enunciated by John XXII that treaties concluded between a pretender to the imperial

---

"possessor": "Quidam abhorrent dicentes papam non posse tollere leges nisi quoad suum forum. Alii vero dicunt papam indistincte quoad utrumque forum posse leges tollere . . . in his autem tenens medium credo, quod papa, ubi non habet talem jurisdictionem, non possit tollere legem quoad forum civile, nisi in his, in quibus vertitur periculum animae . . . in his autem, in quibus periculum animae vertitur, quoad utrumque forum tollit legem. . . ."

[1] Innocent IV in his *Com.* on II.ii.17, fol. 200: "Papa est judex ordinarius omnium," referring to C. IX, q. iii, c. 17. Commenting upon this passage the Archdeacon said that the universal jurisdiction of the pope was based on the grounds of sin; he also referred to Matt. xvi.19.

[2] *Spec.*, lib. I, pars. i, De Legato, § nunc, fol. 50, No. 43: "Appellatur ad eum omnibus mediis omissis."

[3] See *Bullarium Romanum*, tom. iv, pp. 584-85.

throne and another secular power, even if sworn to, were null and void.¹

Now the conception of a Church Militant and a Church Triumphant provided the canonists with one more argument for asserting the sole supremacy of the pope in all temporal and spiritual matters. The Church on earth was to be modelled on that in heaven—the "ecclesia militans" should be the mere reflection of the "ecclesia triumphans".² And just as the Church Triumphant was ruled by one supreme prince only, that is, by Him, to whom every creature owed unquestioned obedience, in the same way the Church Militant was to be ruled by one master whose ordinances every human being was bound to accept.³ Once again, the somewhat amorphous and hardly definable thesis of natural reason was brought into play. Natural reason proved the desirability of superior beings ruling inferior creatures.⁴ Furthermore, in this context the principle of unity was applied specifically to prove the sole supremacy of the pope in all matters. Considering the medieval State, that is, the empire, as an exclusively Christian commonwealth, the canonists rejecting as they did the dualistic principle of government, could not conceive of the State in any other way than as the body of Christ. "Since we form one body in Christ, it would be monstrous, if we had two heads."⁵ According to the conceptions of the medieval canonists, the overlordship of a Christian commonwealth was exclusively in the hands of the

---

¹ ibid., p. 236.
² The conception was derived from Revel. xxi.2-6, and Exod. xxv.40.
³ See Johannes Andreae in his gloss on *Clem*. V.iii.3, s.v. "ecclesiae": "Est enim ecclesia militans exemplata divinitus a triumphante ... cum igitur in ecclesia triumphante sit unus princeps supremus, cuius obedientia tota ipsa ecclesia perfectissime est subjecta, scil. Deus. Necessario sequitur toti militanti unum supremum principem praesidere, scil. papam, cuius praeceptis omnes obedire tenentur."
⁴ Johannes Andreae, loc. cit.,: "Hanc obedientiam probat naturalis ratio, sicut enim operationes rerum naturalium procedunt ex naturalibus potentiis, ita operationes humanae procedunt ex humana voluntate. Oportuit autem in naturalibus, ut superiora moverent inferiora ad suas actiones per excellentiam naturalis virtutis collatae divinutus; sic oportet in rebus humanis, quod superiores moveant inferiores per suam voluntatem ex vi auctoritatis divinutus ordinatae ... istorum autem superiorum moventium unus est supremus, ut praedixi. Omnes igitur sunt subjecti motioni illius, et sunt in illo quasi membra de membro."
⁵ Hostiensis, *Summa*, IV.xvii, col. 1231, No. 9: "Cum enim unum corpus simus in Christo, pro monstro esset, quod duo capita haberemus."

"vicarius Dei". And could a mere emperor or king aspire to that "dignitas", "auctoritas", "potestas" which the biblical arguments and the philosophical speculations on the greater worth of the "anima" bestowed on the pope? Hence, as far as the "majoritas" was to be taken into consideration there was only one Ruler and he claimed to combine the temporal and spiritual mastership of the world in his own hands. "Papa habet utrumque imperium."

This conception of the Church Militant and Triumphant reappeared in the canonistic reflections on the aims of the civil and ecclesiastical powers. Durandus was perhaps clearest in his exposition, and we may briefly outline his ideas, the gist of which was that the secular power pursued aims limited in space and time, whilst the ecclesiastical power's aims were not constrained by limitations of any kind. The prime, if not sole, aim of the civil authority was the creation of such conditions that the citizens were induced to do good and were prevented from doing evil. These objects, Durandus held, belonged to the "present civil and political life", and the civil authority was perfectly capable of realizing these aims. If good civic life were the sole object of man's existence, no other power would be necessary, for "by the prince's prudence and justice" the "vita praesens moralis et politica" of his subjects could easily be directed. From this standpoint, then, no other power was needed. "Ergo praeter potestatem saecularem nulla alia potestas est necessaria ad regendum populum in vita civili et politica."[1]

But in the opinion of Durandus this was not the sole object of man's existence, for "the life of the faithful and of the Christians inclines not only towards the present good, but also and principally towards the good of the future life". The present life was therefore only a preparation for the future.[2] Physical death was not to be feared. What was to be feared, however, was the death of the soul. But the secular power was quite incapable of handling any questions relating to the soul and to the future life: this was the proper dominion of the ecclesiastical authority, and hence the necessity for this second power seemed to be proved. Let us quote the words of Durandus.

[1] Durandus, *De Juris. Eccl.*, Qu. III.
[2] He referred to Matt. vii.21, x.28, and Luke xii.4.

Et quia ad hoc non sufficit potestas saecularis, quae de se nihil novit de donis et praemiis vitae futurae, nec de meritis seu demeritis, quae ad eam perducunt seu abducunt, ideo praeter eam inter Christianos necessaria est alia potestas spiritualis, quam Christus verus Deus et homo dedit Petro, quando ei commisit regimen universalis ecclesiae.

In a Christian State, Durandus concluded, Christians were not subjected to the civil power *qua* Christians, but *qua* citizens.[1] The spiritual power guided the spiritual life of the citizens directly, and their temporal life indirectly, through the medium of the civil power. In other words, the pope possessed both swords.

It is obviously high time for us to consider how the canonists disposed of the two chief obstacles in the Bible, to which the anti-papalists untiringly drew the attention. The one passage concerned the famous "Render unto Caesar...."[2] In general, the canonists, trained, to a certain extent, as they were in theological disputations, declared that these words of Christ were not intended to apply to the division of power or of jurisdiction, but were merely designed to state the obligation of everyone to give his due to God and to the emperor.[3] But even if one adhered to the anti-papalist point of view, the canonists maintained, nothing in that declaration of Christ could disprove their contention that the civil power derived its authority to rule from the ecclesiastical power. For "there is no power but of God,"[4] and the clerics exercised this power directly on behalf of God—"vice Dei". And since this ecclesiastical power embraced all other conceivable powers, because it was superior to them all, they in turn necessarily depended on it for their proper authority. "Ab ipsa (scilicet spirituali potestate) omnis alia jurisdictio depended, quod adversarii invite concederent."[5]

The second obstacle to be disposed of in like manner, presented itself in Christ's *dictum*, "My kindom is not of this

---

[1] "Potestati temporali vel saeculari subsunt Christiani non ut Christiani, quia inter non-Christianos potest esse et est vel fuit illa potestas legitima, sed solum ut cives," Qu. III.

[2] Matt. xxii.21, Mark xii.17, Luke xx.25.

[3] "Loquebatur ergo de redditione debitorum, et non de divisione jurisdictionum, aut personarum, in quas cadunt," Qu. III.

[4] Rom. xiii.1.

[5] Op. cit., Qu. III.

world".[1] This passage, too, was continually held up by the antipapalists as a weapon of defence against the canonists. These, however, were quite prepared to accept the challenge, which they met firstly by pointing out that Christ Himself had said, "All power is given unto me in heaven and in earth,"[2] and that Christ was also spoken of as "the prince of the kings of the earth".[3] So the one utterance was counterbalanced by two others. Then, taking the actual words into consideration, the canonists interpreted them literally. Christ did not say "my kingdom is not *in* this world", but what He said was "my kingdom is not *of* this world", which gave the expression an entirely different meaning. No claim was made by Christ to be a king by reason of election or succession, which would have been the case, if His Kingdom had been *in* this world. Moreover, Christ never denied that He was a king, even when pressed by Pilate himself,[4] but He denied that He had His kingdom given to Him "by men" or "through men".[5] Nor should the educative character of the passage be overlooked. According to the reading of the canonists, by disclaiming all earthly honours Christ desired to give a perfect example of His humility.[6] That Christ, although possessing temporal power, did not exercise it frequently, could be explained by the nature of His mission. "For God sent not His Son into the world, to judge the world, but that the world through him might be saved."[7] But it was indispensable for the government of the Church that it should also have temporal power, and therefore Christ handed to St. Peter both powers. And the popes combined them both.[8]

The resort to historical evidence, in order to prove a case or a claim, has throughout the ages exercised a particularly strong attraction—and never more so than in the Middle Ages. Since historical recording was but in its infancy in medieval times, it was comparatively easy to interpret historical events

---

[1] John xviii.36.
[2] Matt. xxviii.18.
[3] Revel. i.5.
[4] John xviii.37: "Rex sum ego."
[5] "Noluit hoc regnum habere ab hominibus neque per homines."
[6] "Ut nobis, qui puri homines sumus, daret exemplum fugiendi honores mundi."
[7] John iii.17.
[8] Qu. III. On Ptolomy's interpretation see *Det. Comp.*, ed. Krammer, pp. 55ff.

in such a manner as to suit a fixed purpose. It is true that the jurists of the Middle Ages were made responsible for historical errors and that they were charged with want of historical feeling. But we must remember that the utilization of the historical argument was something of a novelty in those days. History is full of excesses, sometimes pardonable, and sometimes unpardonable, all of which were prompted by the onrush of enthusiasm and which cooler reasoning later discarded. And what means had the canonists to check the correctness of centuries old traditions, especially when some of them were enshrined in a body of law that was believed to be a divine ordinance? Historical criticism is of comparatively recent date and was certainly not known in the Middle Ages. Medieval canonistic doctrine was extremely anxious to utilize the recordings of history. In fact as well as in theory, the historical argument was to them of an importance equal to that of the biblical and philosophical argument. This is certainly one more reason why the canonists occupied a far stronger position in political theory than their imperialist brethren. The idea of an historical continuity was fully made use of in papalist disputations. History, the papalists claimed, proved and strengthened the conclusions reached solely on the strength of biblical references and philosophical reasonings.

The first of these historical arguments was the so-called Donation of Constantine, later to be shown an undeniable forgery.[1] It does not seem worth while going into the details of this alleged Donation, because the canonists virtually added nothing new to the well known facts. It was agreed on all sides that the emperor Constantine had handed over to the pope all the provinces possessed by the Roman emperors in the occident including Rome and Italy. By this imperial act the pope, it was maintained, had acquired the temporal plenitude of power, hitherto held by the emperors alone.[2] However, the canonists added some important points to the theory of the Donation.

[1] For a survey of the influence of the Donation on medieval literature, especially in the political field, see G. Laehr, *Die Konstantinische Schenkung in der abendländischen Literatur des Mittelalters bis zur Mitte des 14. Jahrhunderts* Berlin, 1926, and supplementary literature in the review by W. Levison, in *Zeitschrift, kanon. Abt.*, vol. xvi, p. 447.

[2] Cf., for example, Zabarella, in his *Com.* I.vi.34, fol. 149 verso: "Unde in urbe Romana et Italia et provinciis occidentalibus attenta ista donatione papa habet potestatem in temporalibus."

We have just seen that canonistic political doctrine asserted the transfer of all power by Christ to St. Peter and, consequently, to his successors. Christ had handed over the "jura utriusque imperii" to Peter. Now, according to the canonistic teachings, the significant point of the Donation was that Constantine recognized this transfer of power by Christ to Peter, and therefore renounced the power which he had held, in favour of Pope Silvester. In other words, Constantine admitted, explicitly and implicitly, that there was no lawful kingdom or empire, unless it originated in the Church: nobody could legitimately wield any temporal power which was not conferred by the pope. That was the significance of the Donation.[1] And from this it was only a small step to the general thesis of the canonists that no empire was legitimately ruled that could not claim the derivation of its power from the Church. Applied to the case of the medieval empire the idea was expressed in the epitome: "Imperium dependet a papa."

This was certainly an interpretation of history which suited the papalist purpose. But the canonists had to reckon with the very stiff resistance and reasoned objections of the civilians. For the civilian denied the validity, but not the fact, of the Donation. The civilians maintained, firstly, that Constantine had no authority to hand over a whole empire to a pope, secondly, that no emperor could validly bind his successors to recognize a transaction of this kind, and thirdly that whole empires could be frittered away if once this principle were generally recognized.[2] Nearly every one of the great civilians took this line, except those, like Bartolus, for whom the geographical nearness of Rome was an impediment to freedom of speech.[3] This denial

[1] Cf., for instance, the Archdeacon, on *Dist.* x, c. 8, fol. 12 verso: "... nullum imperatorem exercuisse rite gladium, qui illum non accepit a Romana ecclesia, praesertim postquam Christus concessit jura utriusque imperii beato Petro, quod intelligens Constantinus, in resignatione regalium resignavit beato sylvestro gladium, respondens non legitime se usum fuisse gladii potestate nec legitime se habuisse, cum ab ecclesia non recepit."

[2] These reasons were conveniently set out by Accursius in his gloss on the *Authenticum, collatio I*, tit. vi, praefatio. Dante's refutation of the Donation appears like a paraphrase of the civilian's statement, see *Monarchia*, lib. III, cap. 10.

[3] Discussing the validity of the Donation Bartolus said in his lecture on the *Dig. Vet.* Rubrica, No. 13 (fol. 3 verso of the edition of Lugdunum, 1523): "Videte, nos sumus in terris amicis ecclesiae, et ideo dico, quod ista donatio valeat ... volens favere ecclesiae, dico, quod illa donatio valuit."

of the validity of the Donation was based upon juristically sound reasons and might, if not checked, tear asunder the canonistic edifice. Yet it is interesting to see that the canonists met this challenge by developing a theory which successfully resisted this dangerous attack of the imperialists. And out of this opposition grew one of the most cherished papalist arguments in favour of the superiority of the pope over the emperor. The imperialistic thesis became a very resourceful papalist antithesis. If it is said, the canonists retorted, that Constantine had no authority to hand over the empire, one would be bound to say that the people, from whom the emperor originally derived his power, had also no authority to give the emperor the right to rule them. For the basis of the emperor's power was the transfer of power from the people to him. As this transfer was obviously beyond dispute, the right of the emperor to hand over the empire, was practically also indisputable.[1]

The reference made by the civilians to the lack of the emperor's authority made the canonists enquire into the basis of the power which the pope and the emperor exercised. Here the canonists killed two birds with one stone. Firstly, they showed that the emperor's power rested upon the people, whilst the pope's was divinely conferred. Secondly, the serious obstacle innocently put forward by Justinian in his *Novella*, namely, that both the *sacerdotium* and the *imperium* proceeded from God, was rendered innocuous. For the canonists maintained a democratic basis of the emperor's powers and a theocratic basis of the pope's. Surely, in medieval days, he who claimed a divine authority for his power was on a higher pedestal than he who was only able to boast of the will of the people as the source of his authority. And once again the superiority of the pope was proved. It was through the challenge of the civilians that the canonists set about to consider the respective bases of power and thereby reversed the situation.

This leads straight into the realm of the much discussed *Lex Regia*. The general consensus amongst the civilians, who were always eager to confer as much power as possible upon the emperor, was that through this *Lex Regia* the people had transferred all power to the emperor and that this transfer was irre-

---

[1] See, for instance, Hostiensis, *Summa*, IV.xvii, col. 1231, No. 9: "Si dicas, Constantinus non potuit illa concedere, respondeo ergo nec populus potestatem suam in principem transferre, quod tamen falsum esse constat."

vocable. The canonists also relied on the *Lex Regia*, but considered the transfer of power to the emperor revocable, that is to say, according to the common opinion of the canonists, the people were still in a position to revoke the mandate given to the emperor.[1] From the standpoint of the canonists this transfer of power was a "concession" on the part of the people. But a concession, they declared, did not imply irrevocability; delegation, for instance, did not imply that delegated powers could not be withdrawn. However wide were the powers which a delegation conferred, the delegating authority necessarily retained something of its basic original power. And the same was true with regard to the people's transfer of power to the emperor: they still retained some basic powers, above all, they had the right to withdraw the authority granted to him. In fact, said the canonists, Roman law showed at least one example in which this grant was withdrawn from the prince by the people.[2] Some canonists, notably Goffredus de Trano, went so far as to declare that the people's power to legislate was still in existence.[3]

Now, provided that we follow the reasoning of the canonists, this basis of the emperor's powers and authority was incomparably weaker and less stable than that of the pope. Leaving aside all other considerations, who, then, could reasonably say that pope and emperor were of equal rank and power? The canonists pressed this point home, a point which we must remember was originally worked out as a means to counteract the civilians' forceful argument. In the last resort the empire, and the emperor's authority, rested on the people—"imperium

[1] One of the first papalist writers to conceive the theory of people's sovereignty in this sense that the people could depose the emperor and transfer his powers to someone else, seems to have been the German monk, Manegold of Lautenbach. In his "Liber ad Gebhardum" (written between 1083 and 1085) he claimed this right for the people. He compared the emperor with a swine-herd: the farmer who employed a swine-herd would be justified in dismissing him, if he were found pilfering, slaughtering and scattering the swine. All the more reason there would be for men to depose the emperor who proved himself a wicked prince. See *Mon. Germ. Hist.*, *Libelli de Lite*, tom. i, p. 365.

[2] *Dig.*, I.ii.2, 3; see Hostiensis, *Summa*, I De Constit., § Quis possit, col. 19, No. 9: "Dicitur translata, id est, concessa, et sic non omnino a se hanc potestatem populus abdicavit, sicut nec delegans delegando abdicavit a se jurisdictionem."

[3] See Goffredus de Trano, *Summa*, I De Const., fol. 2 verso: "Item populus Romanus legem etiam hodie condere potest . . . licet dicatur potestas in principem translata."

habet auctoritatem a populo Romano" as Innocent IV lucidly put it[1]—whilst the pope's power and authority were derived, not from the people's transfer of power, but from divine ordinance.[2] Perhaps the clearest presentation of the differences between papal and imperial powers was given by the great glossator, Laurentius, whose dictum was quoted over and over again. "The people," he said, "can deprive the emperor of his power, but all the churches taken together could not do the same to the pope, since he does not receive his power from them, but they from him."[3] The canonists used the weapon directed against them in an ingenious manner and thereby turned the tables on the civilian. Instead of showing the equality of pope and emperor, the civilians were shown the inferiority of the emperor, and this by the use of the very same argument by which they had attacked the canonistic doctrine. And the very plausible objection based upon Justinian's *Novella* that the *imperium* also came from God, was brushed aside by declaring either that even the lowest official received his powers from God,[4] or that the empire only indirectly descended from God and therefore depended on His vicar, the pope.[5] The papal

---

[1] I.vii.1, fol. 87, No. 1.

[2] See the Archdeacon on *Dist.* iv, c. 3, fol. 7, No. 6: ". . . cum ipse (scil. papa) non ex translatione populi, sed ex dominica jussione et conciliorum auctoritate suam habet jurisdictionem."

[3] *Id.*, on *Dist.* ii, c. 1, fol. 5, No. 2: "(Laurentius) dixit, quod populus Romanus potest auferri auctoritatem imperatori, sed omnes ecclesiae non possunt papae, quia non habet ab eis, sed ipsae ab eo," see also Zabarella, loc. cit., No. 8. This was foreshadowed, though with an emphasis on the theological aspect, by Gratian himself, when he incorporated the pseudo-Isidorian passage in *Dist.* xxi, c. 2. But here again a more moderate view prevailed amongst the older generation of canonists. Huguccio, for instance, glossing *Dist.* xvii, post cap. 6, § Hinc etiam, contradicted the opinion that the "Roman church" had derived its authority from Christ, and not from the councils. In his opinion the primacy of the "Roman Church" was based, in the first place, on Christ, and, in the second place, on the decrees of the councils. "Dicitur, quod ecclesia Romana habuit primatum a domino et non a conciliis, sed dico, quod a domino principaliter, et per auctoritatem habuit a conciliis vero secundario." Individual churches had submitted themselves "per voluntariam concessionem" to the Roman church's judgment. In order to corroborate this view Huguccio referred to C. IX, q. iii, c. 14, fol. 126 verso of P 72.

[4] Usually with a reference to Christ's reply to Pilate: "Non haberes in me potestatem ullam nisi data esset tibi desuper."

[5] See *Decretales*, I.xxxiv.6; IV.xvii.13; II.i.13, and Zabarella, on I.xxxiv.6 fol. 149: "Imperium dependet a Deo, et cum hoc ab eius vicario, scil. papa."

government was infused by God, the canonists were convinced.[1]

It would be idle to underestimate the forcefulness of this canonistic doctrine and its contribution to the momentary ascendancy of the papalist point of view. And yet, the introduction of the idea of a people's sovereignty was bound to prove fatal to the whole conception of papal monarchy: one could hardly conceive of a more glaring contrast than these two concepts. By the end of the fourteenth century the principle of people's sovereignty made an entry into the discussion concerning papal power within the Church. The Conciliar Movement was but one offspring of the introduction of the concept of popular sovereignty, and it was from this quarter that the structure of the papalist edifice was most vigorously assailed.

The second historical thesis which the canonists employed was that of the so-called Translation of the Empire. There is no need for us to recapitulate the numerous accounts which we find in the medieval chroniclers and annalists. We must concentrate on the canonistic version of the famous transaction performed in Rome in the year 800 when Charlemagne received the imperial crown at the hands of Pope Leo III. This Christmas-day ceremony is an established fact, but when we come to examine the canonistic narration we shall find some discrepancies. Innocent III must be credited with the invention of the Translation of the Empire. The idea seems first to have appeared in the now famous, but then secret, *Deliberatio* held at Christmastide 1200 when Innocent's thoughts might have turned back four centuries to the coronation of Charles. To Innocent's mind the Christmas-day ceremony of the year 800 signified not only that the emperor received his crown at the hands of the pope, but also that by this first coronation of a Frankish king the Eastern empire had been transplanted (or translated) to the West. "The empire was translated by the Church and through the Church from Greece, so that she might

---

[1] See Panormitanus, in his *Com.*, II.i.13, fol. 26 verso, No. 11: "Principatus papae est infusus a Deo." The imperial government was derived from men; therefore the divine government had precedence over its human counterpart. "Principatus temporalis ab homine; ergo principatus Dei debet praeesse principatui hominis." This was also the opinion of jurists who were not thoroughgoing canonists, such as Johannes de Lignano.

be better defended."[1] This idea was given its final expression in the decretal "Venerabilem" issued in March 1202,[2] henceforth repeated several times, namely, that the Church had translated the empire from the East to the person of Charlemagne.[3]

The incorporation of the decretal "Venerabilem" in the official *Compilatio Tertia* forced the canonists to express themselves on this Innocentian interpretation of history. Instead of maintaining (as Innocent apparently did) that coronation and translation were simultaneous acts, the canonists divided the translation chronologically from the coronation. They antedated the translation and thereby entangled themselves in appreciable chronological difficulties. If we take Tancred's *Apparatus* on the *Compilatio Tertia* as a representative product of contemporary canonistic thought, we shall find the statement that the translation was effected a considerable time before 800. He had read in chronicles, he said, that firstly the translation was carried out in the year 766, and secondly that the actual coronation did not take place until fifteen years later when Pope Leo III put the crown on Charles's head (781). According to Tancred, the Roman Church was oppressed by the Lombard king, Aistulph, and the pope after having vainly tried to enlist the help of the Eastern emperors, successfully appealed to the Franks. Because of the importance of this gloss of Tancred, not only for canonistic scholarship, but also for post-thirteenth-century papal policy and historical writings, we may quote the passage in full.[4]

---

[1] *Deliberatio Domini papae Innocentii super facto imperii de tribus electis* in Migne, *Patr. Lat.*, vol. ccxvi, cap. xxix, col. 1025; cf. also the letter to the archbishop of Cologne, cap. xxx, col. 1032; this was clearly foreshadowed in a communication to the archbishop of Mainz, Raynaldus, *Annales Ecclesiastici*, ad annum 1200, § 27, and in the letter to the German princes of 3 May 1199, *Registrum de negotio Romani imperii*, Migne, loc. cit., cap. ii, col. 998 ("ut per nos, ad quos ipsum negotium *principaliter et finaliter* noscitur pertinere. . . .").

[2] Potthast, *Regesta*, No. 1653; *Decretales*, I.vi.34.

[3] Amongst others, repeated in the letter to Philip of which a MS. copy is in LB 105, fols. 219-220 verso. Potthast dates this letter 26 March 1202 (No. 1649), but the MS. has: "nonis kalendis Aprilis pontificatus nostri anno quinto," which is 24 March 1202. The letter as printed by Migne, loc. cit., cap. lxiv, cols. 1068-71 is not complete; the MS. seems to have the full text.

[4] Tancred in his *Apparatus* on *Comp III*, I De elect., c. venerabilem, s.v. "transtulit", fol. 113 of D 4.

Legitur in chronicis, quod cum Romana ecclesia opprimeretur ab aistulpho, rege Lombardorum, petiit auxilium a constantino leoneque, filio eius, imperatoribus constantinopolitanis, et cum nollent patrocinari ecclesiae Romanae, Stephanus papa II transtulit imperium ad Karolum magnum, qui filius Pipini, quem Zacharias praedecessor eius substituerat Ludovico regi Francorum, quem deposuerat, sicur legitur XVI q. VI, alius, et translatio illa facta est anno domini septingentesimo LXVI, qui Karolus coronatus fuit a Leone papa III elapsis post hoc XV annist.

Tancred's gloss formed the backbone of later canonistic political thought. It was literally incorporated in the *glossa ordinaria*, and in fact reappeared in nearly every commentary, lecture, gloss or tract written during the thirteenth and fourteenth centuries. It is only too understandable that when a story is re-told so many times, the details become blurred until at the end there remains nothing but a caricature of the original. Cardinal Zabarella's account at the end of the fourteenth century is a particularly good example. He hopelessly confused the story. Berengarius and Aistulph were made contemporaries, and the latter was asked by the pope for help against Berengarius: the translation of the empire appeared to Zabarella to date from the time of Otto I.[1]

Before we proceed to a further examination of canonistic thought, a few points should be here noted. In the first place, the dates of the translation and of the subsequent coronation were not identical in all narratives. For instance, the printed gloss of Bernardus Parmensis has the date 776 which puts the coronation back to 791, whilst a manuscript copy of the gloss has still another date, i.e. 761, and an interval of eleven years.[2]

---

[1] Zabarella in his *Com.* on I.vi.34, fol. 149, No. 2. The publicists counted two translations, one to the Franks, the other to the Germans, see Ptolomy of Lucca, *De Origine . . . Romani Imperii*, ed. Krammer, p. 71 f.

[2] Fol. 25 of LC 173: "Translatio illa facta est anno domini septingentesimo LXI, qui Carolus coronatus est a Leone papa III elapsis post hoc XI annis." The gloss bears the siglum of Bernardus. Another discrepancy of dates is to be found in Alvarus Pelagius, *De Planctu Ecclesiae*, lib. I, cap. 41, fol. 19: Charles's coronation was performed in 800, but the translation took place seven years earlier: "Translatio imperii a Graecis in Germanos facta fuerat antea jam septem annis per Stephanum papam secundum." Dante also confused dates and persons, see *Monarchia*, lib. III, cap 11: Pope Hadrian crowned Charlemagne.

In the second place, Leo III did not become pope before 795, and therefore cannot have crowned Charles in 781. In the third place, Stephen III was pope from 752 to 757, that is to say, before the canonists would have the translation. Nevertheless, it was in fact Stephen III who had asked Pepin for succour against Aistulph: Pepin was informed that the protection of the Roman Church and of the Roman people was to be entrusted to him and his sons.[1] The most likely explanation of this antedating is that the canonists saw the actual translation of the empire in Stephen III's anointing and blessing of Pepin, his wife, Charles and Carloman. The appointment of Pepin and of his sons as patricians of the Romans by Stephen III and the pronouncement of the anathema on the Franks, if they ever should choose a king from any other family, may have appeared to the canonists as the act of the translation. The mentioning of Pepin and of Pope Zacharias's activity in Tancred's statement may be a confirmation of our hypothesis.

The alleged chronological separation of the translation and coronation lent additional force to the canonistic argument that it depended on the pope whether or not he would put the crown on the Frankish king. The time lag was to bring the coronation into clear relief: the coronation was to be considered a specific concession on the part of the pope, a point of view clearly upheld by Innocent himself in the *Deliberatio*.[2]

Hence, the government of world—the "regnum mundi"— was transferred from the Eastern emperors to the Teutons. The canonistic interpretation of this translation attempted to show that the East Roman empire had thereby ceased to exist,[3] since there could be no empire outside the church. "Nullum

---

[1] See *Mon. Germ. Hist.*, *Epistolae*, tom. iii (Merow. et Karolini, tom. i). pp. 495-97; cf also *Liber Pontificalis*, ed- Duchèsne, tom. i, pp. 450-54.

[2] "... finaliter, quia ipsa (scil. sedes apostolica) *concedit* coronam imperii," Migne, loc. cit., col. 1025. It would be fascinating to enquire into the composition of the consistory of which the *Deliberatio* was the outcome. A high percentage of canonists appear to have attended the consistory. In his letter to Philip, Innocent III also advised him to surround himself with "juristae" and to take their advice when considering Innocent's proposal to enter into negotiations with Otto IV, see fol. 220 of LB 105. M. Krammer, *Das Kurfürstenkolleg* (in *Quellen und Studien zur Verfassungsgeschichte*, ed. Zeumer, vol. v), pp. 30-31, believes that the archbishop of Cologne had great influence on the deliberations of the consistory.

[3] "Et sic patet, quod imperium non est apud Graecos," *glos. ord.*, but see Johannes Teutonicus *supra* p. 146.

imperium extra ecclesiam." Two questions may reasonably be asked, and in fact were asked in medieval canonistic literature. Firstly, upon what authority the pope proceeded when he transferred the empire, and secondly, why the empire had been transferred to the Teutons and to no other people. According to the younger Bernardus Compostellanus, the answer to the first question was contained in Christ's *dictum*. "I will give unto thee the keys of the kingdom...."[1] The uses to which this over-quoted utterance could be put, appeared inexhaustible. Several answers were given to the second question, amongst which were the following, namely, that the Teutons had deserved this translation on account of the effective help they had given to the pope, that their wanderings to Rome showed their devotion to St. Peter and Paul, that they were a braver, more virtuous and adventurous people than other European races and, lastly, that they were selected by the Church, presumably, as Johannes Teutonicus, himself a German, put it, because of their fecundity and also because of the nobility which they represented. But Johannes Teutonicus's judgement, though continually quoted, was frequently suspected, "quia Germanus erat".[2]

In this context it may be apposite to refer to two passages in canon law containing statements which, if canonistic interpretative skill had not exerted itself, would surely have played havoc with canonistic political ideas. The two passages[3] intimately associated with the alleged translation of the

[1] Matt. xvi.19. Bernard's *Commentaria in Decretales* is in LC 167. The passage referred to is fol. 1, on I.ii.3: "Quaeritur, per quae verba (scil. imperium translatum fuit)? Solutio, per illa verba, 'tibi dabo' permisit sibi potestatem solvendi et ligandi." The Incipit of the Commentaries reads: "Hactenus ut loquar cum Seneca meam ignorantiam ignoravi" (wrong transcription of this Incipit and wrong description of the MS. in the catalogue). This MS. which seems to have been unknown, contains only a fragment of the *Commentaria*, i.e. fol. 1—18 verso to I.vi.7. In the prologue the author says: "Ego magister Bernardus Comp. domini papae capellanus ad laudem Dei ac utilitatem studentium...." The pope was Innocent IV whom he had mentioned earlier in the prologue: "Sperans etiam per dominum meum Innocentium papam IIII de cuius laboribus...."

[2] Johannes Teutonicus seems to have been imbued with a good deal of nationalistic spirit, for in the gloss referred to (p. 146 n.4), although he at first supports the extremist claims of the papacy, he continues with an eulogy of the emperor: in fact, reading the latter part of the gloss alone, one might almost think that Johannes was an imperialist.

[3] *Dist.*, lxiii, c. 22 and 23.

empire referred to the *Historia Ecclesiastica*, presumably of Eusebius, in which it was stated, firstly, that Pope Hadrian I had conferred upon Charlemagne and his successors the right to elect the Roman pontiff[1] and, secondly, that Pope Leo VIII had reiterated and confirmed this imperial right of papal election.[2] How did the canonists interpret these two passages of which the latter merely represented the much contested "Privilegium of Otto I"?[3] Two lines of explanation were chosen. Either it was said, for instance by Laurentius and the author of the *Glossa Palatina*, that these popes had no authority to confer the right of papal election upon an emperor, because the cardinals had not been consulted[4] and because it was their prerogative to elect a pope; or it was maintained, for example by Stephen of Tournay, and Huguccio that Charlemagne had been given the right, but other emperors had later renounced it and that in any case Hadrian I and Leo VIII were forced to comply with the wishes of Charlemagne and of Otto I and that therefore their concessions were extorted.[5] This second line of explanation later became common.[6] Compared with the

---

[1] c. 22.   [2] c. 23.

[3] See Baronius, *Annales Ecclesiastici*, ad annum 962; Goldast, *Constit. Imperiales*, vol. ii, p. 44, these two rejected the authenticity of the document. Th. Sickel, *Das Privilegium Ottos I*, established the authenticity of the document which is in *Mon. Germ. Hist.*, *Leges*, vol. ii, p. 29.

[4] "Non poterat hoc papa dare, sine cardinalium consensu, cum cardinalium sit eligere." *Glossa Palatina* on Dist. lxiii, c. 22, fol. 25 verso of D 8. The author of this gloss went a step further and asked the question, whether, on the basis of this canonical text, the pope could grant the emperor the right of deposition after the consultation of the cardinals: this was a privilege which the emperors once had, but which they themselves had renounced: "Num possit papa ei concedere, ut deponeret eum, sic in haeresi tantum, et de consensu cardinalium? Haec autem privilegia hodie non tenent, quia imperatores eis renuntiaverunt, et quia hac potestate abusi sunt," fol. 25 verso.

[5] Stephen of Tournay, *Summa*, on *Dist.* lxiii, c. 22, p. 91 of the edition by Schulte: "Quod hic legitur Adrianus concessisse est ex necessitate; cessante causa debet pariter cessare, quod urgebat." It was a privilege specially bestowed upon Otto I, according to Huguccio, *Summa*, on *Dist.* lxiii, c. 22, fol. 121 verso of LC 2: "Hoc autem fuit speciale privilegium in persona eius et quorundam aliorum sicut hodie est in persona regis apulie, et male ... item quia talibus privilegiis abutebantur, et ita meruerunt ea amittere ... item quia per sequentia decreta sunt eliminata et abrogata." The personal character of the "privilege" was also touched upon by the *Glossa Palatina*, on *Dist.* lxiii, c. 23, fol. 25 verso of D 8: "Non dico primo regi, sed primo ottoni."

[6] See, for example, Bartholomaeus Brixiensis in his glosses on *Dist.* lxiii, cc. 22, 23, and Panormitanus, *Com.* on I.xxxiv, 6 No. 18, fol. 115 verso: "Nam impera-

often tedious and repetitive explanations which we find in so many canonistic writings, the brevity of the interpretations of these two passages is certainly welcome.

The assurances given by the two popes regarding the imperial nomination of the pope, had thus been disposed of by the canonistic skill of interpretation. But once again the canonists utilizing to the full the alleged historical events, gave the thesis a different turn, so that the problem did not concern papal elections by the emperor, but imperial elections by the pope. The thesis was not of course presented as a crude demand for a nomination of the emperor by the pope. The thesis appeared in a subtler shape, demanding the approval, confirmation and coronation of the emperor by the pope.[1] And this leads us to the function of the electoral college, and herewith to the third historical element in the canonists' attempted proof of the dependence of the empire on the papacy. Although present-day historical scholarship is still only tentatively suggesting the origins of the electoral college, the medieval canonists possessed an enviable certainty of knowledge about the origin of this institution. Although modern researches have proved that the electoral college was not firmly established before Frederick I, the canonists went back two centuries further and maintained that the seven electors were instituted by the pope himself during the reign of Otto III. In order to show his appreciation for the help which Otto III had rendered to the pope in driving out Crescentius, the pope "instituted the electors". They were, the canonists stated, the officials of the imperial curia, that is, the four lay princes and the three ecclesiastical princes. This was the canonistic presentation of the story relating to the origin of the electoral college.[2]

---

tori olim praebendi auxilium ecclesiae satis oppresse tribuit papa cum consensu concilii potestatem eligendi papam et alios pontifices, sed illud privilegium postea fuit revocatum, cum ab eo abuteretur."

[1] It should be borne in mind that Innocent III went much further than this; in the secret "Deliberatio super facto imperii de tribus electis" of Christmas 1200 he boldly claimed that the emperor received his empire by papal investiture: "ab eo (scil. papa) benedicitur, coronatur, et de imperio investitur," see *Registrum de Negotio Imperii*, cap. xxix in Migne, *Patr. Lat.*, vol. ccxvi, col. 1025. In the decretal "Venerabilem" this was tuned down to: "unctio, consecratio et coronatio". On the implications of this difference see M. Tangl, "Die Deliberatio Innozenz' III" in *SB d. Preuss. Akad. d. Wiss.*, 1919, p. 1024.

[2] The narration conveniently omits the fact that Otto III nominated a second

It therefore became the common opinion amongst the canonists that the seven electors had acquired their right from the Church.¹ The right was founded upon the papal concession and fourteenth-century canonists could justifiably point to the firm establishment of the custom. But we should bear in mind that the custom thus developed was alleged to have been based upon a papal concession.² Hence, the canonists were anxious to point out that the electoral power was not derived from the people or conferred by any earthly prince, but granted by the pope.³ The part which the pope played in imperial elections, was therefore fully explicable, for the electoral college was a purely papal creation. Consequently, if the electors chose an unworthy candidate for the office of the emperor or if there was a double election, the pope was claimed to be the legitimate and rightful authority to reject the candidate or to tip the balance in favour of one of the elected.⁴ Moreover, if the electors were alleged to be negligent in the performance of their electoral functions, the pope was again considered the authority to nominate an emperor.⁵ The logical sequel of this theory would

---

pope in the person of Gerbert, who significantly called himself Silvester II. The motives of Otto's activity in Rome may in reality have little in common with those attributed to him by the canonists.

¹ See, for instance, Zabarella, ibid., fol. 149 verso, No. 8: "Electores praemissi hanc potestatem adepti sunt ab ecclesia Romana, quae sic transtulit imperium a Graecis, ita et electores constituit."

² *Id.*, ibid.: "Papa recognoscit potestatem eligendi regem, in imperium postmodum promovendum, pertinere ad electores memoratos de jure et antiqua consuetudine, et subdit, quod ad eos jus et potestas huiusmodi ab ecclesia Romana pervenit, sicuti tamen legitur in historiis. Institutio istorum non fuit facta tempore translationis imperii factae a Graecis, sed postea mortuo Ottone III." Cf. also *Registres de Boniface VIII*, No. 4328.

³ Cf. Panormitanus, *Com.* on I.xxxiv.6, No. 18, fol. 115 verso: "Isti electores hanc potestatem habuerunt non a populo Romano, vel ab aliquo imperatore, sed a papa." See also Ptolomy in *Det. Comp.* ed. cit., p. 30 f.

⁴ Before canonistic theory was fully developed, the only basis of the pope's decision in double elections was the Translation of the Empire. In fact, Innocent III based his right to decide the issue between Philip and Otto on the Translation, see *supra* p. 168.

⁵ See, for instance, Innocent IV, *Com.* ibid., No. 4, fol. 65 verso: "Sed eis (scil. electoribus) negligentibus eligere imperatorem papa eligit, et si plures elegerunt, papa de jure cognoscet inter eos et definit." See also Panormitanus, loc. cit., No. 20: "Si electores imperii omnes eligunt scienter indignum, potestas providendi devolvitur ad papam . . . quia ex quo istam potestatem habeant a papa, debet ad ipsum redire potestas, si ea abutentur."

have been that the pope was endowed with the right to deprive the electors of their electoral powers. But this papal right was denied by the majority of the canonists, presumably to make allowance for the actual circumstances and possible consequences. Johannes Andreae, for instance, discussing a papal withdrawal of the electoral power, said that no such right could be conceded to the pope, unless the electors were unwilling to act or could not agree on a candidate.[1] In fact, there was no need for any specific withdrawal, as the cases of negligent electors and unworthy candidates, and so forth, were fully covered by the canonistic thesis that in such eventualities the power to appoint an emperor rested with the pope. A minority, however, proclaimed this papal right and argued, logically enough, that whatever the pope had given, he was also entitled to take away. But even this minority was deterred from following up its opinion to the logical conclusion, and declared that it would not be expedient—"non expediret"—for a pope to do so: the scandal created thereby for the princes involved was too great to justify this last step;[2] also the immemorial custom was against the acceptance of the conclusion.

The basic principles relating to pope and emperor are now before us. For philosophical, biblical and historical reasons the pope was considered by the canonists to be superior to the emperor. It may now be desirable to review briefly some of the more important consequences which followed from these principles. The threat of excommunication hung not only over the humblest individual in the Christian commonwealth, but also, and perhaps to a greater extent, over the person of the emperor or of a king. Although the power of excommunication was not primarily an application of the foregoing principles, but rested upon the spiritual supremacy of the pope over every Christian, it is nevertheless advisable to touch upon this question, because indirectly the pope was able to exercise pressure on a recalcitrant temporal prince.[3] With the caution and reticence that is proper to a diplomat and pope, Innocent IV declared that an

[1] Johannes Andreae, gloss on *Sextus*, II.xiv.2, s.v. "privamus": "Sed numquid papa possit principes electione privare, et per se eligere imperio vacante?" The pope could not do this "dummodo ipsi velint eligere, secus videtur, si vellent eligere vel concordare non possent."

[2] Cf. Alvarus Pelagius, Lib. I, cap. 45, fol. 24.

[3] This was clearly realized by Huguccio, *Summa* on *Dist.* xcvi, c. 6, fol. 171 verso of LC 2.

excommunication of an emperor should be decreed only in cases in which "notorious excesses" of the culprit could be proved.[1] Of course, the exact determination of what constituted "a notorious excess" was left to the trial judge, not necessarily to the pope himself: an episcopal sentence sufficed.[2] Other canonists merely adopted and elaborated the provisions of the third chapter of the Fourth Lateran Council. Thus Goffredus de Trano, Innocent's contemporary, taught that not only heresy of the prince himself, but also of his subjects made him liable to excommunication, provided that he neglected to stamp out the heresy committed by his subjects. The excommunicate prince was to be expelled from his realm which should be occupied by "catholici viri". The same course should be adopted, if the prince failed to enforce justice within his domain, or if he was found wanting in efficiency and capability.[3]

The link between excommunication and deposition of an emperor was very close, although deposition, and not excommunication, was a concrete application of canonistic political thought. Once again, the canonists made use of certain historical events and interpreted them in such a manner that they served the fixed purpose. Canonistic doctrine was, in fact, able to refer to some specific cases, in which a pope had effected the deposition of a secular prince. And yet it is the canonistic interpretation which arouses our interest. We find the first actual example of such a deposition in Gratian's collection. The monk excerpted[4] a statement of Gregory VII[5] in which the

---

[1] See Innocent IV in his *Com.* on I.xxix.1, fol. 147 verso, No. 1: "Dicimus, quod rex vel imperator semper post monitionem canonicam excommunicatur pro notoriis excessibus nisi pareat."

[2] Cf. *Decretales*, I.xxxiv.4, and *gl. ord.*, eod. tit., cap 6. The gloss asks, to which bishop the secular ruler is subjected, if there are more than one? Typically dialectical divisions try to answer the question. The first excommunication by a bishop of a king appears to have been King Charibert's by Bishop Germanus, 567, see Hinschius, *Das Kirchenrecht der Katholiken und Protestanten*, vol. iv, p. 842, note 2.

[3] Goffredus de Trano, *Summa*, De haereticis, fol. 200, No. 12: "Unde diligenter attendes, quod principes saeculi et domini temporales non solum propter suam haeresim, sed propter haeresim aliorum, quos, dum possunt exterminare, neglexerint, sunt excommunicandi ab ecclesia et expellendi a terris et terrae ipsorum exponi possunt catholicis occupandae. Et idem est, si princeps contra regnum et justitiam faciendam negligens inventus fuerit insufficiens et ineptus."

[4] *Decretum*, C.XV, q. vi, c. 3.

[5] See *Mon. Germ. Hist.*, *Scriptores*, vol. ii, n.s., "Das Register Gregors VII", ed, E. Caspar, p. 554.

great pope referred to the deposition of the last Merovingian king, Childeric III, by Pope Zacharias in the year 751. Gregory VII declared that this king was deposed not on account of his injustices, but because he was "useless".[1] Zacharias allowed Pepin to take the place of Childeric, whose subjects were simultaneously released from their oath of fidelity to Childeric. The operative words in this very important and not always properly appreciated papal action were "iniquitas" and "inutilis". This, I believe, was the first concrete political action of the papacy in the secular field, an action which moreover was instigated by the secular power, Pepin. These two terms were to form the backbone of the later canonistic theory. A second example was provided by Innocent III's deposition of Otto IV.[2] The explanation offered by the canonists was that Otto IV had not adhered to the oath of fidelity which he had sworn to his former protector. The pope effected the deposition because Otto, the Guelf, had turned into Otto, the Ghibelline. The third, commonly adduced instance (which was certainly the application of canonistic theory) was Innocent IV's deposition of Frederick II during the first council of Lyons. In the realm of deposition we have a classic example of the degree to which canonistic theory was influenced by papal action and of how much papal activity stimulated canonistic thought to expand the scope of papal rights. The history of the Middle Ages may well be considered as the result of this interdependence between papacy and canonists—a continual circulatory process.

The *glossa ordinaria* of Bartholomaeus Brixiensis on Gregory VII's statement explained that Zacharias deposed the king, because he was weak and effeminate; moreover, the glossator said, he was quite useless. If Childeric had been merely inefficient ("insufficiens"), a "co-adjutor" would have had to be provided, "sed dissolutus erat cum mulieribus et effeminatus". This interpretation, although it attempted to provide a moral basis for the passage, was nevertheless in contradiction to the explicit declaration of Gregory: the deposition was grounded, Gregory said, not in any lack of moral qualities, but in the

---

[1] See the text in cap cit.

[2] Cf. *Decretales*, I.vi.34; see also the remarks of P. Joachimson, "The Investiture Contest and the German Constitution" in *Medieval Germany*, ed. G. Barraclough, p. 119, and F. Kern, *Gottesgnadentum und Widerstandsrecht*, p. 67, note 115.

political uselessness of this king.¹ The earlier interpretation of Benencasa, therefore, came much nearer to the truth. Childeric was deposed, because he had proved himself useless as a king, not because he had committed any crimes.² Very properly has it been remarked that this deposition was irreconcilable with the thesis that the pope could depose a king "ratione peccati" only.³ On the contrary, sinful conduct was implicitly rejected by Gregory as a legitimate reason for deposing a king: the suitability of a prince was more important than his moral qualifications.

There were, however, some other interpretations of this Gregorian passage. And these interpretations were still less reconcilable with the temper of Gregory's view than the one propounded by Bartholomaeus Brixiensis. But they also show that the earlier generation of canonists at least was reluctant to face the full implications of this passage. They did not maintain that Pope Zacharias deposed King Childeric by virtue of his own power. For instance, Huguccio said that the deposition of the king by the pope merely implemented the will of the princes who had accused and convicted the king. Huguccio concluded that only if a king after his conviction by the nobles refused to abdicate, he should be excommunicated by the pope. The king's expulsion by armed force and the election of a successor was only then legitimate.⁴ Going a step further, Huguccio flatly rejected the opinion that the pope had any right to depose a baron or a count: being dependent on a king or an emperor, a baron could not be summoned by the pope and hence not be deposed by him. Huguccio saw a parallel in those provisions in canon law which denied the metropolitan bishop the right to summon clerics under the jurisdictional power of a bishop: bishops alone could be summoned by the metropolitan, but not their clerics.⁵

---

[1] See *Mon. Germ. Hist.*, loc. cit., and c. 3, C. XV, q. vi.

[2] Benencasa in his *Casus ad Decretum*, on C. XV, q. vi, c. 3, fol. 134 verso of W 159: "Hoc probat Zacharias papa, qui regem Francorum deposuit, non tamen propter sua delicta, quantum pro eo, quia inutilis erat, et loco eius pipinum, patrem caroli magni substituit, et omnes francigenas a fidelitate eius absolvit."

[3] F. Kern, op. cit., p. 58, note 103, and pp. 298-99.

[4] "Credo verum esse de voluntate et assensu principum, si coram eis accusatur et convincatur, quod tunc demum intelligo, si convictus et admonitus non vult cessare et satisfacere, tunc debet excommunicari . . . recte expellitur armata manu et alius legitime eligitur," *Summa* on *Dist.* xcvi, c. 6, fol. 171 of LC 2.

[5] *Summa* on C. XV, q. vi, c. 3.

Quaeret aliquis, an papa possit similiter deponere comites et alios barones, qui sunt sub regibus et imperatoribus, sine consensu illorum, quibus subsunt. Credo, quod non, quia non debent sub eo conveniri vel accusari, sed sub suo rege vel imperatore. Simile est de metropolitano, qui licet possit judicare episcopos suos, ut II q. VII metropolitanum, non tamen eorum clericos, ut IX q. III etiam conquestus.

The interpretation of Zacharias's step by the author of the *Summa Cantabrigiensis* was very similar to that of Huguccio. He declared that the pope deposed Childeric "de consilio baronum", because the barons who elected him, should also depose him: "quia barones debent deponere, qui debent eligere." After all, this *Summa* pointed out, any prelate could be deposed by reason of his uselessness.[1] And proceeding a step further, the assertion was made that the pope could not depose an emperor, unless acting upon the decision of the empire—"nisi de consensu imperii".[2] A remarkable interpretation of this Gregorian passage is to be found in the *Apparatus* of Bernardus Compostellanus Junior on the Constitutions of the First Council of Lyons (1245). Commenting on the decree "Grandi non immerito"[3] the Spaniard reduced Pope Zacharias's activity to a mere consent to the decision of the barons: they, not he, had deposed King Childeric, and the pope merely consented to the deposition effected by the barons. What is perhaps still more remarkable is that this glossator claimed the support of the "Doctores" and above all of Huguccio.[4] At the same time Bernardus would have no doubts about the legitimacy of a deposition of an emperor by the pope if the latter had taken this step without even consulting his cardinals.[5]

---

[1] "Propter inutilitatem potest praelatus deponi, C. De prof. et med., contrarietas . . ." on C. XV, q. vi, c. 3, s.v. "regno", fol. 78 of T O.5.17. This passage is not in LC 137, fol. 109, but the one quoted in the text is here as well as in the Cambridge MS. There are some variants in reading.

[2] "Non potest imperator deponi a papa, nisi de consensu imperii. Papa autem nullo modo potest judicari a principe, ut IX, q. III aliorum," on *Dist.* xcvi, c. 6, fol. 32 of T 0.5.17.

[3] The later *Sextus*, I.viii.2.

[4] "Notatur ibi (scil. C. XV, q. vi, c. 3) per doctores, quod papa non deposuit, sed depositioni consensit, ut legitur in historia francorum, ut dixit Huguccio in summa," fol. 286 verso of LC 173. On the *Apparatus* and its author, see Appendix.

[5] See *infra* p. 181.

This latter view of the Spaniard fitted into the general pattern of later thirteenth and fourteenth century political doctrine, for it claimed that the secular prince could be deposed by the pope alone. To rely on the "consensus imperii" would have been tantamount to a severe restriction of papal power. Iniquity alone and uselessness alone were considered to be sufficient causes of a king's deposition. "For any grave crime" an emperor could be deposed, declared the Speculator, Guilelmus Durantis; he added that this in fact amounted to a deposition "propter iniquitatem".[1] When commenting upon the decree of Frederick's deposition, Bernardus Compostellanus Junior said that the pope could depose any secular prince because of his iniquity: "Patet, quod papa potest deponere imperatorem et alios principes propter suas iniquitates, XVq. VI alius."[2] But this author uttered a warning. There must be very compelling reasons for deposing an emperor—"magna causa debet subesse depositioni imperatoris" —because the greater the risks and the greater the scandal created, the slower should one proceed: "quia ubi majus scandalum et periculum timeretur, benignius est agendum." In other words, papal policy should adapt itself to circumstances. The "ratio peccati" as such was no specific reason for the emperor's deposition by the pope: iniquitous conduct alone sufficed. Next to this ground of deposition, the unsuitability of the emperor was an adequate reason for deposing an emperor.[3] Canonistic doctrine therefore went considerably further than Gregory VII originally had intended to go, for to him mere iniquity of a prince was no sufficient reason for deposing him.

The importance of an Innocentian decretal for the development of this theory should not be overlooked. In the most

---

[1] See *Spec.*, Lib. I, pars i, De Legato, No. 17, fol. 46, and Lib. I, pars ii, De Accusationibus, No. 3, fol. 200. This was maintained although Alanus to whom the chief credit for this political theory must go, had said that the emperor could not be deposed for *any* crime, but only for those crimes which he had committed as a persistent offender. Nor was this enough for Alanus: the crime of the emperor must be one that provoked scandal: "Sed numquid pro omni crimine potest deponi imperator? Respondeo, immo pro nullo, nisi persistere in illo contenderit, sed nec tunc forte pro omni, sed solum pro tali, quod scandalum inducit."

[2] Gloss on the decree "Ad apostolicae", fol. 287 verso of LC 173.

[3] See, for example, Johannes Andreae in his gloss on *Sextus*, II.xiv.2, s.v "privamus", and the common opinion, always taking Gregory's statement as the legal basis.

general terms Innocent recalled in a context irrelevant to this particular topic that "whatsoever is not of faith, is sin": "Omne, quod non est ex fide, peccatum est."[1] Hence, not only private actions of individuals, but above all also the political actions of kings and emperors were subject to "synodal judgment", that is, to ecclesiastical jurisdiction. It is true that Innocent III had in mind the acquisition of property by way of prescription when he promulgated that decretal in the Fourth Lateran Council. But these general terms easily lent themselves to a much wider application in the political field. This decretal was interpreted by the proponents of the older doctrine as a proof that the pope could issue binding regulations about the prescription of laymen. "Ratione peccati statuit hic papa de praescriptione laicorum."[2] From here there was only a small step to the further claim that the pope could interfere with the legislation of the civil power, even if the particular law did not prima facie touch upon a spiritual matter. The glossator of the Constitutions of the Lateran Council had clearly pointed the way: here, he stated, was the salvation of the soul at stake, and therefore the pope was the judge "in everything" by reason of sin.[3] "By reason of sin," said Hostiensis, "the Church can correct civil laws, and can draw civil matters into its own courts."[4] Perhaps still more outspoken was Bernardus Parmensis in his gloss[5] which maintained that not so much by reason of their sinfulness did the Church intervene in these mundane matters, as by its desire to prevent any "danger to the soul": "Canon voluit propter periculum animarum in hoc leges corrigere." It was for this reason that all civil laws permitting usury were "to-day" considered invalid,[6] since they

[1] *Decretales*, II.xxvi.20 initium; see Rom. xiv.23.

[2] See the report of the *gl. ord.*, ibid.

[3] Gloss on the *Constitutiones IV Laterani Concilii*, cap. 41, fol. 173 of LB 139, s.v. "civilis": "Dico, quod hic vertitur anima et ita est judex in omnibus ratione peccati." A later hand added: "Constitutiones principum non praejudicant ecclesiae." For the theoretical justification of the pope's jurisdiction "ratione peccati," see ch. IV.

[4] "Ratione peccati potest ecclesia leges corrigere et causas audire et diffinire," Hostiensis, *Summa*, II.xxvi.

[5] *Decr. cit.*

[6] "Sicut dicitur de legibus permittentibus usuras, quae hodie non tenent," *gl. ord.* cap. cit. Some civilians adopted this canonistic point of view in its entirety. Philippus Decius, for example, declared that a statute directed against the liberty of one individual church, must be considered to have offended the whole Church:

were to endanger the souls. Deposition of an emperor or of a king was therefore merely a logical application of the general principle laid down by Innocent III: in the eyes of the Church the deposed emperor's government would have been a source of danger to the souls of his subjects, and hence that source must be removed. Surely, one would have expected a fundamental tenet like this "ratio peccati" to be elaborated. In particular, one might reasonably have thought that the canonists would have said something on the nature of that sin which justified an emperor's deposition: was that sin to be merely venal or was it to be mortal? What criteria was the pope (or the ecclesiastical trial judge) expected to apply when deciding on the nature of that sin? Was it to concern private or public conduct? Was it to concern conduct prejudicial to the State or to the Church?

In this context a brief reference to the Innocentian conception of high treason appears advisable. In his opinion every heresy constituted the *crimen laesae majestatis*. In this he merely followed the current canonistic doctrine which maintained that heretics were to be punished like those accused of high treason: "Haeretici puniuntur ut rei criminis laesae majestatis."[1] Nobody was more imbued with the idea of the pope's being a celestial emperor than Innocent III, and this idea found concrete expression in the decretal in which he justified the stern measures to be taken against heretics as offenders of his divine majesty. But Innocent omitted an exact definition of what constituted this crime: he merely stated that this offence was

---

Com. in Decretales, Venice, 1576, fol. 43: "Statutum, quod est contra libertatem unius ecclesiae particularis, quia quod facit injuriam uni ecclesiae, totam Dei ecclesiam offendit." Even an emphyteusis of a church, when embodied in a statute, would render this state invalid: "Jura civilia, quae loquunter de emphiteusi ecclesiae, non debent observari." In general, Decius declared: "Unde ratione peccati inter laicos potest papa statutum vel consuetudinem(!) tollere; et ideo, quod dicitur, qui peccat legis auctoritate, non peccat . . . intelligitur de auctoritate juris canonici." One needs little imagination to understand the dilemma in which a law-abiding citizen might be put, if such theories were prevalent.

[1] See the gloss of the first stratum in LB 105, fol. 203 verso. The same view was expressed by the anonymous author of the *Summa* on the *Comp. I* in the Codex 162 of the Cistercian Monastery in Zwettl, Lower Austria, fol. 40, on IV. Qui filii sint legit., c. Causam: both heretics and traitors share the same fate 'Nemo post mortem judicandus est . . . nisi in crimine haeresis et laesae majestatis.'

caused by an aberration from the faith.[1] In this one instance he gave his blessing to the civil laws which demanded the confiscation of the property of those who were convicted of high treason. There was all the more reason, Innocent avowed, for canon laws' inflicting still severer penalties upon those "aberrantes in fide". The ecclesiastical punishment went further than the civil punishment. Not only was their property to be confiscated, as the civil laws demanded,[2] but their legitimate heirs were also to be disinherited ("exhaeredatio"). For "it is far more serious to offend the eternal majesty than the temporal" as Innocent put it in that decretal.[3] And the gloss of Bernardus Parmensis added that the severity of punishment was justified by the consideration of the nature of this crime. By offending against the "divina religio"—the character of this offence was never fully defined—the perpetrator inflicted injury upon all citizens, and therefore by offending the whole community his action was classed as a "crimen publicum". The glossator apparently implied by this interpretation that the crime of lése majesté if committed against the emperor, was one directed against his person only and less severity of punishment was justified.

There is one point that deserves our attention. In the same decretal Innocent III said that, upon his command, the secular princes must enforce this ecclesiastical punishment against the heretics under their jurisdiction. He added the threat that the civil authorities would be compelled to carry out his command "per censuram ecclesiasticam", that is to say, in case of a refusal by the secular power, papal jurisdiction would come into full play. In practical terms this threat implied that the secular justice was expected to execute the sentence of an ecclesiastical tribunal, although this sentence had no basis in civil law. If he refused on this ground—a juristically tenable refusal—the pope would have had no difficulty in construing the refusal as a deliberate disobedience to a command given by the spiritual overlord of the world within his spiritual jurisdiction. When glossing this decretal, Vincentius quite frankly

---

[1] *Decretales*, V.vii.10.

[2] *Cod. Just.*, I.v.4, 13, 19. The property of the heretic was to go to the orthodox children; if there were no children, it went to relatives, provided that they were orthodox Catholics.

[3] *Decret. cit.*

declared that it was not only heresy which caused the removal of a secular judge: any other iniquity on his part might serve as a ground for his dismissal.[1] And whatever juristic scruples of conscience there might have been, they were finally appeased by the avowal of the canonists that the over-lenient civil laws had been corrected by this decretal. That was the opinion expressed by Johannes Teutonicus and Laurentius Hispanus— neither of whom was extreme in his views—in their *Apparatus* on the *Compilatio Tertia*;[2] their interpretation was duly endorsed by Tancred.[3]

Never has a solemnly condemned heretic rendered such signal service to the persecution of heretics as did Frederick II, and never has the extreme papalist cause received such enduring support as it did by Frederick's constitution "Ad Decus".[4] During the short-lived spell of his zeal to exterminate heresy, and in order to alleviate the suspicions of the papal monarch, Frederick II issued a fateful decree in 1220, little more than a dozen years after Innocent had published his own. This Frederician decree was no mere replica of Innocent's, although in parts it employed the very same words, but went considerably further than the Innocentian. For Frederick laid down, firstly, that mere suspicion of heresy ("sola suspicio") was sufficient to declare individuals outlawed ("banniti") for a year and if they still persisted, "we shall condemn them as heretics";[5] secondly, that all imperial authorities must take an oath to the

---

[1] Vincentius in his gloss in *Comp. III*, De haeret., c. vergentis, (c. 1), fol. 200 verso of D 4 (*Apparatus* of Tancred), s.v. "praecipimus": "Et ita potest papa etiam saeculares judices privare dignitatibus, non tantum propter haeresim, sed propter alias iniquitates, ut XV q. VI alius. Nam et imperium transfert de loco ad locum."

[2] *Comp. III*, De haeret., c. vergentis (c. 1), fol. 201 of D 4 (*Apparatus* of Tancred): "Illa decretalis corrigit illas leges."

[3] ibid.: "Ego dico hanc decretalem prevalere legibus supradictis." Whilst the *Apparatus* of Tancred in D 4 distinguishes between the three canonists, the *Apparatus* of Tancred in LC 29 ascribes the whole gloss to Tancred himself, fol. 156.

[4] In the *Authenticum*, collatio X, in fine. On the importance of the decree "statuimus" (contained in the same Constitution of Frederick II) for the trial of clerics before secular tribunals, see Généstal, *Le Privilegium Fori en France*, vol. ii, pp. 38-40.

[5] "Ita, quod si sic per annum manserint, ex tunc eos sicut haereticos condemnamus." Condemnation of heresy would therefore be the business of the secular court.

effect that upon bidding of the Church they would exterminate the heretics in their provinces, and, thirdly, perhaps most notable, that if a civil magistrate neglected to carry out the ecclesiastical tribunal's sentence and order within one year, he would be deprived of his power, and his place taken by "catholici". Since this constitution was a considerable enlargement of the third chapter of the Lateran constitutions, it appeared to have so much satisfied curialist circles that it was incorporated in the following official collection of decretals, the *Compilatio Quinta* (1226). Strangely enough, Frederick's decree did not enter the Gregorian collection—perhaps because Gregory had too great a personal distaste for the author of the decree—but this omission was made good by Boniface VIII. In the full flush of papal power Boniface decreed that in case of a pertinacious refusal by a temporal justice the latter, after the lapse of one year, "velut haereticus condemnetur".[1] One may doubt, however, whether it was necessary for Boniface to say in the preamble that he wished "to approve and observe the laws of the late Frederick, Roman Emperor."

The consideration that God's vicar had the same powers as God Himself seems to have been in Innocent IV's mind when he interpreted his own decree of deposing Frederick II. It occurs not too frequently that statesmen are so generous as to provide later generations with their own commentaries on their own decrees. Innocent's sentence was included in Boniface's *Liber Sextus*[2] where the four charges against Frederick were fully set out. Nevertheless, Innocent as a canonist, and not as a pope, hardly touched upon the actual indictment and based his sentence against the emperor on the precedent of Zacharias and Childeric. But to the canonistic genius of Innocent IV this precedent alone did not seem to carry real conviction. Thus he elaborated the theoretical foundations of his action which he declared was "de jure", because Christ whilst living on earth, was the natural master of the world. And Christ could have flung "de jure naturali" as many decrees of deposition against kings and emperors as He wished. "For the same reason"— "eadem ratione"—Christ's vicar could do this, and the objection that a pope could not possess the same powers as Christ was dismissed on the ground that it would be foolish to assume that

---

[1] *Sextus*, V.ii.18.
[2] *Sextus*, II.xiv.2. Cf. *Mon. Germ. Hist., Constit.*, vol. ii, p. 508.

Christ had instituted one vicar only, that is, St. Peter. The powers conferred upon Peter were also conferred upon his successors, the popes.¹ The juristic mind of Johannes Andreae was somewhat perturbed by the fact that Innocent's decree was issued as a consequence of the deliberations in a council. Was a council necessary, asked Johannes Andreae, to effect a deposition of an emperor? Flatly rejecting the older canonistic doctrine, such as Huguccio and the author of the *Summa Cantabrigiensis*, Johannes Andreae denied the question and observed that Innocent convoked the council, not for reasons of necessity, but for those of decency. The decree would have been just as valid, if there had been no council. Although Johannes Andreae did not refer to the glosses on the Constitutions of the First Council of Lyons, their author, Bernardus Compostellanus Junior, had answered the very same question which Johannes asked. According to this author, the reason for deposing an emperor without a council lay in the papal plenitude of power: "Etiam sine praesentia concilii sufficeret sententia solius papae contra imperatorem . . . ipse enim vocatus est in plenitudinem potestatis."² Johannes Andreae enlarged the doctrine by maintaining that the convocation of the clerics at Lyons only served to re-enforce the seriousness of the case and was an adequate means by which to instil greater fear of the decrees of the Church—"ut magis timeatur ecclesia".³

---

¹ See Innocent IV, *Com.* on II.xxvii.27 (Ad apostol.), No. 6, fol. 317: "Nota, papa deponit imperatorem, et est hoc de jure, nam cum Christus filius Dei, dum fuit in hoc saeculo et etiam ab aeterno dominus naturalis fuit, et de jure naturali in imperatores et quoscumque alios sententias depositionis ferre potuisset et damnationis et quascumque alias . . . et eadem ratione et vicarious potest hoc, nam non videretur discretus dominus fuisse, ut cum reverentia loquar, nisi unicum post se talem vicarium reliquisset, qui haec omnia posset, fuit autem iste vicarius eius Petrus, ut Matt. XVI, ultra med., et idem dicendum est de successoribus Petri, cum eadem absurditate sequeretur, si post mortem Petri humanam naturam a se creatam, sine regimine unius personae reliquisset."

² Gloss on the decree "Ad apostolicae", fol. 287 verso of LC 173. It is interesting to point out that Innocent's decree "Ad apostolicae" (by which Frederick II was deposed) served as the constitutional basis of the first deposition of a validly elected king which the Electors ever effected. By specifically referring to the decree the College of Electors deposed the successor of Rudolph of Habsburg, Adolf of Nassau, on 23 June 1298. For the political implications of the decree see A. Hessel, *Jahrbucher des Deutschen Reichs unter Albrecht I*, p. 56, and P.-J. Kessler, "Die Novellengesetzgebung Innocenz' IV" in *Zeitschrift, kan. Abt.*, vol. xxxi, p. 251, note 258.

³ Johannes Andreae in his gloss on *Sextus*, II.xiv.2.

The deposition of an emperor was merely the effluence of the superiority of the pope over the emperor, based as it was on historical, biblical and philosophical grounds. The pope was in all respects master of the world, and Johannes Andreae put the monarchical principle into a neat, plausible and yet somewhat dangerous formula when he avowed that there must be one prince in the world to whom everybody could take his complaints.[1]

The question of the vacancy of the imperial throne merits a few observations. One might have expected that the canonists saw a parallel between the functions of the college of cardinals and that of the college of electors; and one would have thought that they gave the electoral college the right to act as a collegiate head of the empire for the duration of a vacancy, just as they laid down this function for the college of cardinals. Before Clement V gave an authoritative ruling on the scope of the powers of the sacred college,[2] the college was considered to take the place of the pope: they obtained "vicem curiae" and functioned "vice capitis".[3] Not so the college of electors who were not regarded as the legitimate body to carry on the government of the empire until a new emperor was elected. In fact, I have not found one canonist to whom this possibility would have occurred. The canonists considered an imperial vacancy as a "defectum imperii", and since the empire depended for its existence on the pope, it was he alone who could remedy this defect by taking the rulership upon himself,[4] a claim that was violently repudiated by the imperialists, such as Cynus.[5] Now it is interesting to see that the decretal of Innocent III upon which this claim was based, did not go as far as the canonists made out that it went. For Innocent merely said that in the case

[1] *Id.*: "Unum enim oportet esse principatum, ad quem omnes recurrant." Cf. also *Sextus*, I.viii.2, and *Spec.*, Lib. I, pars i, De Legato, § nunc, No. 17, fol. 46.
[2] *Clem.* I.iii.2.
[3] This point of view seems to have originated with Huguccio and Laurentius, see the Archdeacon, on *Dist.* lxxix, c. 4.
[4] See Innocent IV, *Com.* on II.ii.10, No. 1, fol. 197 verso.
[5] In his lectures on the *Dig. Vet.* Cynus attacked the canonistic point of view maintaining that the empire did not depend on the pope, because it was derived directly from God. But even if it were true, as the canonists claimed, that in the case of an imperial vacancy the rulership was in the hands of the pope, the question of expense and time involved in approaching the ecclesiastical authorities should by no means be overlooked. *Com. ad Dig. Vet.*, De just. et jure, l. ex hoc jure, fol. 4 verso.

of an imperial vacancy the supreme appellate tribunal was to be the pope, because there was no other supreme jurisdictional authority.¹ But the canonists, above all Innocent IV, propounded a "succession" of the pope in the rulership of the empire.² If the vacancy was a "defect", negligence on the part of a secular judge was also a defect, the remedy of which lay in papal hands. Hence, whenever a party felt aggrieved a final appeal could be made to the pope, who acted by virtue of his plenitude of power.³

The term vacancy, however, received a somewhat liberal interpretation at the hands of John XXII whose whole pontificate may well be considered a classic example of how much canonistic political theory was put into practice. His bull of 7 April 1317 rested on the tacit assumption that the empire was still vacant. No reason was adduced for this assumption, although the election of 1314 had produced two claimants to the throne.⁴ Quite in the fashion of canonistic political theory John maintained that, owing to the vacancy of the empire, "no appeal was possible to a supreme secular judge" and that therefore he alone was in a legitimate position to exercise full jurisdictional authority in temporal matters and to take over the government of the empire.⁵ Hence anyone acting as an imperial vicar of either Lewis or Frederick tacitly and implicitly arrogated powers which were not conferred upon him. The acceptance of the position of vicar was threatened with excommunication, because this office would, under the circumstances, tend to diminish honour and law—"diminutio honoris et

---

¹ II.ii.10. See also Baethgen in *Z., Kan. Abt.*, vol. x, p. 174.
² See Hostiensis, *Summa*, II.ii.: "Vacantibus regnis et principatibus quibuscumque et ubicumque papa succeditnon solum de plenitudine potestatis, sed etiam de jure et consuetudine." See also Innocent IV loc. cit.
³ See again Innocent IV, loc. cit., No. 2, and Hostiensis, *Summa*, IV.xvii, Rubrica, No. 9, and *gl. ord.* on II.ii.10, s.v. "vacante".
⁴ It is of course true that Clement V upon the death of Henry VII had declared the empire vacant, but this vacancy was genuine and lasted until the elections of 19 and 20 October 1314. Therefore, Clement V having died six months before this event took place, cannot be said to have pronounced himself on it. The *raison d'être* of his bull was in abeyance. Nor did John refer to Clement's bull. Cf. also Raynaldus, *Annales Eccl.*, ad a, 1313, §16 and Kraus, *Dante*, p. 683.
⁵ *Bullarium Romanum*, tom. iv, pp. 234-36, at p. 235: "Cum in illo (scil. imperio) ad saecularem judicem nequeat haberi recursus, ad summum pontificem, cui in persona b. Petri terreni simul et coelestis imperii jura Deus ipse commisit, imperii praedicta jurisdictio, regimen et dispositio devolvuntur."

juris"—and would also be a source of spiritual danger. Excommunication and interdict were flung against the offenders as well as against kings, States, townships, counts, and so forth, who dared to disregard the political claims ponderously set forth in John's bull.

Naturally, similar causes of friction could be observed in the smaller political units which, by the fourteenth century, had acquired considerable power. Owing to the territorial limitations and the unavoidable local flavour, feeling was apt to run higher than in the larger political units. The "dominus mundi" was exchanged for the "dominus loci". The local bishop taking the place of the pope, tried to oust the local duke or baron, who took the place of the emperor. We can but mention one of the many problems which arose out of the fourteenth-century territorialism, which was always eager to pay particular respect to the sovereignty of the prince (or to use traditional medieval terminology: to the supreme jurisdictional authority), and this problem concerned the right of arresting criminals. Who had the right to arrest them, the ecclesiastical or secular lord? Who was supreme, the bishop acting on the basis of the canon law, or the local duke carrying out the civil law?

The maxim recognized by both the canonist and the civilian was that only the "dominus loci" had the right to imprison. He alone was empowered to arrest a suspected criminal, provided that he acted within his jurisdictional domain. Johannes Monachus said: "Nota, quod judex extra territorium suum non potest citare realiter, pro quo sciendum est, quod citatio realis est captio personae, quae non debet fieri extra territorium judicis."[1] But who was the "dominus loci"? Needless to say the canonists held that it was the bishop, the civilians said that it was the duke. Each of them considered that two could not share in the same overlordship of one and the same territory. The only concession made to the bishop was that he was entitled to arrest a criminal within the precincts of the episcopal palace, because this alone was "suum territorium". According to the civilians, then, the "dominus loci" was the duke.[2] But in

[1] Johannes Monachus in his gloss on *Sextus*, II.ii.1.

[2] He continued: "Ista ratione dicunt domini temporales huius regni, quod cum territorium sit solius principis saecularis et non episcopi vel aliorum praelatorum ecclesiasticorum, quod dominus saecularis est dominus territorii, in quo habet jurisdictionem, et quia duo non possunt esse domini eiusdem territorri soli et insolidum, ipse dominus temporalis debet nude et pure appellari dominus

order to ward off this civilian argument, the canonists referred to a decree of Boniface VIII in which he had laid down that a bishop had full jurisdictional power within the whole of his diocese.[1] This method of argument, however, did not carry much conviction with the episcopal competitors who pointed to the one-sided character of the decree: "Ipsi dicunt, quod viri ecclesiastici fecerunt illud capitulum ad suam utilitatem." The always ready objection which, by that time, must have worn somewhat thin, was the diminution of ecclesiastical rights and hence the invalidity of the secular argument. "Dic," Johannes Monachus said, "quod talia, quae specialiter statuuntur ad diminutionem ecclesiae, non tenent de jure canonico."

Although only remotely connected with the topics upon which we have touched, the following problem may be of some interest, not only from the theoretical, but also from the historical point of view. The problem concerned the question of whether a bishop who had joined battle with a secular prince and had been captured, had the right to appeal to the pope so as to secure his liberation. This case was based upon an actual event, namely, the capture of the bishop of Beauvais by the troops of the English king in 1196.[2] Thereupon the bishop protested to the pope maintaining that a bishop could not be made a prisoner, even if he fought in battle. The author of the *Quaestiones Londinenses* made this case the starting point of some interesting considerations. After referring to the return of Richard I and to the invasion of the episcopal territory by his troops, the author declared that in joining battle "multi sunt occisi, ipse enim episcopus captus et in carcerem detrusus".[3]

---

illius loci . . . ista ratione moti dicunt domini temporales, quod episcopi non possunt facere captionem extra domos episcopales, quia non possunt capere extra suum territorium."

[1] *Sextus*, I.xvi.7: "Cum episcopus in sua tota diocesi jurisdictionem ordinariam noscatur habere, dubium non existit. . . ."

[2] See Matthew Paris, *Historia Anglorum*, vol. ii, pp. 59-60, idem, *Chronica Majora*, vol. ii, pp. 421-22, Hoveden, *Chronica*, vol. iv, p. 16, and Roger of Wendover, *Flores Historiarum*, vol. i, pp. 245-46.

[3] BM Royal 9 E VII, fol. 195. The narration as given in this MS. does not quite agree with that given by the chroniclers enumerated in the preceding note. The MS. states: "Rege postmodum reverso Brebantones terram ipsius episcopi invaserunt." In fact, it was John who led the attack. Only Matthew Paris, *Chron. Maj.*, vol. ii, p. 421, says that "jubente rege" John attacked whilst the other chroniclers (and Matthew Paris himself in *Hist. Angl.*, loc. cit) give the impression that John on his own account invaded episcopal territory.

The question was as to whether the bishop was entitled to appeal to the pope for his release: "petit a papa liberationem. quaeritur, an possit?" The answer seemed at first in the affirmative, for nothing wrong could be seen in taking up arms and in waging a war, even if this was done on an episcopal level,[1] for a bishop too was entitled to defend his territory against invaders. Moreover, this bishop acted in a twofold capacity, that is, as an ecclesiastic and as a warrior. The pope himself knew that armed bishops were fighting in the ranks of the army.[2] Lastly, a bishop could not be made a slave as a consequence of his being taken prisoner, because "episcopalis dignitas servitutem removet".

Nevertheles, the author of the *Quaestiones Londinenses* who, to judge by the siglum, was a certain "Nicholas", impugned the validity of the foregoing arguments and arrived at the conclusion that the bishop of Beauvais had no right of appeal to the pope. Firstly, since the king as a crusader enjoyed the special protection of the Holy See[3] he had a right to take action against those who had impeded him in the performance of his crusading task.[4] A bishop who offered himself to the vicissitudes of a battle, must take the risks involved and if captured could be enslaved.[5] His episcopal dignity was to be no protection against this ill-fortune, because he brought it upon himself.[6] On the contrary, the bishop ought to be unfrocked, because he was instrumental in causing the deaths of many people[7] and because the "qualitas personae" merely made his crime worse.[8] Above all, the bishop had resorted to secular arms, and consequently appeared to have renounced

[1] "Quod possit sic: iste episcopus militavit et militia in se mala non est," fol. 195.

[2] "Item summus pontifex scit ita episcopos in exercitu armari (MS.: amari)", fol. 195 verso.

[3] "Rex qui expugnavit saracenos protectionem habuit sedes Romanae, ut in concilio lateranensi."

[4] It was maintained (fol. 195, see also Hoveden, *Chronica* vol. iii, p. 344, and Walter of Coventry, *Memoriale*, vol. i, p. 357) that the Bishop of Beauvais had injured the interests of Richard I. Here again the dates and aims of the bishop's action differ in the accounts and in the MS.

[5] "Episcopus si captus capientis servus est effectus."

[6] "Eo non obstante quod est episcopus, et hoc propter suum delictum . . . ipse culpa sua in casum hunc ingessit et ideo excusari non debet."

[7] "Degradari debet, quia eius auxilio homicidia erant perpetrata."

[8] "Maxime, cum qualitas personae peccatum aggravare debeat."

the protection afforded by the weapons and privileges of the Church.¹ "He who breaks the law cannot afterwards claim the protection of the law"—in this sense the author of the London *Quaestiones* concluded.² It is however doubtful whether this verdict of the unknown English canonist would have commanded general acceptance. Reading through the case and its treatment one cannot help having the impression that Nicholas's judgment was somewhat coloured by the intrusion of the spirit prevailing at the time.

Many more instances could be cited to show the practical application of the canonistic principle of papal plenitude of power. They all centred in the idea that the emperor was a mere "advocatus" or "servus" of the Church, and the papal plenitude of power enabled the pope to conduct himself as a true master. Of particularly great contemporary interest were the cases of the appointment of notaries and the already mentioned legitimation of illegitimate children. The problem was as to whether notaries appointed by the pope in papal territories were allowed to function outside these territories and whether their documents had validity everywhere. As we might expect, the civilians were fiercely antagonistic to this canonistic claim. And the legitimation of children presented a problem that was not unlike that of the notaries. Relying upon the papal plenitude of power in temporal and spiritual matters, the great majority of the canonists claimed that a papal legitimation of an illegitimate child held good everywhere, whilst the one effected by imperial decree was alleged to be valid only within imperial territory. A second problem of a similar nature was as to whether these children made legitimate by papal ordinance were also to be deemed legitimate for temporal purposes. We have referred to this aspect of the question in a different context. These are indeed questions which cannot arouse a great deal of interest to-day, but they were of greatest importance in the feudal society of the thirteenth and fourteenth centuries, especially in regard to inheritance and other rights solely reserved for children, born in lawful wedlock. The term "lawful wedlock" was not as clear and precise as one might have expected. Surely, to be debarred from inheriting an estate because of one's bastardy made this legitimation of illegitimate

---

[1] "Arma habuit saecularia: unde armis et eius privilegiis videtur renuntiasse."
[2] "Unde cum in leges commisit, frustram legis invocat auxilium," fol. 195 verso.

children an issue of profound political significance in a feudal age. The problem of the conflict of laws was one more that was intimately connected with the canonistic claim to papal plenitude of power. What effects did the canon law display in regard to temporal affairs? What was its authority in imperial lands? What was the secular judge's decision to be, if canon and civil laws flatly contradicted each other? All this may seem very remote to us, but when we realize the great importance that was attached to a statement of one party that the secular magistrate had acted maliciously or negligently and that by this very contention the jurisdiction of the ecclesiastical tribunal became operative—we can then perhaps better measure the portentous political significance of all these problems.

In conclusion we must deal briefly with the function which the canonists assigned to the emperor. The metaphorical appellation of the emperor as the servant and advocate of the pope has in itself little value, but it must nevertheless be classified as a political strategem which allows us a deeper insight into the mentality of the canonists. For the elucidation of the emperor's function we must go back to the general philosophical principles upon which the canonistic political principles were erected. We may recall the differences in dignity and worth which the canonists attributed to the spiritual and temporal. Temporal matters, they declared, had only relative value, whilst the spiritual affairs had an absolute value. The temporal was to be a mere servant of the spiritual. It was the spiritual power who directed and guided the temporalities of life to the end recognized as true and fitting for man. The function of the emperor, then, was merely a specific application of this general principle. He was to be directed and guided by the pope and became his servant.[1] But how, we must ask, was this purely speculative

[1] It was in this context that the allegory of sun and moon was employed, the sun symbolizing the pope's power, the moon the emperor's. But this is so well known that there is no need to dwell on it here. It should perhaps be mentioned that the first mathematical computations about the relative sizes of the sun and of the moon were made by Laurentius in his gloss on c. solitae, De majoritate et obedientia, in *Comp. III*, s.v. "inter lunam", fol. 126 verso of D 4, and fol. 115 of LC 29. Hostiensis then made his now famous calculation about which Johannes Andreae mocked in the following words: "Quod ratione non capio, astrologis relinquo." The *Glossa Palatina*, on *Dist.* xcvi, c. 10, s.v. "fulgorem", fol. 36 verso of D 8, contains only a bare statement with a reference to c. solitae: "Et quanta est differentia inter solem et lunam, tanta est differentia inter imperium et sacerdotium."

idea reflected in canonistic political thought? In what shape did the philosophical idea appear in the canonistic system, so as to fit it into the pattern of the relations between Church and State? What, in other words, was the political terminology which supplanted the speculative terms?

The question throws us back once again to the English canonist Alanus. He it was, it will be recalled, who laid the foundations for the later universally accepted doctrine of Church and State. Alanus maintained that the pope's plenitude of power comprised both the spiritual and temporal spheres. But he drew an all-important distinction. Within the compass of the spiritual the pope possessed plenitude of power and exercised it; within the scope of the temporal the pope also possessed plenitude of power, but did not exercise it. In the typically scholastic language of the Middle Ages, Alanus distinguished between powers held "in habitu" and those held "in actu". The pope had spiritual plenitude of power "in habitu" and "in actu", whilst temporal plenitude of power he had only "in habitu". It was the emperor who exercised temporal jurisdiction "in actu". Christ, too, had spiritual and temporal plenitude of power, but the exercise of temporal power was denied to St. Peter (according to Alanus), since Christ said to him: "Put up thy sword into the sheath."[1] Whether or not influenced by Alanus, the *Glossa Palatina* held a point of view very similar to that of the English canonist. According to its compiler, the pope had "nuda potestas" but he did not exercise it, especially in matters affecting blood.[2] But the power of the secular authority to exercise these judgments was clearly derived from the pope.[3] One of the statements in the *Glossa*

---

[1] John xviii.11.

[2] This was apparently the meaning of the cryptic (and otherwise contradictory) passage of Huguccio in which he also distinguished between the "jus executionis" (which rested with the pope) and the "actus exequendi" (which was not in papal hands). He also envisaged the possibility of the handing over of the "sword of blood" to the emperor: "Ecclesia potest concedere gladium sanguinis, licet per illum agitare non debeat, sed saepe per alios possumus, quod non per nos ... sed credo, quod papa et potestatem talem habeat et executionem, id est, jus executionis, scil. non actum exequendi, per singulas provincias, ergo et in hyspania et in anglia, etc., et est argumentum, quod omnes reges debeant subesse imperatori Romani, ut VII, q. I in apibus," *Summa* on *Dist.* lxiii, c. 22, fol. 121 of LC 2. I had no opportunity of comparing this passage with another Huguccio MS. On Richard's view see App. H.

[3] "Argumentum ecclesiam posse concedere ... et dicendum, quod papa

Palatina said: "Uterque gladius petro fuit concessus, non autem utriusque executio."¹ In somewhat graphic—and drastic—terms the same source declared that the pope after handing over the temporal sword, could say to the emperor: "Go, kill and punish the wrong-doers."² The canonists, however, associated this doctrine with the name of Alanus and maintained that "the Church had committed the exercise of temporal power to emperors and kings",³ because otherwise the ecclesiastical status would be most gravely perturbed, as Alanus thought: "Et praeterea ecclesia ex hoc plurimum turbaretur."⁴ And the ceremony of the emperor's coronation was merely the outward, visible act by which this so-called "temporal commission" was effected. In other words, the emperor had no temporal power before he was crowned—this was the opinion of all thirteenth and fourteenth-century canonists.⁵ It was through the coronation and the preceding examination of the person of the candidate that he received the temporal sword and herewith the per-

---

nudam habet potestatem et non eius executionem, et eam nudam concedit, sed ea concessa alicui statim ei conceditur executio, quae ex ea pendit," on *Dist.* lxiii, c. 23, fol. 25 verso of D 8. The inconsistency and vacillation of the *Glossa Palatina* is noteworthy. In the gloss on *Dist.* x, c. 9, fol. 3 verso, the glossator first says: "Liquet omnem principem regnorum a judice ecclesiae confirmationem et executionem consequi", and after quoting the usual "contra" arguments, states: "Ego non credo unam ex alia pendere", and enumerates the "contra" arguments, especially the decretal "Per venerabilem". But in *Dist.* x, c. 4, fol. 3 verso, we find this statement: "§. immo nec papa posset leges tollere nisi quoad forum (suum), imperium enim et sacerdotium ex eodem principio prodierunt, auth. quomod. oport. episcopos," whilst in *Dist.* lxiii, c. 23, fol. 25 verso this statement is contained: "Dominus papa habet maximam potestatem in imperio."

¹ *Glossa Palatina* on *Dist.* xxii, c. 1, s.v. "coelestis", fol. 8 of D 8. The *Summa Cantabrigiensis* also had in mind this distinction, see *Dist.* lxiii, c. 30, fol. 24 of T 0.5.17, s.v. "concedo": "Ergo patet, quod papa habet jus gladii, sed non executionem."

² On C. XV, q. vi, c. 2, fol. 91 of D 8: "... argumentum quod dominus papa cum tradit potestatem gladii principi dicere posset, 'vade, interficias et punias sceleratos'."

³ See the gloss of Bernardus Parmensis on II.i.13: "Potestatem suis successoribus transmisit, XL dis. c. 1, verum executionem gladii temporalis imperatoribus et regibus commisit ecclesia et tamen jurisdictionem causarum civilium aliquando per sacerdotes exercuit". See also *Decretum*, C. XII, q. ii, c. 27.

⁴ Alanus in *Comp. I*, De Appellat., c. si duobus.

⁵ And also of curialist historians, such as Ptolomy of Lucca. Speaking of the election of Lothar III the annalist says: "Quae quidem electio non statim dat jus imperii, nisi prius acceptetur per papam et ab ipso coronam suscipiat," *Mon. Germ. Hist., Scriptores*, n.s., vol. viii, "Die Annalen des Tholomeus von Lucca",

mission by the pope to exercise in practice—hence "in actu"—temporal powers. Therefore, the election of the "King of the Romans" by the college of electors did not confer any powers on the elected individual. The election was considered to be merely the proposal of the seven princes to the pope to approve of their choice.[1] The concrete divergence between imperialists and canonists emerged especially strongly in this particular topic, for the imperialists and earlier canonists declared that the elected became Ruler of the Holy Roman Empire as a result of the election, whilst the majority of the canonists made him Ruler only after he had been approved and crowned by the pope. The imperialists, not unlike Huguccio and those following him, saw in the coronation merely a formal ceremony, which changed the title of "King of the Romans" into that of an Emperor, whilst the canonists attributed genuinely constitutive effects to the coronation. The point of view of either was understandable: the imperialists (and the generation of canonists before Alanus) held that the emperor derived his powers without intermediary directly from God, the canonists avowed that the emperor's powers were based on papal mastership of the world.

My aim in this survey has been to present the basic trends of the political theories of the medieval canonists. The ground has sometimes been stony and mountainous, sometimes ascending in steep gradients to heights and dimensions of desired papal power which our age shrinks from clearly visualizing. I do not say this in any partisan spirit nor do I wish to decide upon the rightness or wrongness of this issue which was easily the most profoundest of the whole Middle Ages. However much we may dissociate ourselves from canonistic political tho6ght, we are not called upon to proclaim judgment upon it. For about the ideological undercurrents and crosscurrents continually bursting forth and shaking the somewhat flimsy structure of medieval Europe we know as yet far too little to sit in judgment. As the late occupant of the Cambridge medieval chair so truthfully said in his Birkbeck lectures, "it seems far more important

---

ed. Schmeidler, p. 43. On Ptolomy's views on the function of an imperial coronation, cf. *Determinatio Compendiosa de Jurisdictione Imperii*, ed. M. Krammer, in *Fontes Juris Germanici*, pp. XIX, XXVIII, 17, 61 f.

[1] This was not the opinion of the earlier generation of canonists, see *supra*, p. 143 f.

to understand than to judge". What we can and should do is to throw open the gateways to the medieval mental laboratories, so as to be able to explain and understand that period in its richness. One such gateway the canonists alone are able to unlock for us. Their vocation and life task it was to build the foundations upon which the imposing papalist edifice was to be erected. The political theories of the canonists constituted an integral part of the medieval European thought and contributed in a large measure to the formation of the Western mind. Has the Western political mind really discarded its ideological ancestor? Centuries and cataclysmic events may separate us from those days, but they are merely the yesterday in the realm of the development of ideas.

APPENDIX

A. NOTE ON THE *Glossa Palatina*: DURHAM C III 8.

I. It appears that there exists only one complete MS. of this very important compilation of glosses, that is, the one listed by Kuttner, *Repertorium*, p. 81 (Vatican, Pal. lat. 658). For C III 8 is certainly not complete, despite Kuttner's assurance, p. 81. Large portions are missing:

(i) from C XXI, q. iii, c. 3, s.v. "inhonestos" to C. XXIV, q. i, c. 33, fols. 104 verso—105; on bottom of fol. 104 verso in later hand: "hic deest magna pars. . . ." rest illegible.

(ii) from C. XXVI, q. vii, c. ult. to De poenitentia, dist, i, c. 21, fols. 109 verso—110; note in left hand corner of fol. 109 verso in fifteenth century hand: "Desunt glossae VIII causarum usque materiam de poenitentia."

(iii) from De consecratione, dist. iv, c. 12 to De consecratione, dist. v, c. 2 on fol. 131; marginal note on fol. 131b: "Ab hoc capitulo Non rat., quod est capitulum XI, IV dist. deficit usque ad secundum capitulum quintae dist."

II. The *Glossa Palatina* in Trinity College, o.10.2, is misbound, see fol. 92, and has also omissions in the text itself, e.g. from De consecratione, dist. ii, c. 12 to c. 45.

III. There are some variants in reading between Kuttner's *Glossa Palatina*, i.e. Vat. Pal. Lat. 658, and C. III 8, so, for instance,

(i) The quotation of Kuttner in *Zeitschr., Kanon. Abt.*, vol. xxi, p. 173 note 2, C. IX, q. i, c. 6, does not agree with D 8 on that passage: *Comp. IV* is not quoted here, but simply: "extra de sent. et rejud., ad probandum," fol. 71 verso.

(ii) There is no quotation of Aristotle, etc. (*Traditio*, vol. i, p. 291, note 68), in C. III 8 on De poenitentia, *Dist.* ii, post cap. 14, and nothing indicates that the gloss was written by Alanus. The same holds true of De poenitentia, *Dist.* V, c. 4: in C. III 8 the gloss is signed "l"; cf. note 74, Kuttner, art. cit., p. 291.

(iii) The authorship of Jacobus de Albenga (art. cit., loc. cit., note 69), is not shown in C. III 8, on C. IV, q. i, c. 18, fol. 65 verso: "jo et az dicunt, quod si sacramentum habet . . . sed videtur esse magis canonica opinio."

(iv) The siglum "b" does not occur in C. III 8 on C. II, q. vi, c. 21: the gloss is unsigned.

(v) The quotation in Kuttner's article in *Zeitschr.*, *kan. Abt.*, vol. xxi, p. 171 (bottom) does not agree with C. III 8, on *Dist.* lxiv, c. 1, fol. 26 verso: "Nihil refert an praesentes consensum exprimant et est argumentum. . . ." This would tally with the *gl. ord.* of Johannes Teutonicus, as transcribed by Kuttner, art. cit., loc. cit.

B. NOTE ON THE *Quaestiones Londinenses*: BRIT. MUS., ROYAL 9 E VII, FOL. 191—FOL. 198 VERSO. INC.: "HOSPITALARIIS INDULSIT PAPA HUIUSMODI PRIVILEGIUM." EXPL.: "VISUS EST PRODUCTIONEM TESTIUM."

I. These *Quaestiones* contain a great number of practical cases. English authorship is certain: the case mentioned in the text (pp. 191 ff). the tone and tenor of its treatment and solution the reference to the appointment of the archbishop of Canterbury as papal legate (obviously Hubert Walter, fol. 197 verso), the reference to the incident in Gisors (fol. 195 verso), the numerous practical problems connected with the impetration of writs (papal and royal), the reference to the appointment of the Bishop of Lincoln as a judge delegate in a specific case (fol. 196 verso)—all these leave no room for doubt that the work belonged to English canonistic scholarship. Moreover, the treatment of the cases and their solution is reminiscent of disputations in a school, not unlike a seminar. The fact that this MS. once belonged to the Benedictine abbey of St. Augustine in Canterbury (see Catalogue, and Neil Ker, *Medieval Libraries of Great Britain*, p. 28) should also be borne in mind.

II. So far no clue could be found as to the author. A number of solutions bear the siglum "nich" or "nichol" (fol. 195 verso, 196); frequent reference is made to a Magister Simon (fol. 191 verso, 197 verso, "in libro mag. symonis": fol. 195), to the solutions propounded by "jo. de chent." (fol. 196), the "decisio j. c. t." or to the "solutio jo. d. t." (fol. 195), or the "decisio jo. de. ce." (*ibid.*) and the "solutio magistri N." (fol. 197 verso, 193 verso); in two cases I could find the siglum "a" (fol. 192 verso, 193).

III. The time of its composition most likely falls between

1196 and 1199. The *terminus a quo* is fixed by the incident of the bishop of Beauvais's capture, which occurred in 1196. The *terminus ad quem* is fixed by the reference to Richard I as the "rex Angliae" which would not have been the case, if the work had been written in John's reign; moreover, decretals of Alexander III and Clement III are quoted, and it is reasonable to presume that Innocent III would have been mentioned, had the composition been made during his pontificate.

C. NOTE ON THE *Novellae* OF INNOCENT IV AND THE *Apparatus* OF BERNARDUS COMPOSTELLANUS JUNIOR: LINCOLN 173.

The Innocentian *Novellae* are of great importance for the history of the sources of the *Liber Sextus*: and the glosses written on them are of equal importance for the history of canonistic literature. A complete analysis of this hitherto unnoticed MS. cannot be undertaken within the framework of an appendix, but a few essential points should be made.

I. Innocent IV published three collections of (mainly his own) Constitutions and decretals.[1] The first collection was published on 25 August 1245 and introduced by the bull "Cum nuper"; it contained twenty-two chapters.[2] The second collection containing eleven chapters was published eight months later, on 21 April 1246, and introduced by the bull "Cum inter". The third collection, introduced by "Ad explicandos nodos", was promulgated on 9 September 1253, but, unlike its two predecessors, this collection did not contain the decretals themselves, but only a list of the "incipits" of decretals which were eventually to be incorporated in the *Corpus*: this list contained the chapters of *Collectio I*, *Collectio II* and eight other decretals, hence forty-one chapters.

[1] Cf. Schulte, "Die Decretalen zwischen den Decretales Gregorii IX und dem Liber Sextus Bonifacii VIII" in *SB d. kais. Akad.*, vol. lv, (1867), pp. 701 ff.: *id.*, ibid., vol. lxviii (1871), pp. 55 ff.; E. Fournier, "L'accueil fait par la France du xiii siècle aux décrétales pontificales" in *Acta Congressus Juridici Internationalis, 1934*, Rome, 1936, pp. 247 ff.; *id.*, *Questions d'Histoire du Droit Canonique*, Paris, 1936; S. Kuttner, "Decretalistica" in *Zeitschrift, kan. Abt.*, vol. xxvi, pp. 436 ff.; *id.*, "Die Konstitutionen des ersten Allgemeinen Konzils von Lyon" in *Studia et Documenta Historiae et Juris*, vol. vi (1940), p. 71 ff.; P.-J. Kessler, "Die Novellengesetzgebung Innozenz' IV" in *Zeitschrift, kan. Abt.*, vol. xxxi (1942), pp. 142-320, vol. xxxii (1943), pp. 300-83; vol. xxxiii (1944), pp. 56-128.

[2] The first really satisfactory computation was made by Kuttner, "Decretalistica", pp. 440-41.

Few MSS. containing the *Coll. I* and *Coll. II* separately are extant.[1] But a fairly great number of MSS. containing the combined *Coll. I* and *II* is known. The collection of thirty-three chapters (*Coll. I*: 22 plus *Coll. II*: 11) was, however, soon enlarged by private collections in which a considerable number of varying *extravagantes* was inserted.[2] These *extravagantes decretales*, therefore, were not part of the official collections, and some of the *extravagantes* were incorporated in the third collection (1253), but before this date they did not belong to the two official collections. Several stages can be distinguished.[3]

LC 173 belongs to the later stages of the enlarged *Coll. I + II*: it contains a number of *extravagantes* which were not later incorporated in *Coll. III*, but, on the other hand, it does not contain four chapters which formed part of *Coll. III*, namely, "Grandi non immerito", "Dilecto filio decano", "Ad apostolicae", and "Abbate sane". These four chapters appear as an appendix to the main body. The *Apparatus* and the text itself do not always show that they were written contemporaneously: the hand of the glosses changes on fol. 281 va, and it seems that this is a later hand than the preceding (gloss) hand; the ink used by this second hand is different too, it is a pale-brown ink. The first gloss hand reappears fol. 284 va, but both text and gloss hand change in the appendix (fol. 286 verso onwards): they appear to be written by the same hand which is identical to that of the gloss from fol. 281 verso—283 rb.

Whether or not this enlarged *Coll. I + II* is of English origin must await closer investigation. Nevertheless, there is an indication that it is of English origin, because the chapter "Attendentes" does not appear in any of the known MSS.[4] containing the enlarged *Coll. I + II*. This chapter contains the letter of Innocent IV to the bishops of the Canterbury diocese concerning the exemption of parish churches from procurations: its date is tentatively given by Potthast (No. 14628) as 8 June 1252.[5] The incorporation of this letter would

---

[1] See Kuttner, art. cit., pp. 443-44, and Kessler, vol. xxxi, pp. 235-38, 239-42.
[2] A very helpful survey is given by Kuttner, pp. 451-52.
[3] These stages were well analyzed by Kessler, loc. cit., pp. 253-75.
[4] They are listed and examined by Kessler, loc. cit. A collation of Durham C II 2 set v, C I 9 set ii, Brit. Mus. Royal 9 F II and 11 B V would perhaps show some affinity with LC 173.
[5] This letter is printed in Matthew Paris, *Chron. Maj.*, vol. vi (Addidamenta), pp. 228-29, and in the *Annales Monastici*, vol. i, pp. 302-3. Luard gives the date

not only indicate the English provenance of this collection, but would also enable us to fix a term within which it must have been made, always provided that the date 1252 is correct. This collection would have been made not before 1252 and not later than 1253, the year in which the *Coll. III* was published, since the four above-mentioned chapters were not yet included in this Lincoln codex. None of the three bulls of promulgation is reproduced here. Rather curiously the bull "Cum nuper" is written in the margin, as if part of the *Apparatus* of Bernardus Compostellanus Junior, but it has here no preamble.[1]

The following table shows the distribution of chapters as they appear in our codex, in the last official collection (*Coll. III,*) and finally in the *Liber Sextus*. A "G" denotes that the particular chapter was glossed; a "b" after the "G" denotes that the gloss was signed by Bernardus.

	LC 173		Coll. III	Sextus
De rescriptis				
Cum in multis	1	Gb	1	I.iii.2
Praesenti decreto	2	Gb	2	—
Dispendia	3	Gb	3	I.iii.3
De electione				
Statuimus ut si quis	4	Gb	4	I.vi.1
In electionibus	5	Gb	5	I.vi.2
De supplenda neglig. praelati				
Romana eccl. & infra :edictum	6	Gb	6	I.viii.1
De officio vicarii				
Romana eccl. & infra: cum archiepisc.	7	G	8	I.xiii.1
De officio et potestate jud. del.				
Statuimus ut conservatores	8	G	9	I.xiv.1
De officio legati				
Officii nostri	9	Gb	10	I.xv.1
De officio ordinarii				
Rom. eccl. & infra: prohibemus	10	Gb	11	I.xvi.1

1252 in both places. A collation of the printed texts with our MS. shows some slight, but inessential variations.

[1] The text of this bull is printed in Denifle, *Chartularium Universitatis Parisiensis*, vol. i, p. 188, No. 153.

	LC 173	Coll. III	Sextus
De judiciis			
Juris (MS.: Jure) esse	11	Gb 12	II.i.1
De foro compet.			
Rom. eccl. & infra: Ne(c) in appellat.	12	Gb 13	II.ii.1
De litis contestatione			
Exceptionis peremptorie	13	G 14	II.iii.1
De restitutione spoliatorum			
Frequens	14	G 15	II.v.1
De dolo & contumacia			
Actor qui	15	G 16	II.vi.1
De eo qui mittitur			
Eum qui	16	Gb 17	II.vii.1
De confessis			
Statuimus ut positiones	17	Gb 18	II.ix.1
De testibus			
Ad haec … praesentium	18	Gb 20	II.x.2
Rom. eccl. & infra: in app. causa	19	Gb 19	II.x.3
De exceptionibus			
Pia consideratione	20	Gb 21	II.xii.1
De sententia			
Cum eterni tribunal	21	Gb 22	II.xiv.1
De appellationibus			
Cordi nobis	22	G 25	II.xv.1
Legitima	23	Gb 26	II.xv.2
Rom. eccl. & infra: cum suffragan.	24	Gb 27	II.xv.3
De censibus			
Rom. eccl. & infra: statuimus ut quilib.	25	— 30	III.xx.1
Attendentes quod provincia Cant.	26	— —	—
Ad memoriam et observat. perpet.	27	— —	—
De concessione praebendae			
Quia cunctis	28	Gb 28	III.vii.1
De rebus ecclesiae			
Dudum	29	Gb 29	III.ix.1

	LC 173	Coll. III		Sextus
Significasti nobis	30	—	—	—
Gravem nobis	31	—	—	—
Non solum	32	—	—	III.xiv.2
Nullum eorum	33	—	—	—
De homicidio				
Pro humani	34	—	31	V.iv.1
De privilegiis				
Volentes	35	Gb	32	V.vii.1
De poenis				
Rom. eccl. & infra: Licet autem	36	Gb	33	V.ix.1
Rom. eccl. & infra: Quaestoribus	37	Gb	34	V.x.1
De sententia excommunicationis				
Cum medicinalis	38	Gb	35	V.xi.1
Solet	39	G	36	V.xi.2
Statuimus ut nullus	40	Gb	37	V.xi.3
Quia periculosum	41	Gb	38	V.xi.4
Rom. eccl. & infra: ceterum	42	G	39	V.xi.5
De verb. signif.				
Veniens	43	—	41	V.xii.1
Perlectis literis	44	—	—	—
Appendix (without title headings)				
Grandi	(45)	Gb	7	I.viii.2
Dilecto	(46)	G	40	V.xi.6
Ad apostolicae	(47)	Gb	23	II.xiv.2
Abbate (fol. 288)	(48)	G	24	II.xiv.3

II. The *Apparatus* of Bernardus Compostellanus Junior.[1]

(1) The chapter "Pro humani" (fol. 283 va) shows only a fragmentary gloss without siglum; it is the only gloss in this margin and finishes: "... quod supplicio corporali aut." The

---

[1] Whether the *Casus "Papa existens"* are also the work of the Compostellan further investigation alone can show. For a discussion see Kuttner, "Decretalistica", loc. cit., pp. 465-66, and Kessler, vol. xxxiii (1944), pp. 99-101. A thorough examination of Durham C II 2 set ii may throw further light on the possible authorship. Inc.: "Papa existente in concilio lugdunensi didicit ex relatione multorum...." (quoted from Th. Rud, *Codicum MSS. Ecclesiae Dunelmensis Catalogus Classicus*, 1825, p. 267).

full gloss is given by Kessler, art. cit., vol. xxxii (1943), p. 349.

(2) The absence of a reference to Alexander IV's decretal "Quia pro qualitate" (of 18 August 1255) in the gloss on the chapter "Quia cunctis", s.v. "excommunicari non potest" indicates that the Spaniard wrote this *Apparatus* before 1255. The assumption of an early redaction of this *Apparatus* is furthermore supported by the following observations.

(*a*) The gloss in the later redactions of the *Apparatus* on c. "Statuimus ut si", s.v. "personam" makes use of some considerations of Innocent IV himself (see Kessler, loc. cit., p. 335), but the gloss in LC 173 does not contain the Innocentian addition, and ends with: "De consuetudine, c. Cum dilecti." The early redaction of our *Apparatus* is also shown by

(*b*) the gloss on c. "Praesentium" which finishes: "... quod fuit verus dominus. *Sufficeret:* ...." The later redaction, as shown by Kessler, p. 331, has a substantial addition before v. "sufficeret".

(3) In view of the early redaction of this *Apparatus*, Bernard's method of references and counter-references remains puzzling. Kessler pp. 320 ff. maintains that the later redactions of this *Apparatus* changed the reference "extra" (i.e. to the *Gregoriana*) of the early redaction into a "supra" or "infra" according to whether the reference applied to a title before or after the one in which the *Apparatus*-reference occurs (p. 324). Now, our *Apparatus*, though belonging to the early redaction, has not "extra", but, like the later redactions, "supra" and "infra". So, for instance,

> Gloss on c. "Cum in multis", s.v. "quatuor" in fine: "infra de off. del., super eo, arg. et infra tit. prox., c. 1."
> (Cf. the passage in Kessler, p. 326.)

The same applies to

> Gloss on c. "Romana ecclesia, et infra: Cum archiepiscopus," s.v. "rationabili causa": "Infra de jud., et si clerici, cum suis concordantiis, et infra c. 1 i. fi." The word "Romana" is here interpolated after c. 1.

(4) The gloss in at least one place is entirely at variance with the established reading. Instead of the gloss as given by

Kessler, p. 331, we read here: fol. 278 ra, gloss on c. "Eum qui", s.v. "vitiosus" (the identical words are italicized):

"Et ita si mitteretur in possessionem causa rei servandae petiit(?) beneficii(?) *sine canonica institutione*, haberet malam fidem, et ita non prescriberet, etiamsi post annum non recuperaret reus possessionem."

D. NOTE ON THE CONSTITUTIONS OF THE SECOND COUNCIL OF LYONS (1274) AND THE *Apparatus* OF GUILELMUS DURANTIS: LINCOLN 173.

(1) The *Apparatus* begins fol. 290 verso: inc.: "Gregorius iste priusquam papa fieret, vocabatur Theobaldus." The text begins fol. 291, and ends fol. 301 verso: "explicit textus constitutionum Gregorii X." The *Apparatus* ends fol. 302 verso: expl.: "sed videtur quod non sit privandus sepultura...."

(2) As there is not one siglum throughout the *Apparatus*, and as Durantis as well as Garsias wrote a commentary on these Constitutions, the ascription may not be without its pitfalls, especially as the scribe in one place made the author say: "De hoc dixi in speculo ecclesiae, eod. tit." (on cap. Fideli, s.v. "ignorantia", fol. 290 verso). But a comparison of this *Apparatus* with the gloss of Johannes Andreae on the *Sextus* shows that this *Apparatus* was the work of Guilelmus Durantis.

Sextus I.vi.4

Apparatus Conc. II Lugd. s.v. "auctenticis", fol. 293.

Debet enim tangere librum dicens juro secundum haec sacra Dei evangelia per me corporaliter tacta, etc., nisi forte jurans fuerit episcopus, qui tangere non debet, ut XI q. I nec honore, C. de episc. et cler., auten. sed judex.

Johannes Andreae s.v. "corporali".

Per hoc dicas secundum Guil. et Gar. quod si juret praesente textu evangeliorum et non tangat quod huic constitutioni satisfactum non est ... quid si sit episcopus qui appelletur, quaero an teneatur tangere sacra, dixit Gar. quod sic, quia generaliter loquitur haec decretalis ... Guil. contradicens quod episcopus tangere non

> tenetur, XI q. I nec honore,
> C. De episc. et cler., authent.
> sed judex . . . et hoc credo
> verius, idem jo mo et archi.

Any remaining doubt about the authorship is removed by the dictum, *ibid.*, fol. 293, s.v. "praestito" where the author, after referring to Innocent V and John XXI, says: "Et dixi in speculo judiciali in titulo De exceptionibus, § viso."

E. NOTE ON THE *Summa Cantabrigiensis*: TRINITY COLLEGE, O.5.17.

This work seems to be largely based upon the *Apparatus* "*Ecce vicit leo*" (discovered by Kuttner, *Repertorium*, p. 59). I do not think that there is any identity between these two, mainly because of the many variants. The *Apparatus* in LC 137 contains the original work, as a comparison between it and the St. Florian MS. clearly shows. All that can safely be said is that the *Summa Cantabrigiensis* has a close affinity to the *Apparatus*. I am inclined to attribute this *Summa* to an English school, and the fact that this MS. originally belonged to the Augustinian priory at Bradenstoke, Wiltshire (Neil Ker, *Medieval Libraries of Great Britain*, p. 7) should be borne in mind in this connexion.

F. NOTE ON THE *Apparatus* ON *Compilatio Prima* IN LAMBETH PALACE MS. 105.

This very interesting gloss composition would warrant close study. It is difficult to say to what extent this *Apparatus* is based upon Bernardus Papiensis's material and to what extent upon that of Richard de Lacy: both figure prominently in it. It is obvious that this *Apparatus* consists of several layers of glosses. One might be inclined to see in Bernard's glosses the groundwork of the *Apparatus*, because the prologue "Libellus iste...." bears his usual siglum, as also does the very first gloss on fol. 137 and numerous other glosses. In some glosses of the evidently first layer of glosses we also find "b. dicit . . .", cf., for instance, II.i.c. de adult., s.v. "deserviunt", fol. 154, etc. But against this must be set the fact that the first layer of glosses also contains a great number of Richard's glosses, although not all signed. For a number of glosses Richard's authorship can be confirmed by collation, so for instance, for the gloss on *Comp. I*, De jurejur., c. si vero, s.v. "aliquis", fol. 161: "Hic plerique erraverunt et ab utroque locuti sunt falsa. . . ." Now, in a gloss of Vincentius on the same passage (in MS. Lips. 983, fol. 17, with which passage Professor Kuttner very kindly supplied me) we read: "Hoc capitulum fortiter impugnat opinionem baziani . . . vel responde secundum Ri. in glossa ibi posita, quae incipit 'Hic plerique erraverunt a vero et ab utro locuti sunt falsa dicentes. . . .'"

A noteworthy feature of this *Apparatus* is the frequent reference to legists, such as Johannes Bassianus and Martinus and to a master "p". The first layer of glosses was written under the pontificate of Innocent III, cf. the gloss on V. De sententia excomm., c. Parochianos, s.v. "evitari", fol. 212 verso: "Innocentius cotidie admonet. . . ." This layer was strongly influenced by Huguccio, as the frequent references testify, cf. fols. 191, 203 verso, 205 verso, 207 verso, 211, 213 verso, etc.; these glosses also contain a number of original glosses by Bernardus Papiensis himself. References to a Master g°, ham, are not infrequent in this stratum.

The outstanding feature of the indubitably second layer of glosses is the very frequent reference to Master p. B. who also appears as p. B^i. Master Bernardus (Compostellanus Antiquus?) is not infrequently juxtaposed to Master p. B., cf. fol. 205 verso, gloss on V. De cler. pugn, in duello, c. Porro, s.v. "diminutio": "§ B' hic intelligit duo sequentia capitula. . . p. B. intelligit generaliter de quolibet;" fol. 192, gloss on IV. De eo qui duxerit, c. Ex, s.v. "alterius": "B' simpliciter concedit . . . p. B^i dicit idem esse. . . ." There is a strong case for assuming that p. B. (or p. B^i) is the siglum of Master Petrus Brito who glossed the *Compilatio Prima* as late as the second half of the second decade of the thirteenth century (cf. Kuttner, *Traditio*, vol. i, p. 317, note 54). If our identification be correct, this second stratum of glosses would contain some very essential doctrines of this canonist who appeared to belong, not to the Bolognese school, but to one of the Western, perhaps even to one of the English schools. One reference to Spanish conditions should not of course lead to the assumption that the gloss of the second layer is of Spanish origin: fol. 202, V. De Judeis, c. Judei et Saraceni, s.v. "excludantur": "Ergo hic intelligendum de bonis provenientibus ex antiqua haereditate, non ex fenore vel labore, ut in hyspania." This second layer ends on fol. 208.

One might think that the gloss of the second stratum was merely a "reportatio" that is to say, a reproduction of the lecture as given by Master p. B. (or p. B^i), since in nearly every case the gloss has: "p. B. concedit", "p. B. intelligit", "p. B^i legens", "p. B. exponit", and the like. But against this must be set the fact that the gloss also contains opinions contrary to those of Master p. B., e.g. fol. 192: "Ego credo ... p. B^i dicit...." In another case this gloss refers to a *Summa* of p. B^i (fol. 193, where Master p. B^i is alleged to have adhered to Laurentius).

G. NOTE ON THE *Collectio Quaestionum* IN VIENNA, NATIONAL BIBLIOTHEK, MS. 2163 (FOLS. 75-100); INC.: "AGITATA EST CAUSA CORAM EPISCOPO."

This MS. was first made known and described by Professor Kuttner in *Traditio*, vol. i (1944), pp. 322-25, but the following observations appear to be justified.

I. It seems that there are two collections of *Quaestiones*, and not one, as Kuttner stated: the first collection from fol. 75 to fol. 90 verso, and the second from fol. 91 to fol. 100. Kuttner correctly observed that "the rest of that page (fol. 90 verso) is blank", but incorrectly maintained that "on fol. 91 the anonymous *Quaestiones* are taken up again by another hand" (art. cit., p. 325). Now, a consultation of the MS. 162 of the Cistercian Monastery in Zwettl, Lower Austria (which MS. belongs to the same family as the Viennese MS.) proves that the *Quaestiones* of Vienna 2163, fols. 75–90 verso, form one separate group and that fols. 91-100 contain another group of *Quaestiones*. For Zwettl 162, fol. 178 verso, ends with the same words as Vienna 2163, fol. 90 verso, i.e.: "Dic, quod si alias non erat ... ff, de furtis, in furti actione, § recte." In Zwettl 162 this collection is immediately followed (fol. 179) by the *Summa Quaestionum* of the English canonist Honorius (to fol. 213), whilst fol. 91 of Vienna 2163 begins: "Ad tempus secus, ubi hoc in sententia exprimitur...." There does not seem to be any connexion between fol. 90 verso and fol. 91, except that the two writings belong to the same literary species, the *Quaestiones Disputatae*. That this second collection of *Quaestiones* (fol. 91 onwards) is not a mere continuation of the preceding is borne out by the absence of the siglum "ber" and by the occurrence of a siglum that does not appear in the first collection: f' bar., on fol. 93 verso, and f' bar. col.' „ on fol. 99.

II. This MS. preserves one of the few sayings of the English canonist Robertus Anglicus. The case in which the person of the English king figures prominently (fol. 86 verso–87: "Rex Angliae concessit quandam villam cum omni jure suo cuidam monasterio, sed adjecit. . . .") was, naturally enough, submitted to Master Ro. for its solution: "Dicit Ro. cum solvit contrarietates istarum. . . ." fol. 87. I was unable to extract any more details from the text. But it seems almost certain that it was King John whose transaction aroused canonistic interest. Kuttner who also noticed this case (p. 326, note 32) but who doubts that Ro. is Robertus, does not, therefore, think that this question was treated in the school of Vicenza (1204-1209). It is, however, unfortunate, that we have preserved no opinion of a contemporary English canonist on the famous case of the monks of Christ Church against the archbishops of Canterbury; the opinion of the Spaniard, Bernardus Compostellanus, is preserved (fol. 88 verso: "Cantuariensis archiepiscopus vult constituere quandam ecclesiam et instituere ibi canonicos saeculares et assignare eis de provenientibus quarundam ecclesiarum . . . ber. sentit pro monachis").

III. No other collection of decretals is made use of but the *Compilatio Prima*, and hence the *Quaestiones* of both collections were discussed before 1210, the year in which the *Compilatio Tertia* was published.

H. RICHARD DE LACY ON CHURCH AND STATE,[1] MS. 162, ZWETTL, CISTERCIAN MONASTERY.

In his *Summa Quaestionum*[2] Richard de Lacy also came to speak of the controversial relationship between the empire and the papacy (fol. 147vb–148ra). Had the pope also supremacy in temporal matters? "Quaeri solet, an summus pontifex utrumque gladium habet, materialem scilicet et spiritualem?" (fol. 147vb). Richard's theory was uncompromisingly dualistic and

---

[1] See *supra* p. 145.
[2] Incipit: fol. 145ra: "Circa jus naturale variae quaestiones solent fieri." Explicit: fol. 173ra: "Explentur quaestiones veneriales magistri ricardi super tota decreta." This *Summa Quaestionum* of the English canonist was written during the pontificate of Innocent III, probably not later than 1210. A detailed analysis of this interesting MS. cannot be undertaken here. On the literary form of the *Summa Quaestionum* (which St. Thomas Aquinas later in the century also adopted) to which Professor Kuttner was the first modern authority to draw attention, see *Traditio*, vol. i, p. 321, note 4.

P

could hardly be distinguished from the later anti-papalist views. There is of course no direct evidence that he wished to oppose the scheme of Innocent III and of his fellow countryman Alanus. But that the whole *quaestio* is a denial and refutation of the political ideas as set forth by the curia at that time, is suggested by the tenor of this important passage.

Richard summarized the arguments of those canonists who ascribed to the pope a temporal superiority over the emperor, over and above his spiritual supremacy. He rejected the theory of the so-called commission of the temporalities,[1] since the pope's binding and loosening powers referred only to the spiritual affairs, but not to the temporal matters, of clerics and laymen.[2] Nor could the fact that the emperor on the occasion of his coronation took an oath be interpreted as his voluntary submission to the pope: that oath merely expressed the emperor's willingness to recognize the pope's spiritual superiority, but did not imply any inferiority in other ways.[3] This oath could on no account be put on a footing equal to that of a vassal. "Nec hoc est facere fidelitatem quam fideles faciunt dominis."[4] Nor could the action of Pope Zacharias indicate any powers of the pope in temporal matters. According to Richard, Zacharias merely ex-communicated the king, and the deposition followed then only as a consequence of the excommunication: "Hoc est regem degradare per consequentiam."[5]

[1] *Dist.* xxii, c. 1 (Nicholas I): Christ "beato Petro terreni et coelestis imperii jura commisit".

[2] "Quod autem dicitur utrumque imperium sibi esse concessum, ita exponitur, in causa super clericos quam laicos imperium habet quoad spiritualia, ut si quis ligatur in terra, etiam ligatur in coelo."

[3] "Si autem objiciatur, quod fidelitatem facit imperator dicunt hoc non contingere ratione alicuius potestatis, quam accipiat ab eo, sed illud facit, ut sciatur, quod illi subjectus est in spiritualibus."

[4] This, naturally, was a favourite weapon in the armoury of the anti-papalists. See, for example, King Frederick III's memorandum to Emperor Henry VII (1312?), in *Mon. Germ. Hist., Constit.*, vol. iv, p. 1312, where we find the same argumentation, that is, that the emperor's oath was not a vassal's, but one which was taken "ratione obsequii, quod debet spiritualiter quilibet Christianus ecclesiae et maxime principes catholici, et ante omnes imperator." One might wonder whether the author of this memorandum would have reckoned Richard de Lacy amongst the "canoniste", p. 1315.

[5] "Item si dicatur, quod Zacharias deposuit regem, hoc factum est, sed ideo deposuisse dicitur, quia pro contumacia sua excommunicavit, nam subditos ab eius obedientia subtraxit, quia subditi domino excommunicato non tenentur obedire, ut XV q.VI, juratos, et hoc est regem degradare per consequentiam."

APPENDIX 213

Richard also made an objection which was not pointed out by any other canonist. He perceived an inconsistency in the view that the emperor derived his power from the pope, for then one would implicitly admit that the secular authority exercised its jurisdiction in capital matters by authority of the Church. Relying on C.XXIII, q.iii,c. 7, where St. Ambrose referred to Salomon's "Deliver them that are drawn unto death" (Prov. xxiv, 11), Richard pointed out that the duty of the Church was to save individuals from death, and not to hasten their extermination. Hence, it would be incorrect to say that the secular authority could deliver those individuals to death "by authority of the Church".[1] Furthermore, if the death penalty were executed by the authority of the Church, an appeal from the secular court to the papal court would have to be allowed; this was manifestly wrong according to a decretal of Alexander III,[2] because this kind of jurisdiction was outside the ecclesiastical courts.[3] Lastly, what was the papal court to do with an appeal in a capital case, since the curia could not exercise judgment in these matters? "Si appelletur ad ipsum (*scil*. papam), quid faciet in causa sanguinis: ipse siquidem cognoscere non potest, quia nec cogitare judicium sanguinis?" For all these reasons it seemed safer to Richard to uphold the independence of the empire from the Church: "Videtur nobis securior via eorum, qui dicunt, quod imperator a solo Deo habet potestatem." (fol. 148ra).

These views are interesting enough in themselves, but our interest is considerably heightened when we consider that this *quaestio* of Richard may well have served as a model for later extremist anti-papal pronouncements. For here we find a striking anticipation of those words[4] which made one of Philip

---

[1] "Si enim potestatem habet a summo pontifice, ergo eius auctoritate cognoscit in jurisdictione (MS: juditione) sanguinis. Item alibi dicitur 'eripe eum, qui ducitur ad mortem' ut XXIII, q.III, non inferenda. Si ergo tenetur reos sanguinis defendere ecclesia, non ergo eius auctoritate ultima debet puniri supplicio."

[2] *Gregoriana*, II.xxviii.7. This, incidentally, is the decretal which gave Alanus the opportunity to state his views.

[3] Cf. the wording of Alexander III in decr. cit. with the passage of Richard: "Item, si eius auctoritate debet imperator cognoscere in causa sanguinis, ergo ab imperatore potest ad papam appellari, quod manifeste negatur in decretali Alexandri III Denique."

[4] About the idea itself (Huguccio, Laurentius and Richard himself) see *supra* pp. 144 f.

p*

IV's communications to Boniface VIII so famous: *Antequam essent clerici*. This communication asserted that before there were any clerics the French king had undisputed powers over France.[1] And it is precisely the same idea and the same phrase, coined, naturally, with reference to the empire, that we find here: "Antequam essent summi pontifices, erant imperatores et eandem potestatem habebant quam nunc habent. Unde videtur, quod non ab illis nacti fuerint hanc potestatem, sed a Deo." Should this identity of views and formulation be a mere coincidence?

But in least one more respect we may sense some connexion between Richard de Lacy and later anti-papalists, that is, in his conception of the Church. It has been maintained[2] that Philip IV derived his idea of the "ecclesia"—"ecclesia non solum est ex clericis, sed etiam ex laicis" (also set forth in *Antequam essent clerici*)—from the wording of Frederick II's great anti-papal manifesto of 30 April 1239.[3] In the *Apparatus* on the *Compilatio Prima* of Richard (W 122) we find a discussion as to who was to decide controversial matters concerning the faith. Richard's answer was that clerics as well as lay people should be consulted: "Ubi de causa fidei agitur, tam clerici quam laici debent interesse,"[4] because this was a matter that touched all. Now to understand the import of this gloss we should keep in mind that in the decretal upon which Richard commented, Lucius III excluded lay people from taking part in the formula-

---

[1] Dupuy, *Histoire de differend d'entre le pape Boniface VIII et Philippe le Bel*, Paris, 1655, pp. 21-23. Cf. also my paper in *E.H.R.*, vol. lxi, 1946, p. 183, G. de Lagarde, *La naissance de l'esprit laique*, 2nd ed., 1948, pp. 242 ff. and J. Rivière, *Le problème de l'église et de l'état au temps de Philippe le Bel*, pp. 99-102.

[2] Helene Wieruszowski, *Vom Imperium zum Nationalen Königtum*, Beiheft 30 of the *Historische Zeitschrift*, pp. 21, 91, 179.

[3] Manifesto "Levate" addressed to all European princes (see J. F. Böhmer, *Regesta Imperii*, ed. J. Ficker, vol. v, no. 2431), *Mon. Germ. Hist., Constit.*, vol. ii, p. 298. Frederick II held the same view seven years before, in 1232, see Huillard-Bréholles, *Historia Diplomatica Friderici II*, vol. iv, p. 409. He could have cited canon law itself: *De Cons., dist.* i, c. 8, and C.XXIV, q. i, c. 18.

[4] W 122, fol. 71 verso, De haeret., c. Ad abolendum, s.v. "consilio". See *supra* p. 21. The passage in LB 105, fol. 203, is identical with that in W 122. Although it would not be surprising to find Marsiglio of Padua referring to Richard, Riezler's statement that the Paduan actually quoted "Richardus Anglus" (*Die literarischen Widersacher der Päpste zur Zeit Ludwigs des Baiers*, p. 197), cannot, however, be verified. Riezler's reference to Huguccio can be traced, see *Defensor Pacis*, dictio II, cap. i, p. 112, of the edition by the late C. W. Previté-Orton.

tion of principles of faith.[1] It is not difficult to imagine that a short time afterwards Richard de Lacy would have been stigmatized as an anti-papalist.

[1] *Gregoriana*, V. vii. 9. The gloss also refers to *Dist.* xcvi, c.2, and *Dist.* lxvi, c.1, but it is difficult to see how these two passages can support the statement made in the text.

LIST OF MANUSCRIPTS CITED[1]

CAMBRIDGE
Pembroke College: *72*: 32 n.4, 39 n.2, 41 n.2, 42 n.4, 45 n.2, 46 n.2,3, 59 n.1, 95 n.2, 142 n.3, 143 n.2, 154 n.5, 155 n.3, 167 n.3

Trinity College: *O.5.17:* 146 n.2,3, 180 n.1,2, 196 n.1, 208
O.10.2: 199
R.9.17: 14 n.3

DURHAM
Cathedral Chapter Library: *C III 4:* 21 n.4, 36 n.1, 51 n.1, 51 n.1, 56 n.4, 87 n.2, 3, 93 n.3, 94 n.5, 98 n.3, 100 n.4, 101 n.5, 102 n.1, 105 n.2, 4, 106 n.1, 4, 143 n.2, 145 n.3, 146 n.4, 149 n.1,3, 150 n.4,6, 154 n.1, 169 n.4, 185 n.1, 194 n.1
C III 8: 36 n.3, 95 note, 101 n.3, 126 n.1, 146 n.1, 156 n.3, 173 n. 4, 5, 194 n.1, 196 notes, 199 f.

EDINBURGH
University Library: *Db V 12:* 133 n.3

FLORENCE
Laurenziana: *S. Croce, Plut. V sin.4*: 96 n.4

[1] Only those MSS are listed which I have seen in original or in photostatic copy.

KARLSRUHE
　　Badische Landes Bibliothek: *Cod. Aug. XL*: 147 n.1, 181 n.1, 196 n.4

LINCOLN
　　Cathedral Chapter Library:　　*2*: 51 n.2, 78 n.2, 144 n.1, 149 note, 156 n.3, 173 n.5, 176 n.3, 179 n.4, 195 n.2
　　　　　　　　　　　　　　　　29: 102 note, 185 n.3, 194 n.1
　　　　　　　　　　　　　　　137: 146 n.3, 180 n.1, 208
　　　　　　　　　　　　　　　151: 6 n.3, 12 n.3
　　　　　　　　　　　　　　　162: 34 n.2
　　　　　　　　　　　　　　　163: 102 note
　　　　　　　　　　　　　　　167: 172 n.1
　　　　　　　　　　　　　　　173: 99 n.2, 101 n.3, 103 n.1, 152 n.2, 170 n.2, 180 n.4, 181 n.2, 187 n.2, 201 ff., 207 f.

LONDON
　　British Museum: *Royal 9 E VII*: 13 n.2, 60 note, 74 n.1, 153 n.4, 191 n.3, 192 notes, 200 f.

　　　　　　　　　　Royal 9 E VIII: 13 n.2
　　　　　　　　　　Royal 9 F I: 15 n.7
　　Lambeth Palace: *105*: 6 n.4, 14 n.2,3, 21 n.3,4, 102 note, 145 n.2, 169 n.3, 171 n.2, 183 n.1, 208 ff, 212
　　　　　　　　　　139: 60 note, 64 n.3, 66 n.3, 182 n.3

PARIS
　　Bibliothèque Nationale: *Lat. 3932*: 147 n.1

VIENNA
　　National Bibliothek: *2080*: 97 n.4
　　　　　　　　　　　　2125: 26 n.1
　　　　　　　　　　　　2163: 36 n.4, 210 f.

WORCESTER
Cathedral Chapter Library: *F 122*: 21 n.3,4, 36 n.2, 65 n.1, 102 note, 145 n.1
F 159: 106 n.2,3, 107 n.3,4, 146, n.1, 149 n.2, 179 n.2

YORK
Minster Library: *xvi.D.5*: 39 n.8
xvi.Q.13: 34 n.2
xvi.Q.14: 153 n.6

ZWETTL
Cistercian Monastery: *162*: 183 n.1, 210, 211 ff.

INDEX

Accursius, 141 n. 1, 164 n. 2
Actio spolii, 25
Adams, G. B., 24 n. 3, 72 note
Adolf of Nassau, 187 n. 2
Advowson, see Jus patronatus
Aeneas Sylvius, 4
Aistulph, 169, 170, 171
Alanus, English canonist, 10; influence 14, 112, 142; on corporate consent, 21 n. 4; on matrimony, 62; on study of civil law, 96; on jurisdiction, 100 n. 4, 101; on plenitude of power of pope, 142, 147 ff., 211; on episcopal power, 143 n. 2; on deposition of emperor, 181 n.1; on emperor's function, 195
Albertus, Magister, 3
Alexander II, 5, 148 n. 1
Alexander III, canonist, 3, 12, n. 2, 16, 35, 59 n. 2, 60 f., 63 n. 1, 64 n. 3, 96 n. 2, 136; theologian, 34; legislator, 21 n. 4, 56, 60 f., 64, 65, 69, 76, 122; judge, 73, 101, 155 n. 2
Alvarus Pelagius, 11 n. 1, 15, 79 n. 2, 87, 89 n. 1, 93, 118 n. 4, 120 n. 5, 170 n. 2, 176 n. 2
Andreas de Perusio, 92 n. 1.
Anselm of Lucca, 5
Antequam essent clerici, 214
Antonius de Butrio, 7; on patristic literature, 32 n. 3; on appeals to pope, 78 n. 3; on ecclesiastical jurisdiction, 102 n. 2; on Roman empire, 133 n. 1
Apparatus "Ecce vicit leo", 146 n. 2, 208
Apparatus "Jus naturale", 150
Archdeacon, 10, 18, 93 n. 2; on natural law, 40 ff., 48 f.; on pope's dispensatory powers, 52, 55; on empire's dependence on Church, 84 n.2; on structure of society, 97 n. 6, 98 n. 1; on Donation of Constantine, 164 n. 1; on papal basis of power, 167; on papal vacancy, 188 n. 3
Aristotle, 26 n. 1, 31, 45, 47, 77, 85, 91, 109 ff., 117, 141, 159 n. 4
Arnulf of Lisieux, 11 n. 6
Authenticum, 29, 78 n. 1, 97 n. 3, 139 n. 1, 185 n. 4
Avignon, 4
Azo, 15 n. 1, 99 n. 1

Baldus, 4, 16 n. 1, 99 n. 2, 143 n. 1, 157 n. 1
Barker, E., 21 n. 1
Barons, deposition by pope, 179; and emperor, 180; and bishops, 190 f.
Barraclough, G., 5 n. 5, 7 n. 3, 95 note
Bartholomaeus Brixiensis, 33; see *Glossa ordinaria, Decretum*
Bartolus, 4, 36, 100 n. 3, 103 n. 2, 157 n. 1, 164
Bassianus, 209
Bazianus, 74, 209
Beauvais, bishop of, 191
Benencasa, 107, 179
Bernardus Compostellanus Antiquus, 5, 15, 99 n. 1, 101 n. 3, 126 n. 1, 156, n. 3, 209, 211
Bernardus Compostellanus Junior, Spanish canonist, 5, 15; on Christ's possession of both swords, 152; on translation of empire, 172; on deposition of king Childeric, 180, and of emperors, 181, 187; glossator of constitutions of 1st Council of Lyons, 152, 205 ff.
Bernardus Papiensis, 14, 21 n. 4, 25 n. 2, 34 n. 1, 36, 208

221

Bernardus Parmensis, 55, 69; see *Glossa Ordinaria, Decretales*
Berengarius, 170
Bigamy, 65 f.
Bishop, vicar of Christ, 51 n. 1; dispensatory powers, 70; jurisdiction, 87, 94 n. 5, 177; election, 143 n. 2; territorial lord, 190 f.; in battle, 191 f.; and metropolitan, 179
Bohuslav of Prag, 15 n. 7
Bologna, school of, 3, 5, 6, 11, 12, 150
Boniface VIII, 3 n. 5, 4, 6 n. 3, 9, 10, 16, 24, 90 n. 1, 93, 134, 186, 191, 212
Bracton, 25 n. 2, 26, 100
Brooke, Z. N., 9 n. 1, 11 n. 6, 113 n. 1, 197
Burbach, M., 85 n. 3

Calixtus II, 70 n. 1
Canonistics, value to medieval studies, 7 f., 9, 10, 20 f.; role in papal politics, 79 ff., 178, 189; international character, 13 ff.; characteristics, 16 ff., 77; and diplomatic history, 8 f.
Canonists, mere lawyers? 32 f., 77; not all clerics, 6 f.; English, 10 ff., 13 ff., 200; Italian, 13 f.; German, 14; Spanish, French, Hungarian, 15; and publicists, 2, 9 f., 17 f., 77; and civilians (legists), 33 f., 143, 163, 164, 190; and popes, 2, 3 ff., 7, 16, 178, 189; and St. Thomas, 47; and theology, 26 f.; on canonistic scholarship, 26–37; working method, 77; their role in papal politics, 79 ff.
Canterbury, monks, 4, 15, 211
Capital punishment, 86 f., 211 f.
Cardinals, canonists, 4 f., 16; during papal vacancy, 188
Caspar Calderinus, 7
Celestine V, 6
Charlemagne, 168, 173
Charles IV, emperor, 158
Cheney, C. R., 10 n. 2, 94 n. 5
Childeric, 149, 178, 179, 180, 212 f.
Church, and State, 81 f., 85, 113, 116, ch. VI *passim*, 211 ff.; prior to State, 120, but see 144 ff., 151 211 f.; mother of empire, 113, 141; exempt from State's jurisdiction, 148; possesses both swords, 152 ff.; institutes the 7 electors, 175 f.; concept of, 212. See also Jurisdiction, Pope and Spiritual
Church property, 90, 148, 155
Circumspecte Agatis, 102
Citizenship, 98, 138, 160 f., 184
Civil authority, see Temporal authority
Civilians, 1, 8, 9, 17, 18, 19, 28 f., 33 f., 35 ff., 40, 76, 79, 103, 105, 112, 117, 135, 138 ff., 141, 151, 157 n. 1, 161 f., 164 f., 190, 193
Clement III, 118
Clement IV, 4
Clement V, 3 n. 5, 4, 6 n. 3, 70, 100 n. 3, 122, 188, 189 n. 4
Clement VII, anti-pope, 158
Clementinae, 4, 6 n. 3
Clericis laicos, 24
Clerics, 83, 84, 94 f., 96, 161, 179
Codex juris canonici, 65 n. 4
Codex Justinianeus, 3 n. 2, 23 note, 119 n. 1, 149 n. 3, 184 n. 2
Coeleste arbitrium, 51
Collectio Cantabrigiensis, 14 n. 3
Collectio Lambethana, 14 n. 3
Collectio Romana, 5
College of cardinals, 188
"Commission" of temporal power, 90, 119, 150, 154, 163, 196, 211 f.
Compilatio I, II, 14
Compilatio III, 3, 5, 14 n. 3
Compilatio IV, 14
Compilatio V, 3, 186
Conciliar Movement, 168
Confiscation of property, 93, 136, 184
Conflict of laws, 194
Constantine, Donation of, 44, 107 ff., 119, 128, 132, 163 ff.
Constitutions of Clarendon, 73, 90, 100 n. 6
Coronation, imperial, 84, 85, 143, 145, 171, 196 f., 211 f.
Corporeal, the, 30, 31, 82 ff.
Crescentius, 174

Crimes, jurisdiction in, 103
Criminals, arrest of, 190
Crusades, 120 128
Cynus, 103, 140 n. 1, 141 n. 3, 143, 157 n. 1, 188

Damasus, 15, 43 note, 97
Dante, 18, 28 n. 1, 164 n. 2, 170 n. 2
David of London, 11
Decius, Philippus, 182 n. 6
Decretals, 3, 6; greater force than saints' sayings, 32
Decretum, 14, 17, 18, 38 ff.
De Ecclesiastica Potestate, 17; see Egidius Romanus
de Ghellinck, J., 12 n. 2, 34 n. 1, 43 n. 2, 44 n. 2
de Lagarde, G., 113 n. 1, 212 note
Deliberatio papae, 168 ff.
Denifle, H., 6 n. 3, 12 n. 2, 203 n. 1
Determinatio compendiosa, 162 n. 8, 175 n. 3, 196 n. 5; see also Ptolomy of Lucca
Deusdedit, cardinal, 5
Dionysius, 20 n. 1
Disinheritance, 184
Dispensation, 51 ff.
Distinctiones Halenses, 11 n. 6
Divine law, 40 f., 108, 134, 139, 142
Dogma, virgin birth, 59 n.2
Dominion, theory of, 133 ff.
Dowry, 99
Dualism, 113, 140, 144, 159, 211
Duns Scotus, 85 n. 3
Durandus, 15, 85 n. 3, 86 n. 1, 87 n. 4, 91, n. 1, 104, 117 n. 1, 123 n. 1, 125, 133 n. 2, 152 n. 3, 4, 160
Dynus, 7

Ecclesia Militans, Triumphans, 20, 159
Ecclesiastical authority, see Spiritual authority
Edward I, 24, 103
Edwards, J. G., 21 n. 2
Egidius Fuscararius, 7
Egidius Romanus, 17, 39 n. 8, 49 n. 1, 77, 85 n. 2, 130, 131, 132, 134 n. 3, 135
Egidius Spiritalis, 93 n. 2, 107 n. 2
Ehrle, F., 63 n. 1
Electoral college, 144, 174 ff., 187 n. 2, 197
Emperor, inferiority to pope, 33, 45, 77, 109, 140, 160, 165 f., 193; instrument of papal policy, 76, 85, 86, 88; deposition, 78, 93, 107, 123, 177 ff., 211 ff.; "dominus mundi", 79, 116, 141; needs papal approbation, 84; coronation, 84, 85, 143, 145, 146, 169, 171, 196 f., 211 f.; election, 144, 146 n. 1, 148, 150, 174 ff., 196, 211 f.; excommunication, 176 f.; instituted by pope, 148, 174, but see 144 ff., 151, 211 ff.; symbolizes matter, 82, 140; under ecclesiastical jurisdiction, 103; not bound by his laws, 154 f., 157 f.; territorially restricted in power, 78, 83, 105, 115, 118; treaties concluded by, 157 n. 1; basis of his authority, 165; high treason against 184; the authority conceded to, 194 ff.
Empire, depended on papacy, 84, 161, 164, 167; vacancy, 107, 109, 188; instituted by God, 139; sister of the Church, 144, 145, 164, 212; translation of, 168 ff.; lawful, 164; and papacy, a constitutional issue, 76
England, and the papacy, 4, 9, 102
English canonists, see Canonists
Esmein, A., 65 n. 5
Eubel, S., 5 n. 6, 6 n. 3
Evesham abbey, 13
Excommunication, 79, 123, 176, 189, 212

f'bar. cols., 210
Feudal affairs, jurisdiction, 105
Finke, H., 6 n. 3, 15 n. 4, 17
Fitzralph, archbishop, 133
Flahiff, G. B., 90 n. 2, 102 n. 4, 103 n. 1.
Fliche, A., 5 n. 4

Frederick, I, 174
Frederick II, 102 n. 4, 178, 181, 185, 212
Frederick of Austria, 189
Friedberg, A., 3 n. 4, 14 n. 3

Gandulphus, Magister, 34
Garsias, Magister, 15, 207
Gaufridus Arthurus, 153 n. 6
Gelasius I, 53, 139
Geoffrey de Vinsauf, 153
Gérard Pucelle, 12
Gilbertus, 11, 14, 74
Glanvell, W., 5 n. 2
Glossa ordinaria, Decretales, 23, 54, 56 n. 4, 62 n. 3, 65 n. 4, 69, 74 n.3, 5, 99 n. 2, 101 n. 3, 105, 118 n. 6, 119 n. 4, 122 n. 5, 170, 171 n. 3, 177 n. 2, 182, 184, 196 n. 3
Glossa ordinaria, Decretum, 33, 40 n. 3, 53 n. 2, 84 n. 1, 152 n. 1, 173 n. 6, 178
Glossa ordinaria, Extravagantes, see Zenzelinus de Cassanis
Glossa Palatina, 36 n. 3, 95 note, 101 n. 3, 126 n. 1, 146, n. 1, 156 n. 3, 173, 194 n. 1, 195 f., 199 f.
Goffredus de Trano, 6; on natural law, 41 f.; on papal dispensatory power, 53 f., 55; on matrimony, 59 f., 62 f., 66 n. 1; on expropriation, 136 n. 3; on papal power, 151, 154 n. 5; on legislative powers of the people, 166; on excommunication of princes, 177
Gospels, see New Testament
Government, lawful, 92, see Emperor, Empire
Grabmann, M., 26 n. 1, 47 n. 1, 111 n. 3, 155 n. 2
Gratian, 14, 38 f., 43 n. 1, 45 n. 3, 48 n. 1, 51 n. 2, 59 n. 1, 66, 67 n.1, 84 n. 2, 88, 98 n. 3, 139 n. 2, 142, 167 n. 3, 177
Gregoriana, 6, see Decretals
Gregory VII, 1, 5, 55, 79 n. 2, 152 n. 5, 177, 181
Gregory VIII, 3
Gregory IX, 3 n. 5, 4, 42, 51 n. 1, 186

Gregory XI, 4, 57, 60, 64, 65 n. 4, 73, 123
Guido Brito, 34, 106
Guido de Baysio, see Archdeacon
Guido de Suzaria, 157 n. 2
Guido Vernanus, 155 n. 2
Guilelmus de Amidanis, 55 n. 3, 89 n. 4, 92 n. 1
Guilelmus de Mandagoto, 6 n. 4, 15 n. 6, 35
Guilelmus Durantis, 6 n. 4, 50 n. 1, 51 n. 3, 53 n. 1, 58, 68 n. 2, 69 n. 2, 70, 154 n. 1, 4, 181, 188 n. 1, 207 f.
Guilelmus Vasco, 96 n. 4

Hadrian I, 170 n. 2, 173
Haller, J., 3 n. 2, 139 n. 3
Harnack, A., 7 n. 3
Hefele-Leclercq, 15 n. 4
Henricus de Segusia, see Hostiensis
Henry II, emperor, 7 n. 3
Henry IV, emperor, 152 n. 5
Henry VII, emperor, 189 n. 4
Henry II, king, 25, 90, 100
Henry III, 4
Henry VIII, 10
Heresy, 32, 94, 103 n. 2, 123 f.; of pope, 156 f., 183 f.
Herueus, Magister, 85 n. 3
Heyer, F., 5 n. 7
High treason, 183 f.
Hildebrand, see Gregory VII
Hinschius, P., 95 note, 177 n. 2
Holtzmann, W., 155 n. 2
Honorius III, 3, 69, 96, 185
Honorius, archdeacon, Richmond, 11, 210
Hostiensis, 2, 4, 10, 18, 27, 29, 30 f.; on papal power, 52 n. 1, 89 n. 3, 93, 148, 151; on structure of society, 97 n. 2; on jurisdiction, 100 n. 5, 102 n. 2; on monarchy, 117, 159 n. 5; on conquest of non-Christian countries, 129 ff.; on Donation of Constantine, 165 n. 1; on popular transfer of power, 166; on papal interference in legislation, 182; on

INDEX

imperial vacancy, 189; on sun and moon allegory, 194 n. 1
Hubert Walter, 153 n. 4, 200
Hugh of St. Victor, 44 n. 2
Hugolinus, 4, 51 n. 1
Huguccio, teacher of Innocent III, 3, 68, 142, 144 n. 2; lexicographer, 34; independence of judgment, 35, 60 n. 1; on natural and divine law, 39, 41, 45, 46; on authority of Roman church, 51 n. 2, 167 n. 3; on matrimony, 59 n. 1, 64; on oath, 68; on papal power, 78 n. 2, 142, 154 n. 5, 155, 195 n. 2; on clerics, 95 n. 2; on jus patronatus, 101; on separation of Church and State, 142 f., 148, 150, 151; on imperial coronation, 143, 197; on Christ's powers, 149; on heresy of pope, 156 f.; on deposition of emperor, 173, 179, of pope, 156 n. 3; on excommunication of princes, 176 n. 3; on vacancy of papal throne, 188

Idolatry, 122
Immunity, clerical, 94 f.; see also Clerics, Jurisdiction
Infidels, political power, 84, 131; subject to papal rule, 119, 121, 130 f., 132
Inheritance, jurisdiction in, 99 f., 193
Innocent III, pupil of Huguccio, 36, 68, 144 n. 2; invoked by Honorius, 11; on kingship, 71; supreme legislator, 55, 56 n. 3, 61, 64, 65, 66, 76, 79, 101 n. 1, 109, 154 n. 1, 182, 183, 188; judge 12 n. 1, 13, 18, 21 n. 4, 51 n. 1, 71, 84, 87 n. 5, 100, 105, 108, 118, 168, 174 n. 1, 175 n. 4, 178; and Magna Carta, 71 ff.
Innocent IV, 2, 4, 5 n. 5, 10, 18, 65 f., 68 n. 4, 148, 151, 172 n. 1; on pope's dispensatory powers, 52; on clerical exemption, 95; on ecclesiastical jurisdiction, 99 n. 2, 102 n. 3; on world monarchy of pope, 199 ff.; on papal plenitude of power, 152 f., 158; on the basis of the emperor's power, 166 f.; on electoral college, 175; on excommunication of princes, 176 f.; on deposition of Frederick II, 178, 186 f.; on imperial vacancy, 188 f.; his *Novellae*, 201 ff.
Inquisition, 94

Jacobus Butrigarius, 143 n. 1
Jacobus de Albenga, 199
Jacobus de Arena, 143
Jews, 48 n. 1, 117, 127; subject to papal jurisdiction, 122
Johann von Winterthur, 154 note
Johannes Andreae, 5 n. 5, 7, 15 n. 7, 102 n. 3, 153, 154 n. 5, 155 n. 4, 157, 159, 176, 181 n. 3, 187, 194 n. 1, 207; on natural law, 42, 45 n. 1
Johannes Calderinus, 7
Johannes de Deo, 15, 35, 53, 70
Johannes de Imola, 7
Johannes de Lignano, 7, 34, 168 n. 1
Johannes de Turrecremata, 6 n. 4, 34
Johannes Faventinus, 40, 45, 62
Johannes Galensis, 11, 14
Johannes Monachus, cardinal, 6, 15, 111 n. 3, 134, 190
Johannes Teutonicus, 14, 21 n. 4, 87 n. 2, 94 n. 5, 98 n, 3, 105, 106 n. 4, 146, 172, 185
John XXII, 4, 56, 158, 189
John, king, 15, 21 n. 4, 71, 102, 105 n. 1, 191 n. 3, 211
John Le Cras, 34 n. 2
John of Salisbury, 11, 147
Julian II, 32
Jurisdiction, ecclesiastical, 29, 83, 87, 90, 92, 93, 94 ff., 98 ff., 102 ff., 148, 157 ff., 182, 184, 185, 194, 212
Jury, trial by, 25
Jus gentium, 26, 40, 135
Jus patronatus, 100
Justices, secular, removal by pope, 185 f.
Justinian, 3 n. 2, 19, 29, 139, 141, 142, 150, 165

Kantorowicz, H. U., 3 n. 2, 5 n. 1, 14 n. 4, 15 n. 7, 25 n. 2, 43 note
Kern, F., 2 n. 1, 113 n. 1, 178 n. 2, 179 n. 3
Kessler, P. J., 187 n. 2, 201 f.
King, deposition, 78, 93, 103, 107, 149, 187; excommunication, 176 f; vicar of God, 113 n. 1; and emperor, 145 n. 1, 2
Knowles, M. D., 47 n. 1, 110 n. 1
Köstler, R., 18 n. 2
Kuttner, S., 3 n. 1 and *passim*

Laborans, cardinal, 5
Lajard, 15 n. 4
Lapsley, G., 24 n. 3
Lateran Council, 3rd, 56; 4th, 14, 21 n. 4, 122, 123 n. 1, 124, 127, 177, 182; 5th, 32
Laurence of Somercote, 12
Laurentius, Spanish canonist, 15; on episcopal functions, 51 n. 1; on papal dispensations, 52; on papal plenitude of power, 93 n. 3; on jurisdictional powers of Church, 102, 106 n. 4, 167; on legitimation of children, 105 f.; on independence of empire from Church, 145, 150; on election of pope, 173; on correction of civil laws by decretals, 185; on papal vacancy, 188; on mathematical computation of size of sun and moon, 194 n. 1; otherwise mentioned, 18, 210
Laurentius de Polonia, 15 n. 7
Law, its role in medieval political theory, 1, 8; and dogma, 59 n. 2; see also Political science, Roman law and Civilians
Le Bras, G., 5 n. 2, 18 n. 2, 43 n. 2, 45 n. 3, 48 n. 1, 55 n. 3
Legislation, secular, interference by pope, 157, 182, 185
Legists, see Civilians
Legitimation of children, 105, 193
Leo III, 168, 169, 171
Leo VIII, 173
Lewis of Bavaria, 9 n. 2, 189

Lex Regia, 165
Liber Extra, see *Decretals*
Liber Sextus, 4, 6, 15 n. 6, 201
Liberty, 55 ff., 138
Liberum arbitrium, 39
Lucas de Penna, 11, 99 n. 2
Lucius III, 64, 214
Lyons, Council at, 152, 178, 180, 187

Magna Carta, 22, 71 ff.
Maitland, F. W., 5 n. 1, 9 n. 1, 13, 25, 26, 35, 63 n. 1, 101 n. 1, 102 note, 124 n. 2
Manegold of Lautenbach, 166 n. 1
Margarita Decreti (Martinus Polonus) 15 n. 7
Marsiglio of Padua, 24 n. 4, 113 n. 1, 117 n. 1
Martin I, 65
Martin, O., 15 n. 4, 86 note
Martinus, civilian, 209
Martinus de Fano, 7, 16 n. 1, 78 n. 1, 94 n. 2, 119 n. 1
Martinus Polonus, 15 n. 7
Matrimony, 59 ff., 99
Matthew Paris, 5 n. 1, 18 n. 2, 22 n. 3, 102 n. 3, 191 n. 2, 202 n. 5
McIlwain, C. H., 17, 24 n. 3, 72 note
Melendus, Spanish canonist and bishop, 6, 15, 101 n. 3
Mercati, G., 21 n. 4
Merton, Parliament at, 9
Mind and matter, 81 ff.
Miracles, 45 n. 3
Mirror of the Saxons, 73, 123, 158
Missionaries, 121, 124
Mohammedans, 92, 117, 122, 124, 125, 128
Monarchy, justification, 116, 117, 141, 148, 159 f., 188
Monism, 113, 116, 140, 148
Moral law, 29, 38, 43, 45
Morey, A., 9 n. 1, 12 n. 2

Natural law, ch. II and III *passim*, 121 f., 123 n. 1, 142, 186

Natural reason, 30 f., 39, 41, 159
New Testament, 40, 42, 43, 45, 47 n. 1, 48 n. 2, 52 ff., 55, 62, 63, 65, 66, 67, 68, 76, 77, 79, 83, 88, 111, 116 n. 1, 117 n. 2, 119, 120, 121, 130, 132, 133, 145 n. 1, 149 n. 1, 152, 160 n. 2, 161 f., 172
Nicholas, English canonist? 13 n. 2, 200
Nicholas, papal legate, 21 n. 4
Nicholas I, 58
Nicholas II, 154
Nicholas de Parisiis, 26 n. 1
Notaries, appointment, 193
Novel disseisin, 25
Novellae, Justinian, 29 see *Anthenticum*, Innocent IV, 201 ff.

Oath, 66 ff.; of fidelity, release from, 78, 178
Old Testament, 40, 42, 43, 47 n. 1, 59 n. 1, 67 n. 1, 87 n. 4, 92, 109, 111, 118, 121, 130, 132, 151
Otto I, 7 n. 3, 76, 95 note, 170 173
Otto III, 174
Otto of Brunswick, 68 n. 5, 171 n. 2, 175 n. 4, 178
Oxford, school of, 11, 13

Padua, school of, 11 n. 2
Panormitanus, 6 n. 4, 50 n. 2, 68 n. 5, 89 n. 3, 95 n. 1, 98 n. 4, 100 n. 3, 102 n. 2, 120 n. 3, 140 n. 2, 3, 168 n. 1, 173 n. 6, 175 n. 3, 5
Pantheism, 40, 46
Papacy, see Church, Pope
Parliament, medieval English, 10, 20 ff.
Paucapalea, 63 n. 1
Paulus Hungarus, Hungarian canonist, 15, 106, 107, 149
Peace treaty, 102
Pepin, 171, 178
Perjury, 70, 102
Peter Lombard, 64, 125 n. 1
Peter Quesvel, 13 n. 1
Petrus Beneventanus Collivaccinus, cardinal, 5 n. 7, 15 n. 1

Petrus Bertrandi, cardinal, 6, 15, 86 note, 92, 133
Petrus Boemus, 15
Petrus Brito, 209
Petrus de Ancharano, 7, 111 n. 3, 140 n. 2
Petrus de Bellapertica, 103
Petrus de Cugneriis, 86 note
Petrus de Sampsone, 15 n. 6
Petrus Hispanus, 60 n. 1
Philip IV, 9, 70, 103, 213
Philip Augustus, 71, 102, 105 n. 1, 169 n. 3, 171 n. 2
Philip of Swabia, 68 n. 5, 168 f., 175 n. 4
Philosophers, medieval, 2
Pierre Mauclerk, 102 n. 4
Pius II, 4
Pius V, 94
Plena potestas, 20 f., 24
Plenitude of power, pope, 10, 17 47, 50, 53, 55, 78, 93, 107, 118, 140, 150, 151 ff., 163, 187, 193, 195; emperor, 139, 140
Political science, medieval, 8, 26 f., 31
Politics, Aristotle, 26 n. 1, 31, see Aristotle
Policraticus, 11 n. 1
Pope, vicar of God, 7, 16, 50 f., 55, 79, 89, 95, 107, 118, 121, 150, 153 ff., 160; dispensatory powers, 51 ff.; supremacy in temporal matters, 77, 81, 107, 148, 150 151 ff., 160, 163; but denied, 143 ff., 211 ff.; superior to emperor, 77, 89, 123, 140, 160, 165 ff., 176, 188, and invokes his help, 93 f., 125, and judges him, 150, 158; appeal to, 78, 158, 188, 189, 191, 194, 212; policy of, 80 f.; symbolizes soul, 82, 110 ff., 140, and sun, 194; non-recognition of, 93; world monarch, ch. V *passim*; a celestial emperor. 118, 127, 154, 155, 183; directly instituted by God, 141, 165; institutes emperor, 148, 164, 175; a quasi-imperator, 127 f.; not bound by law, 154 f., successor of Moses, 149, 151; can be charged with heresy, 156 f., and

deposed by cardinals, 156 n. 3; annuls civil laws, 157; is judex ordinarius, 158; judges international treaties, 158; institutes electoral college, 175 f., 197; deposes emperors and kings, 177 ff.; high treason against 183 f.; and the gospels, 52 ff.
Post, G., 5 n. 1, 21 n. 2, 4; 24 n. 3, 4
Priesthood, 108
Poupardin, R., 11 n. 6
Powicke, F. M., 9 n. 2, 20 n. 1, 21 n. 4, 71
Primitive peoples, law, 39
Private property, 129, 135
Privilegium fori, 94 n. 5
Ptolomy of Lucca, 6 n. 2, 72 note, 162 n. 8, 170 n. 1, 175 n. 3, 196 n. 5
Publicists, medieval, and canonists, 2, 9, 17 f., 79

Quaestiones Londinenses, 13 n. 2, 60 note, 74 n. 1, 153 n. 4, 191 ff., 200 f.
Quaestiones Stuttgardienses, 64 n. 3
Quod omnes tangit, 21 f.

Rashdall, H., 12 n. 1, 76
Ranulph Higden, 34 n. 2
Ratio connexitatis, 98 f.
Ratio peccati, 71, 93, 103 ff., 157 f., 179, 181, 182
Raymundus de Pennaforte, 6, 25 n. 2
Raynaldus, 32 n. 2, 57 n. 2, 86 note, 169 n. 1
Realism, 30, 89
Renaissance, twelfth-cent., 76
Representation, 20 f.
Respublica Christiana, 127, 138 f.
Rex-imperator, idea, 145 n. 2
Rex-sacerdos, idea, 7 n. 3
Richard I, 191, 192 n. 4
Ricardus Anglicus, see Richard de Lacy
Richardus de Senis, 6
Richard de Lacy, English canonist, 11, 14; and Bernardus Papiensis, 36; on concept of Church 21 f., 212 f.; on Alexander's matrimonial legislation, 60 n. 1, 65 n. 1; on English jus patronatus, 101; on Church and State, 144 f., 211 ff.; otherwise mentioned, 60 n. 1, 78 n. 2, 87 n. 5, 208
Richard Wych, 13
Richardson, H. G., 25 n. 1, 2
Richmond, archdeaconry, 11
Rivière, J., 17
Robert de Clipstone, 12 n. 1
Robertus Anglicus, 12, 211
Rodulphus Anglicus, 12 n. 1
Roger Bacon, 37
Roger of Hoveden, 11, 191 n. 2
Roger of Wendover, 191 n. 2
Rolandus, see Alexander III
Roman law, in England, 10; position of emperor in, 33, 76, 79, 116, 139, 141; and canon law, 19 f.; and canonists, 28 ff., 38, 118, 154; and *Decretum*, 38 f.; and slavery, 57
Romans, 133, 165, 175
Rufinus, Magister, 15, 35, 39 n. 1, 40 n. 2, 51 n. 2, 59 n. 2, 64 n. 3, 95 n. 1, 147
Russel, J. C., 12 n. 1

Saliceus, Bartholomaeus, 157 n. 1
"Sanior pars", 22 note, 24, 25 note
Savigny, F. v., 3 n. 4, 12 n. 1
Sayles, G. O., 10 n. 1, 25 n. 1, 72 note
Scholz, R., 11 n. 1, 17, 89 n. 4
Schulte, J. F. v., 3 n. 1 and *passim*
Secular authority, see Temporal authority
Self-defence, 40
Sextus, see *Liber Sextus*
Sicardus, 34
Simon, Magister, English canonist? 13 n. 2, 208
Simon de Bisignano, 43 note
Simon de Boraston, 13 n. 1
Sinibaldus, Fliscus, see Innocent IV
Slavery, 55 f.
Smith, A. L., 1
Society, structure, 97 f., see also Citizenship

Sovereignty, 114, 125, 190 f.; of the people, 166 ff.
Soul, 81 ff., 104, 140, see also Pope
Speculator, see Guilelmus Durantis
Speculum Regum, (Alvarus), 11 n. 1
Spiritual, the, 30, 31, 82 ff., 104, 105, 108, 111, 112 f., 139, 194
Spiritual authority, 83, 87, 88, 90 ff., 105, 123, 160 f., see also Jurisdiction
Spiritual matters, 76, 81, 82, 142 n. 3, 144 n. 1, 145
Sponsalia, 63 ff.
St. Augustine 32, 62, 136
St. Bernard, 77, 79, 87, 88
St. Gregory Nazianzenus, 82 n. 1
St. Paul, 30, 53, 54, 79, 88, 104, 172
State, see Emperor, Empire, Barons, Citizenship
Stephanus Polonus, 15 n. 7
Stephen III, 171
Stephen Langton, 11
Stephen of Tournay, 15, 29 n. 1, 41, 43 f., 44 n. 4, 68 n. 3, 94, 97, 137, 173
Stoicism, 40
Stroma Rolandi, see *Summa Rolandi*
Stubbs, W., 24 n. 3
Stutz, U., 44 n. 2, 101 n. 2
Summa "Animal est Substantia", 49
Summa Cantabrigiensis, 144, 146, 180, 187, 196 n. 1, 208
Summa Coloniensis, (S. "Elegantius in jure"), 26 n. 1, 63 n. 2
Summa Lambethana, 60 note, 64 n. 3, 66
Summa Lipsiensis, 39
Summa "Magister Gratianus in hoc opere," 63 n. 2
Summa Oxoniensis, 39, 40 n. 6
Summa "Permissio quaedam", 11 n. 6
Summa Rolandi, 16 n. 1, 34, 63 n. 1, 64 n. 3, see also Alexander III
Sun and Moon, allegory, 194 n. 1

Tancred, archdeacon of Bologna and Magister, 3, 18, 21 n. 4, 25 n. 2, 35; on pope's power, 50 f., 52, 55, 93 n. 3, 150, 154 n. 1; on oath, 74; on translation of empire, 169; on correction of civil laws by canon law, 185; on delegating powers of Church, 87 n. 3
Temporal, the, 30, 31, 83 ff., 104, 105, 112 f., 139, 194
Temporal authority, 83, 84, 86 f., 88 f., 90 ff., 105, 107, 108, 160 f., 184 ff., 194, 195 f.; see Emperor
Temporal matters, power of pope in, 76, 86, 99 ff., 105 ff., 144 n. 1, 145, 152 ff.; t. goods, 90 f., 92, 135
Territorial restrictions of papal power? 78, 83, 105
Teutons, 172
Theiner, A., 4 n. 1, 5 n. 5, 142 n. 3
Theocratic government, 115, 117, 118, 141; see also Pope, Church
Theologians, medieval, 2, 77
Theology, 2; and canonists, 26 ff., 37
Thomas Becket, 90, 97 n. 6, 147
Thomas of Marlborough, 11, 13 n. 5, 15
Thomism, 15 n. 3, 46, 47, 82 n. 1, 85 n. 3, 86 note
Thompson, Hamilton A., 11 n. 4
Thorne, S. E., 10 n. 2
Translation of empire, 20, 168 ff., 175 n. 1, 185 n. 1
Treaties, between kings, 157 n. 1; subject to papal jurisdiction, 158 f.

Ulpian, 38
Unam sanctam, 11, 93, 110 note, 134, 147, 148
Universitas civitatis, 145 n. 2
Urban II, 65
Urban V, 61
Urban VI, 158
Usury, 182

Vetulani, A., 39 n. 8
Vicenza, university, 12
Vincennes, 9, 86 note
Vincentius, Spanish canonist and bishop, 6 n. 4, 15, 209; on corporate

consent, 21 n. 4; on slavery and natural law, 56; on matrimony, 62; on credibility of English canonists 101; on ecclesiastical jurisdiction, 105, 106 n. 1; on priesthood of Moses, 149; on removal of judges, 184 f.

Virgin birth, 59 n. 2

Waldenses, 66
Walter Suffield, 12
Warichez, J., 15 n. 2
Wenger, L., 29 n. 4
Wenzel, king, 158
Wilkinson, B., 24 n. 3, 4
William de Mandagot, 12 n. 3
William of Drogheda, 11, 25 n. 2
Winchester, bishop of, 15
World government, ch. V *passim*
Worcester, bishop of, 12 n. 1, 13, 15
Writ, impetration of, 25 f., 200; of prohibition, 90; summons to parliament, 20, 24

Wyclif, 133

York, statute of, 24

Zabarella, Franciscus, cardinal and canonist, 5; theologian, 34; Aristotelian, 111 n. 3; and political science, 27 n. 1, and legal science, 31 f.; of greater dignity of spiritualia, 31; on papal plenitude of power, 118, 163; on papal jurisdiction over Jews, 122; on admission of preachers into pagan countries, 124; on papal interference in non-Christian countries, 126; on conquest of countries, 129; on dependence of empire on Church 167 n. 5; on translation of empire, 170, on electoral college, 175 n. 1, 2; otherwise mentioned, 167 n. 3

Zacharias, 149, 178, 179, 180, 186, 211 f.

Zenzelinus de Cassanis, 6, 15 n. 6, 56, 57, 97 n. 3, 131 n. 1